THE HISTORY OF
THE TIMES

Published by Times Books

An imprint of HarperCollins Publishers
Westerhill Road, Bishopbriggs
Glasgow G64 2QT

HarperCollins Publishers
Macken House, 39/40 Mayor Street Upper,
Dublin 1, D01 C9W8, Ireland

Volume 8, 2024

Thanks and acknowledgements go to Becky Callanan, Robert Crampton, Nigel Farndale, Jill Fenner, Tony Gallagher, Rana Greig, Jeremy Griffin, Robert Hands, James Harding, Les Hinton, Romina Hopkins, Alan Hunter, Anne Jensen, Tim Levell, Chris Longcroft, Liane MacIver, Nicholas Mays, Robbie Millen, Mairéad O'Donnell, Claire Patchett, Sam Stewart, Pia Sarma, Robert Thomson, Craig Tregurtha, Robert Tyrer, Victoria Watson and Tyrell Willock. Thanks also go to Joanne Lovey, Robin Ashton, Ian Brunskill, Harley Griffiths, Lauren Murray, James Hunter and Rachel Weaver.

A catalogue record for this book is available from the British Library.

ISBN 978-0-00-874363-5

10 9 8 7 6 5 4 3 2 1

If you would like to comment on any aspect of this publication, please contact the Publishers at the above address or online.

e-mail: times.books@harpercollins.co.uk

www.timesbooks.co.uk

Printed in the UK using 100% Renewable Electricity at CPI Group (UK) Ltd

MIX
Paper | Supporting
responsible forestry
FSC
www.fsc.org FSC™ C007454

This book is produced from independently certified FSC™ paper
to ensure responsible forest management.

For more information visit: www.harpercollins.co.uk/green

THE HISTORY OF THE TIMES

2002 to 2022

The Digital Age

Volume VIII

Christopher McKane

CONTENTS

PREFACE

This is volume eight of *The History of The Times*, a project begun in 1935 and telling the story of the paper from its beginnings (as *The Daily Universal Register*) in 1785. The present volume brings the narrative almost up to date. Spanning 20 years from 2002, it covers the editorships of Robert Thomson (2002–07), James Harding (2007–12) and John Witherow (2013–22). It records how *The Times* reported some momentous world events – wars, terrorism, a financial crash, the elections of Barack Obama and Donald Trump, the Brexit referendum, the Covid-19 pandemic, the death of a queen – but its primary focus is closer to home, on the developments and personalities that made *The Times* what it is.

The previous volume opened with an episode of high drama, when Rupert Murdoch moved production of his newspapers to a secretly converted 19th-century rum warehouse in Wapping. The 1986 move transformed the British press – literally overnight – and secured its long-term future by introducing computerised typesetting (with journalists inputting their stories direct to the system) and breaking the stranglehold of the militant print unions. Change was fiercely contested. For months the Wapping plant was besieged by angry pickets, often held at bay by mounted police, as armoured buses drove staff to work in the plant.

This volume contains no comparable moment of drama, no bitter confrontations or violent scenes, yet the transformation it documents in *The Times* (and in the wider media landscape) is if anything more profound. Wapping was a 20th-century equivalent of John Walter II's equally dramatic (and similarly motivated) secret introduction of the steam press for printing *The Times* in 1814. Both developments, in the face of firm resistance, harnessed new technology to change the way newspapers were produced. Both were, above all, improvements in efficiency. They made it possible to produce bigger and better papers and get them to readers faster and at a lower cost. The business of publishing newspapers became more viable.

Far-reaching as those production changes were, what was being produced remained essentially the same. *The Times* was a daily, printed newspaper. A reader from 1814 encountering a copy from 1986 might marvel at the photographs and be baffled by much of the content, but would have no difficulty recognising that this was an edition of *The Times*.

In the period covered here, that ceased to be the case. By the time Witherow stood down, people were reading *The Times* in ways unimaginable even on Thomson's first day as editor. Print circulations for all titles have steadily declined for many years, as lifestyles and demographics change. *Times* digital subscriptions now outnumber print sales by more than three to one. *The Times* still prizes fine, clear writing, but its newsroom is "digital-first", geared up to supplying a constantly updated flow of stories to multiple digital platforms. *Times* journalists still do what journalists have always done, and they do it as well as their predecessors did. But they also make videos, record podcasts, compile email newsletters and post on social media. Today *The Times* is a broadcaster too, with a successful radio station of its own and its journalists forging new careers as radio presenters.

Print remains vital, of course, both to the paper's identity and to commercial success. There will always be readers of all generations who like to wake to the thud of a morning paper on their doormat, or enjoy the walk to the newsagent, or hide behind a printed page at breakfast or on the train. On great national occasions, nothing captures the historic moment as effectively as print. In the days after the death of Queen Elizabeth II in 2022 print circulations soared, just as they always have when princes marry or governments fall or wars break out. As several publishers have learnt the hard way, a title that ceases print publication becomes just another website among many. In an age of content overload and fake news, that's a big risk to take, attractive though the cost savings may seem.

As well as continuing to invest in print, with Murdoch opening three new printing plants at a cost of £650 million in 2008, *The Times* roughly halfway through this book took a decision that set it apart from most other newspaper websites. The introduction in 2010 of a so-called hard paywall, asking readers to subscribe if they wanted to read *Times* content online, was greeted with surprise and even derision by rival publishers. The move flew in the face of an industry consensus that the way to success lay through maximising free visits from passing readers and charging advertisers based on the resulting "clicks".

The paywall decision taken when Harding was editor turned out to be as bold and significant as the introduction of the steam press by John Walter or of new technology at Wapping. The near-universal business model based on volume-advertising proved seriously flawed, while the belief at *The Times* that quality journalism was worth paying for – and that readers would be willing to pay – has helped make the paper profitable in a challenging digital marketplace. Most other publishers have since, of necessity, adopted some version of the same approach.

Confidence in the value of good journalism and commitment to producing it underpinned the *Times* paywall decision. The same confidence and commitment run through the three editorships documented in this volume.

John Walter, in starting *The Daily Universal Register*, explained that "like a well-covered table, it should contain something suited to every palate", including politics, foreign affairs, matters of trade, legal trials, advertisements and "amusements". Walter reserved the right of the newspaper "to censure or applaud either [political party]" and to cover contending issues with respectful "fair argument". The range of "amusements" may have grown beyond Walter's imagining to embrace everything from sudoku to a weekly football supplement (both introduced under Thomson) but the pages that follow show how coverage of business, politics, the law and foreign affairs remain *Times* strengths as they have always been.

As *The Times* celebrated its bicentenary in 1984, a year or two pre-Wapping and several decades pre-internet, the editor Charles Douglas-Home looked forward with some trepidation. "The coming revolution in information technology is a potential threat to newspapers as well as an opportunity," he wrote. Nonetheless, whatever the threats and however seductive the opportunities, Douglas-Home was clear that "they should not so preoccupy us that they lift our attention from the main aim, which is to produce an excellent paper every day, much as our predecessors have done for the past 200 years".

What that meant in practice for Douglas-Home was "embracing a constituency of readership which has some sense of community about it and some almost subliminal connection with the writers and editors on the paper's staff, which is the living organism". The three editors whose work is documented here were doing much the same in a very different world. This book shows how the "living organism" of *The Times* has survived – and continues to thrive – well into the 21st century.

SECTION ONE

ROBERT THOMSON

2002 to 2007

CHAPTER ONE

On the map, Torrumbarry is hard to find, a mere dot on the south bank of the immense Murray River, which bisects southeastern Australia. The town (population around 257) is about 16 miles west of the traditional river port of Echuca, where paddle steamers docked in the 19th-century boom times, before being made redundant by the railway network emerging from Melbourne, 133 miles to the south. In 1961, when Robert Thomson was born, Torrumbarry was the epitome of a small bush town with a typical bush pub, managed by his parents, Jim and Gen, and frequented by local farmers and labourers and travellers, who somehow found themselves thirsty in the middle of nowhere. The family eventually meandered its way to central Melbourne, via rural Fosterville and Bendigo, with his father far more proud of his part-Italian maternal heritage than that of "Thomson". Jim's alcoholic father abandoned his mother, who was half-Italian, a quarter Chinese and a quarter Maori, while Gen was the clever girl in a large Irish-Australian family, the Gaffys. Jim held a succession of jobs of varying duration – collecting payments for the local milkman, driving a food delivery truck and distributing parcels for a regional post office – but his longest stint was as a proofreader for *The Age*, one of the two morning newspapers in Melbourne. Gen, meanwhile, was the rock of the family, raising three sons and working as a bookkeeper, ensuring that there was a consistent flow of money, as her autodidact husband was increasingly gripped by a chronic gambling addiction. The proofreader position meant that there was always a newspaper on the dining table, and Robert read avidly and became fascinated by current affairs. At 17, the media connection was formally made, when Robert became a "copy boy" at *The Herald*, then an afternoon broadsheet newspaper in Melbourne – the "copy boy" and "copy girl" posts were the lowest form of journalistic life, given to promising candidates who missed out on a formal cadetship. They spent much of their first year making tea, buying sandwiches for the real reporters and furnishing milkshakes for those who wanted to line their stomachs ahead of evening sessions at the pub. It was the first step on a remarkable media journey around the globe. Twenty-three years later, the boy from the bush became the editor of *The Times* of London.

"Robert is the ideal candidate," declared Rupert Murdoch, appointing the sixth editor since he had bought *The Times* in 1981. Thomson in his turn said that it was "the best job in world journalism". Murdoch had not only chosen the first non-British editor of *The Times*, but, coincidentally, they shared a birthday, March 11, albeit 30 years apart. Thomson's wife, Ping Wang, was Chinese-born, as was Wendi Deng, to whom Murdoch was married at the time, though the two women had met only once ahead of the appointment. And *The Herald*, Thomson's first paper, was where Sir Keith Murdoch, Rupert's father, had laid the foundations of the family media empire. Murdoch-watchers also noted that Thomson had just lost a tussle for the editorship of *The Financial Times* when approached by Murdoch, who had a knack for finding clever, motivated people with a point to prove. Apart from the personal journey, it was a pivotal moment for media, with the rapid rise of digital platforms and crucial arguments over strategy that would ultimately determine the fate of newspapers, many of which have since succumbed.

When Thomson joined *The Herald* in 1979 other cadets had not thought much of his prospects, according to one of his contemporaries (Mark Baker, Australian Media Hall of Fame). He was tall and quiet, wry rather than rowdy. He lacked the social and journalistic connections that had assisted many of his more polished contemporaries. Editors recognised his talents, however. Within six years, he was Beijing correspondent for the rival *The Sydney Morning Herald*, popularly known as the SMH. That posting brought with it a commitment to file stories for *The Financial Times* (FT), which in late 1988 made him, aged only 27, a correspondent in its Tokyo bureau. To the surprise of many Australian colleagues, Thomson had turned down a seemingly far more prestigious post as Washington correspondent of the SMH to become the third-ranked FT journalist in Japan. He had an instinct that he would eventually work in the US, and he thought the chance to learn about a different culture with a focus on business journalism was more compelling.

As the Tiananmen Square democracy protests erupted, the FT sent him back to China, and Thomson was able to use his connections in the Tokyo embassy to get a rare visa at short notice. And when the Chinese Communist Party sent the army into Tiananmen Square in Beijing on the night of June 4, 1989, to crush pro-democracy demonstrators, Thomson rescued Jonathan Mirsky, an American journalist working for the UK's *The Observer*, who would later report for *The Times*. Mirsky was in the square when troops opened fire on the crowd and started attacking protesters. He was grabbed by soldiers and beaten. Struggling to stay on his feet and fearing that he would be shot, he was clinging to a balustrade when he was spotted by Thomson, who ran towards Mirsky to rescue him from the deadly mayhem. Thomson, who barely knew Mirsky, seized him and hustled him away to the safety of the Beijing Hotel before returning to the square, where he was one of few journalists who actually witnessed the final crushing of the democracy movement.

After covering the tragedy of Tiananmen, Thomson returned to Tokyo and charted the extraordinary rise and gradual decline of the Japanese economy in what were known as "The Bubble Years". At that time, he was diagnosed with a rare form of inflammatory arthritis, ankylosing spondylitis, that calcifies and stiffens the spine and causes a stoop. Sebastian Mallaby, then a Japan correspondent for *The Economist*, said that this added to his allure: "He has a kind of sweet humour. Some people are funny in a cutting way. He managed to be funny but never nasty. You can understand why he stood out to many bosses, including Rupert Murdoch. He has magic dust, which comes from being a self-made guy from a modest Australian background who has this physical stiffness yet is very comfortable."

One of the notable traits of Thomson's character is a lateral wit, a quirky sense of humour: *True Fiction*, published in 1998, is a collection of amusing, ironic, satirical pieces from the *Weekend FT*, including several by him. Thomson edited the collection and wrote a short introduction that confessed that the writing had "a fig leaf of truth, and that's a fact". Another key to understanding Thomson is a Japanese concept: the contrast between *tatemae* (the behaviour and opinions one displays in public) and *honne* (one's true feelings and desires). Thomson is widely read on Japanese society and history. He describes his Japanese as "conversational"; having spent five years in Japan with consistent language, he could read the business paper, *The Nihon Keizai Shimbun*, by the time he left Tokyo and deliver a shortish, mundane speech in Japanese. His Mandarin Chinese is "not quite conversational" and he was entirely dependent on an interpreter when he first went to China, not having been a sinologist by trade.

After five years in Tokyo, Thomson was called to London in 1994 to become the FT's foreign news editor and then editor of the weekend edition. In the former post, he managed the FT's extensive network of correspondents, commissioning stories and overseeing page layout, rewriting and headlines. He had spent almost a year as a caption writer at *The Herald*, which had helped him develop skills in brevity and precision that were useful in the concise approach of the FT. That period was also crucial in forcing Thomson to better understand parts of the world where he had no exposure, in particular Africa and Latin America. The period at the weekend paper was his first experience of directly marketing and remaking a traditional product. Thomson changed the masthead from *Financial Times* to *FT* and oversaw a redesign of the weekend section and the launch of the *How to Spend It* magazine, expanding on the section created by Lucia van der Post, the daughter of Laurens. The logic behind those image changes was that the FT on Saturday had a different personality and that character needed to be reflected and projected clearly on the front page. The result of the overhaul was that the *Weekend FT* became the fastest-growing of all UK newspapers during that two-year period.

In 1998, Thomson was tasked with leading the FT's ambitious US expansion, both in print and digitally through FT.com. Richard Lambert, the paper's editor-in-chief, had already spent a year paving the way for the expansion, and Thomson rapidly expanded the editorial staff, building a New York editing desk that handled stories for the distinct US edition and the website. The New York editorial team rose from six staff to close to sixty, all hired by Thomson, who also appointed correspondents in Atlanta and Houston, among other regional centres. US print sales rose from just over 35,000 to around 150,000 and the FT was matching and beating the much larger *Wall Street Journal* (WSJ) in generating business scoops. Thomson and the WSJ editors were on friendly terms and even played softball matches, which the WSJ inevitably won comfortably – those editorial connections would prove to be crucial when Rupert Murdoch made his bid to acquire Dow Jones in late 2007. Murdoch took close notice of the FT's rise, according to Richard Lambert. "Robert did a lot of hiring and a lot of flag-waving," Lambert said. "Rupert was very interested in what we were doing and rang me a couple of times. He certainly would have watched what Robert did in expanding the paper."

Lambert was on the brink of retirement after ten years in the job, and by then Thomson had achieved enough to see himself as a natural successor as editor-in-chief: he was confident that he knew what the FT needed in its contemporary leadership and that his digital experience would be crucial in building the FT's global reach. But, instead, in October 2001, the Pearson Board chose Andrew Gowers, a Londoner and Cambridge graduate who ran the FT's German edition in Hamburg and had previously been a talented foreign editor. Unlike Gowers, Thomson had not actively campaigned to succeed Lambert, having been told by FT executives that his record spoke for itself. "But there were clearly concerns," he remembered. "I was an outsider. I would have been the first foreigner. I wasn't Oxbridge. My politics were centrist rather than liberal. Andrew was obviously a very capable journalist and a brilliant writer, but, without being arrogant, I thought that I was better qualified. A couple of years later, a Pearson executive told me quietly that they had made an unfortunate mistake."

After this rebuff, Thomson decided to see what other offers might surface and discreetly put himself on the market. Soon he was juggling job offers, including business editor of *The New York Times* and a top editorial post at CNBC, the American business news channel. Meanwhile, the FT offered a significant increase in salary and suggested that he develop an Asian print and digital edition in a similar way to his work in the United States. A return to Asia had genuine appeal to Thomson, given his background and his perception of the region's potential, but the most fascinating prospect was an invitation to edit *The Times*. Murdoch said that he chased Thomson down quickly – "three meetings and it was done".

In an interview a year later with the Wapping staff newspaper *The News* (April 2003, issue 181), Thomson talked about his first day at work, March 6, 2002, just under a week before his 41st birthday. As he sat on the sofa outside the editor's office, he was almost unnoticed by the paper's early-morning staff. He straightened his narrow tie and took a few deep breaths to get his bearings and compose himself. He recalled:

"As I looked up at the brass plate on the door which reads 'Times Editor' I had a moment of reckoning as the enormity and prestige of the job suddenly hit me. I was almost reluctant to walk into the office because I knew the moment I crossed the threshold I would inherit an extraordinary tradition, a paper in very good health and an enormous responsibility – not only for the paper and the people who work on it, but also for quality journalism. I knew *The Times* was a great newspaper before I arrived but the thing that has so struck me [one year on] is the level of passion, commitment and expertise of the journalists and others who work on it. They genuinely believe in the paper and that is obvious every day in both the quality and quantity of what we do. It will take a few more years to get the paper where I want it to be but we are heading in that direction. That's not to say there won't be a couple of bumps along the way, but I am confident in the plan I have.

There were certainly bumps. Thomson had taken over at a challenging time. The digital challenge was rising by the day. By early 2002 sales had slipped to about 700,000, from 821,000 in 1997, when there was heavy discounting on cover price, while the paper's main rival, *The Daily Telegraph*, continued to sell more than a million copies a day. Sharp reductions in advertising revenue – suffered by many media organisations after the 9/11 attacks in America in September 2001 – had also intensified the financial pressure. Within a week of his appointment Thomson was presented with a request from Clive Milner, managing director of Times Newspapers Ltd, to cut his 2002–03 budget by 7 per cent. Looking back 20 years later, Thomson said he had not been particularly fazed. He worked well with Milner and with the amiable, canny, honourable Les Hinton, who was overseeing News UK. His experience working closely with commercial teams at the *Weekend FT* and with the FT in America, and his background as a business journalist, meant that he had an understanding of the commercial imperatives.

Given that background, Thomson was instinctively sympathetic to the business executives, whom he felt did much of the heavy lifting without the social prestige of the journalists – journalistic hubris was not a vice that Thomson respected. As at the FT, Thomson was interested in commercial strategy and felt that newsrooms had to be modernised, but he was viscerally opposed to faddish business decisions. Some in management at the FT had wanted to dispense with the name FT.com and create a generic digital brand separate from the paper's core character – Thomson thought that an absurd devaluing of the FT brand and eventually won that argument. And, at *The Times*, there were already voices suggesting that Times Online be regarded as a separate company, which Thomson insisted was a betrayal of the paper's core identity. At the time, newspapers around the world were in upheaval, with some putting their digital teams in different buildings and considering separate stock market listings. Fortuitously, Thomson, as new editor, was given extra resources and leeway by Rupert Murdoch. He explained: "Rupert is always open to new ideas, and you have a period to prove yourself, so I didn't feel under intense budget pressure at the time. He is incredibly supportive of his journalists."

Thomson envisaged making the paper more contemporary. "We needed to make some changes to the design, to the look, the feel, the sort of subjects we were covering." He had a clear sense of a holistic package across the six publication days, and a pressing need to attract more young readers and more women. "We renovated every day of the week – we redesigned Times 2 [as T2] and increased business and international coverage," he said. The idea of new, separate sections was to give readers distinctive experiences, add value and take them "to a slightly different place and a different pace". It involved thinking about the paper's role in contemporary society and how to empathise with its current readers and develop empathy with new ones. Monday saw the addition of The Game, which focused on the emerging popularity of the Premier League, and used a combination of humorous writing and clever metrics to fashion a different type of sports writing. Thomson later used the same formula in creating the sports pages of *The Wall Street Journal*. There was a luxury Saturday magazine, *Luxx*, and a property section on Fridays, Bricks & Mortar, which again emphasised high-quality writing, quirky graphics and a distinct reading experience. Much of the visual appeal of the new sections was down to the innovative design of Tomaso Capuano, whom Thomson had lured across from *The Financial Times*, where he had designed the *How to Spend It* magazine.

Thomson considered *The Times* to be as close to being a journal of record as it could be "and still is at a time when journalism is being tossed by the narrative of news rather than the news itself . . . I thought that having strong and diverse opinions on the opinion pages combined with reporting that was as factual as possible was a bit of a novelty in itself". Politically, the paper had been in conflict with the Conservative Party in preceding years, and Thomson thought that the mutual hostility had to be brought to an end. "That didn't mean unnecessarily favourable coverage but it did mean ending various legal conflicts and ensuring that we had the objective of being objective in our political writing. We could not be seen as unquestioning supporters of the Blair Labour government, fashionable as that government happened to be at the time." Twenty years on, when the print heyday of his *Times* editorship had given way to the primacy of Times Online, Thomson found the paper still very well put together, with a carefully crafted flow and rhythm. "It's succinct, concise, unpredictable – I mean predictable in its reliability and its integrity but unpredictable in what you find on the next page." He added that, like *The Sun*, *The Times* exemplified "the craft of papers for different demographics, and there is an art to that craft".

Often described as enigmatic, Thomson was in fact more watchful than inscrutable. A degree of detachment was essential in a journalist, he felt, and especially in an editor. "Journalists have to cultivate contacts," he said:

> "It's crucial as a means of getting information that could be the foundation of a scoop or of insights to enlighten readers. Cultivation does not mean being co-opted or compromised. Journalists, including editors, are conduits for delivering information and insight and judgment to the public, so having a sense of the personality and psychology of those in power is a potential advantage. Some journalists do mistake that privileged access for friendship as do some political leaders, but it is very difficult for an editor to have actual friends in government. I've always aimed to have a wide range of contacts, but presumed that none could really be a friend. It's easier for an editor to do his/her job efficiently and purposefully if friendless. Actually an editor also cannot be close friends with the journalists on his/her paper as it inevitably creates the impression of favouritism. There are, hopefully, strong, vibrant professional relationships, which, later in life, become personal but not in the newsroom. Newspapers should be the ultimate meritocracy – the best story on the day must prevail. Friendship is no foundation for news judgment.

When he started at *The Times*, Thomson operated from an apartment in the Athenaeum Hotel in Piccadilly and remained late at night in the office. His wife, Ping Wang, had just had their second son, Jack, and had remained in New York for the moment with their other son, Luke. Thomson spent many evenings sitting behind the backbench simply observing the night editors' modus operandi.

He listened more than he talked. John Wellman, home news editor, observed that it was possible to emerge from his morning news conference no wiser about his views on the news schedules than before. Thomson said he gave colleagues a good amount of autonomy: "I get involved in things when I feel I need to. But with such a complex organism it can't just be Thomson by diktat.". His calm demeanour could be deceptive; although he described himself as "not very loud except when I have to be professionally", there would be occasional flare-ups, but never public personal castigations in the newsroom. He was fiercely proud of the people at *The Times*, "proud of the paper and proud of the effort of so many individuals who go to make up the paper each day".

That calmness also belies a fierce and relentless competitive streak, and Thomson's initial focus included beating the FT. The battle between him and Gowers was personal and inventive, even though the two remained friends in succeeding years. Ken Auletta wrote in *The New Yorker* (April 4, 2011): "A van turned up outside the FT's offices in London with a sign saying 'Buy *The Times*. *The Times* is the best business newspaper in England.' It drove Gowers nuts." The FT's advertising slogan since 1986 had been "No FT . . . no comment". Thomson responded with "No FT . . . no problem". He also set about poaching staff from his old paper, declaring: "There are a great many good journalists at the FT and we will hire them all eventually." Among his phalanx of recruits were Emma Tucker, later editor of *The Sunday Times* and *The Wall Street Journal*; the now distinguished author Sathnam Sanghera, "who brought real emotional intelligence to business"; James Harding, the future *Times* editor, who joined as business editor; Gerry Baker ("a brilliant writer with a formidable intellect"), also a future editor of *The Wall Street Journal*; Ashling O'Connor, the FT Media writer who became one of the first journalists to cover the business of sport; the aforementioned Tomaso Capuano ("a design genius"), who came as art director; and Anne Spackman ("a savvy property journalist and an even better leader"), who launched Bricks & Mortar. The astute Camilla Cavendish became a *Times* columnist and leader writer, while Richard Lambert, the former FT editor, even wrote a column for the business pages. Anoushka Healy arrived as editorial communications director and later became chief strategy officer of News Corp and oversaw the crucial negotiations with Google, Facebook and Apple. Looking back, he didn't think there was anyone he particularly wanted to recruit from the FT who didn't join *The Times* – he joked that he had taken only their best people. They were drawn to *The Times*, he said, not as a personal favour to him but by a perception of what the paper could be and the impact they could have. When he moved to the WSJ, Thomson again went on a hiring spree of FT journalists, including a team, led by the thoughtful Thorold Barker, from the august Lex column to write for the rival, recast Heard on the Street.

As editor, Thomson wrote occasional signed commentaries on topics with which he felt comfortable, such as economics and China, but did not trumpet them. A comment piece headlined "Inscrutable Mr Hu may be Tony Blair in disguise", marking the highly significant transition from Jiang Zemin to Hu Jintao as general secretary of the Chinese Communist Party in November 2002, was not flagged up on page 1 or even in the page 2 What's Important index. It appeared on page 18 and carried a note at the end: "The author is editor of *The Times*". None of the other bylines on the page – William Rees-Mogg, Ann Widdecombe or Tim Hames – had to be so amplified. Thomson felt that "excessive ego is inappropriate for an editor . . . I am allergic to the self-aggrandising stuff".

Thomson recalled deferring somewhat to his deputy, Ben Preston, and the news desk team on human interest crime stories, because he had no background in UK general news when he arrived. "In retrospect, I would certainly cover those stories. Ben just had a much better feel for the ebb and flow of general news. Ultimately, my instinct was to include more foreign and business news, and be the best in the land on political coverage. Preston, for his part, thinks the editor's big set-piece interviews with world leaders in politics and business were one of his defining characteristics. "Thomson made *The Times* one of those global newspapers and he made sure it was outward looking. He did that by personal example – people were thrilled that they had a working editor who was going off and opening doors to presidents and important people and then doing interviews alongside correspondents – even though he wrote most of them. It gave the paper a shot of self-confidence. He was very aware that he was an ambassador for the paper, both for individual readers and presidents." Behind Thomson's push for business news was not just competition with the FT, but a realisation that a higher, trusted profile in the business community was commercially beneficial at a time of increasing competition with digital sources.

CHAPTER TWO

In Thomson's first year, amidst the day-to-day flow of breaking news, two extraordinary stories landed on his desk: a tabloid-beating scoop and a build-up to war. In great secrecy, Brian MacArthur, an experienced *Times* executive adored by the publishing world, had learnt that a sensational political diary was on the market. Written by Edwina Currie, a former high-profile Tory health minister, the diary revealed that she had had a lengthy and passionate affair with John Major, a politician the public had generally presumed was passion-free. Their frisky relationship had started when she was a backbencher and he was a whip in Margaret Thatcher's government; both were married at the time. Currie had since left politics. Major had become prime minister, serving from 1990 to 1997. It was the great political scoop of 2002 with an extra serving of spicy sauce. Thomson snapped up the rights to publish diary extracts for £75,000. Tabloid and mid-market rivals would have bid much more, had they known, but MacArthur cannily emphasised the respectability of *The Times* in convincing the publishers that money wasn't everything when it came to serialising a book that other titles might exploit shamelessly and salaciously. They also knew that they could trust MacArthur to keep a secret while the book was prepared for publication. He was, Thomson said, "a trusted person in the literary world who would keep a confidence. It wouldn't have happened without him – he came to me with the idea."

Only a tight circle was in on the secret, as MacArthur explained in his Paper Round column (October 4, 2002). Jonathan Lloyd, managing director of Curtis Brown and Currie's agent, had known for a year. Alan Samson, Currie's editor at Little, Brown, had read the diary in January 2002. Ursula Mackenzie, Little, Brown's publisher and David Young, its chief executive, had been aware since May. MacArthur had struck the serial deal in August. At *The Times*, the loop had to be widened: Pat Burge, an in-house lawyer, had to draw up a contract. Andrew Mullins, marketing director, had to be told. A date was set for Ginny Dougary to interview Currie. Sandra Parsons, Dougary's editor at Times 2, also had to know, as did Bob Kirwin, the picture editor, and Chris Harris, the photographer. Barry Turner, the serial editor, had to select the most pertinent extracts, and Trevor Jones, the adept circulation manager, was involved in overseeing the printing and distribution logistics.

Thomson told one executive the story was so fantastic that if he said a word about it to anyone he would have to kill him. When Thomson wanted to impose discipline, it was clear to all around that there would be severe consequences for any breach of trust, no matter how amiable the editor may have, at times, appeared. There was a real risk that if there was a leak, Major would seek an injunction to block publication of both the serialisation and the book on privacy grounds. If he did so, *The Times* would have to pay the full cost of the serialisation deal in compensation to Little, Brown. Major still had to be asked for a comment, however. Pulling off the coup meant putting Currie's claim to him late enough to minimise the chances of an injunction but early enough to deal with an outright denial.

Publication of the diary extracts was set for Saturday, September 28. The task of approaching Major was handed to Philip Webster, the political editor, who wrote later in his memoir, *Inside Story*, about his increasingly desperate efforts to raise the former prime minister. He started early on the evening of Friday, September 27, and was told Major was in a meeting. Webster reluctantly gave a summary of the allegations to Major's office to be passed on to him. By then it was 6.30pm. The security was so tight that Simon Pearson, the joint executive editor, and his backbench were putting together Saturday's news pages completely oblivious to what was going on behind their backs. Their first edition had a story about Jeffrey Archer stripped across the top of page 1. They were unaware that this was a spoof to mislead competitors, that the full page ads for Curry's electrical stores on pages 4 and 5 were a bravura joke, and that upstairs in the *Times* building Christopher McKane, the other executive editor, and David Driver, head of design, had been working in a secret room laying out and subbing a second edition front page carrying the Edwina Currie scoop and the two pages of the Dougary interview with her.

The first edition went to press with still no word from Major. At last, just after 9.30pm, he issued a statement confirming "the one event in my life of which I am the most ashamed". It turned out that he was in Chicago. Fortunately he sent his statement only to *The Times*; if he had sent it to the Press Association for general distribution, as more vengeful politicians might have done, all the other papers would have got the story. Once Webster had inserted Major's statement into the Currie splash, the new front page and pages 2, 4, 5 and the leader page were sent to press. Ben Preston oversaw the flipping of editions and the presses were running again by 9.36pm. Only 18,000 copies of the spoof had been printed and nearly 650,000 with the Currie story were circulated over most of the country. The headline was simple and restrained: "Edwina Currie's diaries disclose her four-year affair with John Major." The puff accompanying it was more eye-catching: "Do you still love him? That's difficult . . ."

A leader, "Time and Truth" (Saturday, September 28), presented the public interest case for publishing. It said the diaries gave an intimate and telling perspective on the practice of power in British politics. Their interest went beyond mere curiosity and compelled a reassessment of Major and his premiership. His later years in office had been pockmarked by scandals. An ill-fated "Back to Basics" campaign had promised a return to traditional Tory standards with a focus on family values, but distrust of the government intensified and contributed to the heavy electoral defeat of the Conservatives by Tony Blair's modernised "New Labour" party in 1997. The revelation of Major's own adulterous affair before he was prime minister with a colleague who had remained a candidate for ministerial preferment after he entered No 10 "places the atmosphere of the era in a new light". The diaries would give readers "a deeper understanding of the conflicts, strains and tensions which eventually brought Conservatism to humiliating defeat and haunt it still".

National newspapers used to have couriers in their opposition's press halls ready to collect early editions and rush them back to the office, where newsdesks would look for missed stories and lift them for their own pages. That night the first-edition spoof fooled most of them, but the fleet-footed *Sun* and *Daily Mirror* managed to get the Currie story into their last editions. Piers Morgan, editor of the *Mirror*, recalled being woken up at 2am by his news desk with the classic words: "Are you sitting down?" Jaws had dropped all over Fleet Street. It was, as Morgan said, a story to rate with Elvis Dead and Man on the Moon. Not all *Times* readers were amused. Frances Stott, writing to the editor from Devizes in Wiltshire, was outraged that a "supposedly serious, responsible broadsheet newspaper" had published Currie's diaries and profited from them. Others wrote in a similar vein, but Thomson had no regrets. He believed that the story, far from being tawdry and inappropriate, was a fascinating political diary that revealed an unexpected side of the former prime minister's character and the contradiction between public utterances and actual behaviour.

The Currie and Major infelicities proved to be a diversion from a weightier matter dominating the news that year: the build-up to war in Iraq. This looming conflict had its roots in the "war on terror" declared by President George W Bush after al-Qaeda's 9/11 attacks in America in which nearly 3,000 people had been killed. Having initially hammered al-Qaeda and the Taliban in Afghanistan, Bush had turned his attention to Saddam Hussein. The Iraqi president had a long history of murdering his own people and defying the international order. His invasion of neighbouring Kuwait in 1990 had led to the first Gulf War, in which his army was routed by America with the support of Britain, but he had remained in power and, for more than a decade, had defied western attempts to constrain him through United Nations sanctions.

Bush wanted to finish the job by invading Iraq. In the absence of evidence that Saddam had conspired in 9/11, the potential *casus belli* was his suspected possession of weapons of mass destruction (WMD) in breach of UN sanctions. Tony Blair, who had committed British troops to Bush's Afghan campaign, supported the Iraq venture. On Tuesday, September 24, four days before the Currie extracts appeared in *The Times*, parliament was recalled at Westminster to discuss a dossier entitled "Iraq's Weapons of Mass Destruction – The Assessment of the British Government". It included sections on chemical, biological, nuclear and missile programmes, and on UN inspectors' attempts to find them. It was Blair's case for war. In a foreword he wrote: "The document discloses that [Saddam's] military planning allows for some of the WMD to be ready within 45 minutes of an order to use them."

Opinion on this September Dossier was divided. In parliament, 56 Labour MPs voted against Blair's Iraq policy and *The Times* published a column by Simon Jenkins, the former editor, dismissing the dossier as an "act of desperation". Saddam, he wrote, had become "the object of a Third Crusade in the holy war on terror". Meanwhile, a *Times* leader called on Saddam to allow UN weapons inspectors immediate and unconditional access to facilities within Iraq. It added that the chances were that he would refuse, or that he would allow inspectors in and obstruct them. By his willingness or not to embrace the inspectors, Saddam would prove whether he could change the character of his regime or whether regime change by other means was needed. The clear message was that, given the intensifying international pressure, Saddam Hussein's destiny was in his own hands. He had repeatedly used chemical weapons (mustard gas, tabun and sarin) during the Iran–Iraq war (1980–88) and the onus was on him to provide hard evidence that those weapons were destroyed.

The Times continued to support Blair while he sought to overcome doubters by going to the UN, where in November the Security Council passed Resolution 1441 giving Saddam "a final opportunity" to comply with his disarmament obligations or face "serious consequences". Saddam let in the weapons inspectors, who found nothing of note, prompting official claims that he had taken evasive action by hiding his arsenal. A new British dossier issued to journalists in early February 2003 by Alastair Campbell, Blair's communications director, asserted that "prohibited materials" were being hidden "beneath hospitals and even mosques". Investigative journalists subsequently discovered that key elements of this dossier had been cobbled together by junior Downing Street staff or copied from work by a 29-year-old Iraqi-American academic, but the progress to conflict proved unstoppable – while resistance to it grew.

On February 15, *The Times* estimated a million people took part in an anti-war demonstration in London, but the paper remained supportive of the prime minister. In a leader it said that Saddam had not produced as complete an audit of his arsenal as required. "The Security Council must now uphold Resolution 1441," it declared. "Mr Blair can contend with confidence that he has followed international law."

The Times also reported on the physical impact the stress was having on the prime minister. "I have never seen a man more burdened by power, more acutely conscious of the burden of responsibility, as he prepares to go to war, whatever may happen in the United Nations, the Labour Party or the country," Ben Macintyre wrote alongside a photograph by Jack Hill of a haggard premier. "His face is grey and thin. His hair has died from exhaustion. A bump has appeared on his forehead . . . His expression was that of a saint-martyr on a stained glass window: ascetic, drained and brittle. He is no longer living on plaudit and soundbite but on raw adrenalin, self-belief and the knowledge that disaster and humiliation are as likely as the success that has always come so effortlessly. He is living in a place of trial and tension that he has never been to before."

An eight-column headline "War dawns on Iraq" ran across the front of a 4am edition of *The Times* on Thursday, March 20. This was the first of 23 consecutive days on which news from Iraq led the paper. Operation Iraqi Freedom initially involved a force of about 130,000 Americans with 46,000 British, 2,000 Australian and 194

Polish troops. A single leader that day, headlined "War and after", ran the full depth of the page. It explained the stance of *The Times* and, by definition, that of the editor. It described the inevitable costs and consequences of the tragic conflict, including civilian casualties and losses among Iraq's conscripted troops, who would be innocent victims. "Mr Blair is, though, right, to have taken the fateful step and initiated this campaign. He has sought with admirable resolve to work through the UN." *The Times* also consistently made clear that while planning for war was crucial, it was imperative that there be a coherent plan for postwar Iraq. President Bush had asserted that post-Saddam Iraq would be a "beacon of democracy", but that Middle Eastern precedent would not happen spontaneously.

The Times assigned 24 writers and photographers to the Iraq region. Two had almost comically contrasting wars. Chris Ayres, by his own self-deprecating admission a coward, saw more than enough frontline action in southern Iraq. Anthony Loyd, an action man in thrall to the highs of the battlefield, saw none. An early-morning phone call from Martin Fletcher, the foreign news editor, catapulted Ayres from Hollywood correspondent in Los Angeles to an "embed" with the US 2nd Battalion, 11th Marines, an artillery force known as the Long Distance Death Dealers who addressed each other as "Devil Dawgs". By the time he had had the order to CSMO (marine jargon for Clear Shit and Move Out) over the LOD (Line of Departure) in a Humvee with a broken door through which he almost fell at speed, he felt as though he had been at war for a year. On day seven, blasted by a sandstorm in the marshes of central Iraq, Ayres was the only *Times* reporter anywhere near the frontline and was certain that death was imminent. He had done his best for professional pride and the paper, but the battlefield was not for him. Ben Preston told him from London: "If you want to leave, no one's going to think less of you. You can say I ordered you out, if you want," and added: "It's your call. No one's going to second-guess you." When Ayres's Thuraya satphone was confiscated, allegedly because the Iraqis could trace its signals, his mind was made up and he asked for transport back to Kuwait City.

His finest hour had been his picture-bylined page 1 splash from al-Diwaniyah, about 90 miles south of Baghdad. Now it was back to the JW Marriott hotel for a bath followed by the Wagyu beef and a dozen Gulf prawns with lobster tail. He wrote a long T2 confessional piece, headlined "I made my excuses and left" (April

11, 2003) and expanded it into his book *War Reporting for Cowards*, an open account of his emotions that would be a vivid parody of conflict journalism if it were not also a chronicle of life and death.

Anthony Loyd had fought in the first Gulf War as a soldier with the Royal Green Jackets when he was 24, having joined up to "fulfil his dreams of glory". He had subsequently reported for *The Times* from Kosovo in 1999, from Sierra Leone and from Afghanistan, his favourite country and people to cover. His frequent visa applications were supported by a list of "battle honours" that also included Northern Ireland and the Gulf as a soldier and Algeria, Albania, Bosnia, Croatia, Chechnya, Ethiopia, Kosovo, Kyrgyzstan, Liberia and Macedonia. With 18 years of war experience behind him, he was scornful of embedding and being spoon-fed by military press officers. Noting that the coalition's strategic plan involved a twin-front nutcracker squeeze on Baghdad from the north as well as the south, he headed north before the start of the war to wait for the US 4th Infantry Division, which was supposed to move through Turkey and into northern Iraq on its push to Baghdad.

Loyd was sure he had chosen the best jumping-off point when he reached his advance base in Sulaymaniyah, 230 miles by road from Baghdad. A few days before the invasion began he moved southwest to Chamchamal, populated by Kurds and shadowed by a ridgeline held by Iraqis. It was the gateway to the main road to Kirkuk and on to the capital. But for Loyd it was the road to nowhere. Turkey refused the Americans overland passage and the US 4th Infantry never materialised. "I might as well have been on Mars for all the relevance my situation had to the bigger picture," he wrote as news of the fall of Baghdad filtered through. The fall of Kirkuk was no consolation – a damp squib "like the shy squeak of a spinster's fart". The aftermath of the brief war was tumultuous and tragic. In Iraq, anarchy spread as it emerged that the US was unprepared for the task of running the country after removing its leadership, and the ideal of creating a democracy disintegrated in the dust.

In London, recriminations flew. Had *The Times* been too hasty in supporting the war? Tim Hames, chief leader writer at that time, felt that the paper had been overcommitted and was left exposed by the aftermath – but then, in fairness, most people were. *The Times* had not been a cheerleader for the invasion, Thomson said later. "We were very late on our judgment . . . It was a difficult decision and ultimately the way [the war] was handled did a lot of damage . . .

it wasn't just about the war, it was about what happened after the war. If you make the difficult decision to go to war and then, having won the war, you lose the war, that is a tragedy, particularly for the people of Iraq.".

As the pretext for the invasion started to unravel and no WMD were located in the months that followed, recriminations grew louder – as did the government's attempts to rebut them. In subsequent years, US troops found large caches of abandoned chemical weapons (*The New York Times*, October 14, 2014), but not the battle-ready armaments described by the British government. Peter Stothard, Thomson's immediate predecessor as editor, had been given access to Downing Street to follow the war from the prime minister's perspective. His eyewitness day-to-day account became a book, *Thirty Days*. In May, *The Times* magazine published extracts that included an arresting statement from Blair: he believed he would be called to account for the war before God, and could justify to his "maker" decisions that had led to hundreds of deaths. Ominously for Blair, however, late in May the BBC journalist Andrew Gilligan made an incendiary allegation against him on the *Today* programme. Gilligan claimed that, according to a well-placed source, the government's September Dossier, in which Blair had helped to build the case for war, had been "sexed up" by his spin doctor Alastair Campbell to include the prime minister's claim that Iraqi WMD could be prepared for firing in only 45 minutes. The spin doctor dismissed the allegation as chaff; but the story gained traction – with tragic consequences.

Blair and Campbell became ever more agitated as a vicious blame game broke out over who was responsible for the contents of the dossier. Discrediting Gilligan's story – which involved identifying the source – became an overriding imperative in Downing Street. *The Times* followed Campbell in pursuit of the source. On July 10, along with other newspapers, it named him as David Kelly, a British expert in biological weapons who had led several inspection missions in Iraq and had been advising the UK government. Kelly was summoned to appear before the parliamentary foreign affairs select committee at Westminster on July 15. He told the MPs he had helped to draft a background section of the dossier and he had discussed the 45-minute theory on a non-attributable basis with Gilligan, but he thought he could not have been Gilligan's main source as the broadcast story bore little relation to their discussion.

The MPs decided that he was not the source but, amid further claims and counterclaims, Kelly walked five miles to a beauty spot near his home in Oxfordshire where he was found dead on July 17 with a slit wrist and having taken an overdose of painkillers.

Kelly's MP, Robert Jackson, said the BBC had killed him as it should have confirmed the select committee's finding that he was not the source of the story. Tom Baldwin, assistant editor of *The Times*, who was known to have particularly intimate links with Labour and would himself become the party's director of communications in 2010, weighed in with an onslaught on Gilligan and the BBC in the Thunderer column. Baldwin wrote that he would choose Campbell over Gilligan on a question of trustworthiness. The foreign affairs select committee had found Gilligan unreliable, and just about everyone with any responsibility for the dossier had denied his claim. The BBC, however, "would not admit that the allegations were false", Baldwin wrote.

A *Times* leader said that Kelly "was a bit player in a conflict between two of the country's most powerful institutions. He was guilty of nothing more than lunching with a gung-ho journalist". In a statement the same day the BBC said Kelly had been the principal source of Gilligan's story; it had protected Kelly's anonymity but now, with his family's consent, wanted to end the speculation. *The Times*, in another leader, (July 22, 2003) considered that institutional flaws had been exposed at the BBC, adding: "An institution, whose function is, in part, to be the voice of the nation, has a duty to explain itself."

At Blair's request, Lord Hutton, a former Lord Chief Justice of Northern Ireland, held a judicial inquiry into the affair and concluded that Kelly had committed suicide because of a loss of self-esteem and the threat to his reputation. Blair was cleared of any "dishonourable, underhand or duplicitous" conduct in the lead-up to Kelly's death. Hutton also concluded that the government had not "sexed up" intelligence and that Gilligan's allegation broadcast by the BBC, that the government knew the 45-minute claim was false, was unfounded. Gavin Davies, the BBC chairman, and Greg Dyke, its director general, resigned. Gilligan had already gone. It was a pyrrhic victory for Campbell – he had also quit during the inquiry.

For some, the Kelly affair fuelled criticism that *The Times* was too close to No 10. Blair had won a second term in 2001 with the endorsement of *The Times*; the paper had supported the Iraq war;

it had attacked the BBC through Baldwin, a Campbell confidant; and Philip Webster, the political editor, also had a close working relationship with Campbell. Thomson felt that the political coverage had, at times, become too innately hostile to the Conservative Party and its recent leaders, including William Hague, who became a columnist at *The Times* two decades later. Following Thomson's direct outreach, an outstanding legal conflict with the former Tory party treasurer, Michael Ashcroft, was resolved and the Labour-leaning "Islington influence" waned.

Phil Webster was deftly diplomatic and, with Peter Riddell, was part of a duopoly that ran the parliamentary office of *The Times*. Riddell had briefly been the political editor before handing the reins over to Webster, who had covered Labour in opposition for a decade before the Blair election landslide of 1997 and was the obvious choice to cover the party in government. Riddell had stayed on as chief political commentator with an unrivalled network of contacts across the senior civil service. Webster and Riddell enjoyed what was in the main a friendly and productive partnership. The former was tiggerish, the latter more cautious. Each indulged in a judicious amount of teasing of the other but quickly closed ranks against upstart juniors and incursions from head office. For more than a decade they were a constant as others in the *Times* parliamentary office came and went. In the early autumn of 2006, Webster hurried back from interviewing Blair at Chequers, the prime minister's official residence, to play Riddell the tape. Both knew that the interview would trigger an explosion in the duopoly running Britain. Blair and his formidable chancellor of the exchequer, Gordon Brown.

Iraq had inflicted significant damage on Blair and he had been forced to say that his victorious general election campaign in 2005 – his third – would be his last as prime minister and party leader. The implication had been that the impatient Brown would take over at 10 Downing Street, but Blair's form of words had begged the question of when, precisely, he would quit. This unstable ambiguity lasted for a year but, as the party's annual conference approached in 2006, Brown's team stoked expectations that Blair would use the gathering to announce a departure timetable. Certainly Webster thought that's what he would hear from Blair when he was summoned to Chequers for the interview before the party conference. Instead, a defiant prime minister appeared determined to preserve his position. Using

The Times as his vehicle, Blair told his party to "stop obsessing" about the leadership and let him "get on with the job".

The interview was duly published (although not before a nervy moment when Webster and Riddell accidentally deleted a portion of the interview while playing back the tape). It was a potent front-page story and precipitated the final Brownite push to drive Blair from power. Blair had chosen to make his intervention in *The Times* because of its authority and trustworthiness. Sometimes political journalism is at its most devastating when providing space for politicians to be the authors of their own downfall. The strong reaction meant that Blair was not allowed to get on with the job and, on June 27, 2007, he bequeathed power to Brown.

Blair used his last major speech as prime minister (June 13, 2007) to castigate the British media, saying that it demolished reputations for commercial advantage. Sensationalism was subordinated to accuracy: "The fear of missing out means that today's media . . . hunts in a pack. In these modes it is like a feral beast, just tearing people and reputations to bits." He also defended his relationship with Rupert Murdoch, with whom he had had a dialogue since becoming opposition leader in 1994, saying that the relationship was necessary for a politician "in the real world". The speech prompted a *Times* leader asserting that Blair had conceded New Labour, in its early days, paid inordinate attention to the media, courting and assuaging it. He was not its victim: his attempts to use the media were at least as intense as his efforts to respond to its demands. The leader conceded, however, that his critique of the media conveyed harsh truths. The press should recognise that most politicians entered public life out of a sincere desire to improve the lives of their fellow citizens and that they often had to make decisions with less time and less information than they would wish: "None of us is perfect in this respect." Objectivity should always be the ambition of news. "The tendency of some so-called serious newspapers to act as viewspapers (a swipe at *The Independent*) would have a profoundly negative effect if universally followed . . . Intelligent readers are not fooled by an individual article or an individual politician, but if the traditional media exist as a separate, self-serving universe, then the distance from readers will grow and the size of the audience will shrink." Those words, personally crafted by Thomson, unfortunately, came to pass for many newspapers in many countries in succeeding years.

CHAPTER THREE

Robert Thomson was keen on sport, which was an almost obligatory part of working class life in Australia. His first love was Australian rules football, and he was signed by a professional club, St Kilda, just after starting life as a copyboy, but could not balance the two obligations, and subsequently played for pleasure at amateur level. His sport of choice in the UK was football and his team Arsenal, for which he had a faint, distant interest in his youth. In his first summer as editor of *The Times* he fervently embraced the sporting event of 2002, the FIFA World Cup in Japan and South Korea, both countries of great interest to him. He took to drifting into the sports department to chat and encouraged the editors to think creatively about sports writing and presentation. His instinct was that traditional sports coverage was hackneyed and lacking in imagination and vitality.

England's hopes were high. Eight thousand English fans, many without tickets, were expected to fly to Sapporo in Hokkaido, the most northern of Japan's main islands, for the crucial game against Argentina. Ian Cobain, one of the nine-strong squad covering the tournament for *The Times*, reported that the Japanese authorities, worried about bad behaviour, planned to detain up to 630 fans on a converted ferry, the Sunflo.

Bill Bryson – the American-born former *Times* business news sub-editor whose book about Britain had made him a renowned author – was an inspired addition to the World Cup reporting team by Keith Blackmore, the sports editor. He had form of sorts as a sportswriter, having "covered" the Sydney Olympic Games of 2000 in his inimitable way, marvelling at an apparatus that could fill 32 beer glasses in seconds and observing that the Australians would rather win an Olympic gold medal than a Nobel prize. In an eight-page special section in *The Times* on May 31, previewing the tournament, Bryson answered readers' questions from his base in Seoul. One suggested that, if the first football match he had ever attended was the England–Korea friendly a few days ago, this was a "serious omission for someone who writes cultural observations about the countries he lives in". "Yes," agreed Bryson, "and what's more, I've still never been to a cricket match." Why had he become involved in the World Cup? Simply because some nice people at *The Times* invited him to go: he had accepted "for obvious reasons".

He did, however, file a more substantial piece reminiscing about half-forgotten names from football's glory days – the Dutch back line of Phlegm, Floss, Snorkel and Kerfuffle; the brooding giant Uruguay centre forward Cyclops, his career tragically cut short by a mistimed header; the lamentable 1928 cash-for-tango-lessons scandal in Buenos Aires. When he took to the streets he found Seoul abuzz with anticipation. Once he had evaded the motorists who "accelerate to a halt", he had become enchanted by Seoul, the charming people, the absence of tipping and the "unceasingly splendid" food, like Chinese cuisine but with aspirations to be a blowtorch. The word "football" appeared in the last paragraph (Saturday, June 1).

Bryson then moved on to Tokyo and, after wandering for hours, reached the suburb of Saitama, where England drew 1–1 with Sweden. He admired England's "curious determination to keep the outcome as exciting as possible until the final whistle. It was just dazzling. I am giddy yet." A June heatwave overcame him. Sweating and bedraggled, he asked at the front desk of his smart hotel in one of most efficient and orderly cities in the world if he could borrow an iron for his crumpled clothes. The receptionist said he would ask housekeeping but looked doubtful. Later, a note was slipped under his door which said: "We are so sorry mistake information. We don't have any iron. Other guest use now. If they finished use iron. We let you." After visiting Ueno Park in the centre of Tokyo, where hundreds of victims of the recession were living in immaculately tidy cardboard boxes, with polished shoes and pressed clothes, he returned to the hotel to find an iron and a board with a note. "We find for you iron. Enjoy please!"

"I went straight to work in my last clean shirt. If I say so myself, I am looking awfully sharp now. I can't wait to see what the guys in the park make of me," Bryson reported.

His distinctly football-light Notes From the World Cup ended on the eve of England's most important game: the quarter-final against Brazil. It was not that he had lost interest: his son was getting married in Chicago and his presence and his chequebook were needed there.

> It has been worth it all, the constant travel, the anonymous hotels, the 27 straight days of living on noodles and hedge clippings, the scary toilets, the pain of watching Germany advance to the quarter-finals . . . The only hooliganism has

been by Japanese fans and it was only hooliganism of a mild Japanese sort ... Soon, I suppose, the 2002 World Cup will feel almost as if it never happened. It's already beginning to feel a bit that way to me. But gosh, it was good while it lasted.

In his absence, Brazil knocked England out of the tournament on June 21. Cobain reported that, after the defeat, countless teenage Japanese girls in their David Beckham shirts "sat and sobbed, row after row of trembling little No 7s".

A *Times* leader the next day maintained that there was much to be learnt from the World Cup experience. There had been worse moments in English history – the Roman Conquest, the Black Death, the Civil War, the fall of France in 1940 and virtually the whole of the 1970s, but there would be modest spinoffs. Collective understanding of the Far East should have been enhanced. But the Football Association needed to look at domestic arrangements – some players still bore the scars of 60 matches ending only a fortnight before the tournament. With more choir practice a roster of national songs could be devised. And for anyone who thought that it was only a game, the leader cited Bill Shankly, the former Liverpool manager: "Some people think football is a matter of life and death. I can assure them that it is much more serious than that."

Within weeks, *The Times* had a brand-new Monday supplement reporting and analysing football, The Game, which was launched on August 12. It promised to cover: "Every kick. Every pass. Every tackle. Every save. Every goal. Every Monday." There had been debate within *Times* staff over whether to create a supplement covering the fringe sports ignored by other newspapers, but Thomson was insistent that the paper and website cover the most popular sport more cleverly and compellingly than other newspapers. He was pleased with the sports team's work and told staff on launch day that it was "just a tad cool". Blackmore said it was replete with its own style and lexicon and "great fun". Features included a fantasy league competition with a first prize of £100,000. Continuing the self-consciously hyperbolic self-promotion, The Game claimed to give fans "two halves and a whole lot more", with "facts, figures, flair, fantasy and fun" – a nod to the editor's affection for alliteration. The first issue offered an exclusive interview with the Republic of Ireland's fiery former captain Roy Keane, who had walked out of the team's World Cup training base before the tournament after a furious verbal assault on the manager, Mick McCarthy. The cover was a graphic mugshot of a shaven-headed Keane headlined "Why I quit the World Cup" and the back page was the intimidating rear of said shaven head headlined "Game over". The two framed pages adorned the walls of Thomson's office.

Football was by far the most important sport in the battle for readers, and resources were devoted to the cause. Star writers included Tony Cascarino, Ken Bates, Matt Dickinson, Simon Barnes, Frank Skinner, Martin Samuel and Oliver Kay. Thomson also wanted an English footballer who could write for The Game. He insisted that the paper wouldn't pay for someone who would simply phone half-baked thoughts from the golf course or cede most of the task to a ghost writer. Blackmore discovered Aki Riihilati, of Crystal Palace. He was, in fact, Finnish and had a slight touch of English as a second language but his intellect and introspection were perfect for *The Times*. Blackmore had misgivings about introducing him to the editor at a party for The Game but quickly discovered that they had hit it off and were discussing investing in the Japanese stock market – at which point he left them to it.

"Aki was writing incredibly candid reports about the team and insights about the various goings on and I thought this might get him into trouble," Thomson recalled. "I said: 'Aki, I think what you're doing is brilliant. You're a lovely writer, very thoughtful but very revealing and I hope we're not causing you any grief at Crystal Palace.' Aki smiled and replied: 'Robert, absolutely not, I can assure that there's no one else at Crystal Palace who reads *The Times*'".

The sports department proved a breeding ground for editorial talent. Jeremy Griffin, later to be executive editor, made his name as a creative football editor, driving The Game when it launched. Innovations included Sicknote, a column about common injuries, and Daniel Finkelstein's Fink Tank column, which used academic analysis of data to divine unreported trends – his column was the harbinger of a later obsession with sports metrics. When Griffin moved up to be deputy sports editor, he was succeeded as football editor by Craig Tregurtha, later managing editor of *The Times* and *Sunday Times*. He brought a former tabloid editor's eye for fun to the supplement, with a Spot the Pie competition, conceived in the

Old Rose pub up the road from the office in Wapping, in which a small delicacy was hidden in one of The Game's photographs. Hundreds of readers entered every week, hoping to win a month's supply of pies. Even when, as happened on at least one occasion, the picture editor forgot to include a pie, readers still wrote in with the certain belief they had seen a pasty in a smudge.

Soon the effort was being overseen by Tim Hallissey, a thoughtful, unflappable figure who took over after Blackmore, with his eye on the surging significance of digital publishing, became sport online editorial director. It was a time of large budgets, big-name columnists (Michael Owen, Jonny Wilkinson, Shane Warne and many more) and ample pagination. This allowed occasional special series that ran across a spread, such as on the greatest sports books or the best sports films, for which they enlisted the movie critic Barry Norman and held the judging at the Odeon in Leicester Square.

The sports department also had the luxury and advertising income to produce regular supplements to promote leading events, from the Six Nations rugby in the spring to the World Match Play golf in the autumn as well as a monthly Football Handbook, edited by Richard Whitehead. In 2004, Euan Blair, the prime minister's 20-year-old son, came to *The Times* on work experience and was handed to Whitehead, who set him the task of writing a headline on a feature to mark 40 years of the BBC's *Match of the Day*. Blair duly transliterated the programme's famous signature tune: "Der-der-der-der, der-der-der-der-der, der-der-der-der-der-der."

Cricket had its moments too. The visitor whom everyone at Wapping remembered best was Shane Warne, the legendary Australian leg spinner, who arrived at Wapping on the day before the deciding Fifth Test at the Oval between England and Australia in September 2005. England was ahead 2–1 in the series, with one match drawn, and only had to draw again to take the Ashes for the first time in 16 years. Warne was crucial to the Australian attack, but Thomson asked Blackmore if the bowler could pay a visit on the eve of the opening session. To Blackmore's surprise, Warne said he would come if his captain, Ricky Ponting, agreed. Thomson's driver took Blackmore to the hotel in Kensington where the Australians were staying. He had been there half an hour when Warne appeared and said: "Come on, quick, we've got to go, we've got to be back here in two hours."

Blackmore continued: "We jumped in the car and drove back to the office. He chatted with Robert and then walked round the staff. He went to T2, everywhere signing everything people put in front of him. He was very sweet and a terrible flirt with all the girls, who were thrilled." When he was prised away, Blackmore shepherded him to the street and Warne said: "I can't go for a minute, I'm gasping for a fag." At the time he was being paid by Nicorette for an anti-smoking campaign. Warne leant against the editor's car smoking and told Blackmore not to tell anyone. Blackmore replied: "I won't tell anyone about it – but look up there." The balconies overlooking the street were packed with *Times* staff waving as he smoked. The crucial match ended in another draw and England took the Ashes, but Warne was Australia's man of the series. His final haul of 40 wickets was an Australian record for a five-match series and a reminder that it was Australia every bit as much as England who had made this the best Ashes series of them all. *The Times* next day, Tuesday, September 13, carried ten pages of sport and the promise of a 24-page supplement to come. Design for most of this expanded sport coverage was done by Tomaso Capuano, who worked with Blackmore and Preston, a diehard Millwall fan and enthusiast who wanted to cover more than "in the eighth minute the forward came through and hit the post" – there should also be "the laughs and the jokes". Thomson said years later the original *Game* (he considers its originality has been somewhat diluted by competitors mimicking the innovations) sparkled with wit and vivid writing.

Innovation was not confined to the sport pages. On becoming editor, Thomson had inherited a reconfiguration of the paper codenamed Project X that was completed less than a month before he inherited the chair. Controversially, for traditionally minded readers, it positioned a new Register section between Business and Sport. This created space for a Letters overspill "debate" section, more room for obituaries and a new Lives Remembered feature. It was devised and edited by Ian Brunskill, who said his aim was to make it feel like it had always been there. Project X was also a feast for the technically minded. The main typeface was changed from Millennium, the digitised font which had been in use since 1991, to Times Classic. David Driver, head of design, and David Wadmore, his deputy, were delighted with the result. Classic, Driver said, had more character and its style was elegant (Brian MacArthur, *The Times*, February 15, 2002).

The detailed style guide for Classic ran to 38 pages: the new font's first objective was to improve legibility and it had been designed "to give a familiar appearance to the reader, retaining a 'Britishness' in the shapes of its characters."

This reorganisation was partly a byproduct of reverting to collect printing, which forced the paper into two broadsheet sections of equal pagination. Each section was printed separately and then collected together just before it came off the press. (Straight printing has the capacity for an uneven split of the sections.) The presses were capable of only 50 per cent colour, mainly on left hand pages and then only at the optimum pagination of 24 + 24. The relaunch issue of two 24-page sections therefore maximised the use of colour sites for both editorial and advertising purposes. The maximum section size was 32 pages, which could be further subdivided into 24 plus 8 and 24 plus 8 to accommodate special eight-page sections on events such as the budget.

At the end of the month George Brock, the managing editor, reported that he had seen 200 letters and emails from readers. Twenty approved of the changes and 180 were complaints, some of which were "the usual scattergun moans which react in barely coherent ways to any change at all". The largest category concerned the positioning of the Register. "Put obituaries back in *The Times* where they belong" was the refrain of older readers, who considered sport and business to be barely part of the paper proper. But even while complaining about the positioning of obituaries, some correspondents conceded that more was better. Brock's impression was that more people would get used to the change than would defect. He wrote thanking Dave Farey and Richard Dawson of HouseStyle, who had designed Times Classic: "The highest compliment that I can pay to our new typeface is to say that many people have noticed it but very few of them are quite sure what has changed. This seems to me to show that we have, with your help, hit the target at which we were aiming." In reality, much had changed and would go on changing.

CHAPTER FOUR

Early in 2003, Thomson was in Japan considering how to beef up reporting of a region that was personally important to him as well as to the paper. While he was away, George Brock was thinking about matters closer to home. Awaiting Thomson on his return to London were several proposals from Brock for persuading the "No 1 Reader in New York" (Murdoch) to step outside the "confining space of projects that are mostly low cost, low profit-or-loss and low risk". Among them was "a commuter/ urban/evening or morning edition which breaks the mould of the market". This became the blueprint for a project called Sputnik, which never got off the ground but turned out to be the launchpad for the transformation of *The Times*.

Sputnik was aimed at Ireland, where *The Times* had a problem that Brock's proposal might fix. *The Times* was perceived in Ireland as a British establishment newspaper and News International, its UK parent company, had been losing £3 million a year there. A new product was needed if the company was to compete in Ireland as effectively as in the UK. There was no Irish mid/upmarket tabloid, so Brock got to work on creating one in a closed room on the sixth floor at Wapping. The result was *The Irish Day*, a proposed 64-page tabloid with 33 per cent colour. It would use *Times* material and some stories from *The Sun*: it would be strong on aggregation and links from news stories to online. A full 64-page dummy was printed and, although *The Irish Day* was then shelved, it gave Thomson the confidence that a "squat product a little above square could be made to look half decent", according to Clive Milner.

Brock produced a discussion paper, "What Project Sputnik tells *The Times*", which proposed a "wittily distilled version of *The Times*" aimed at an untapped pool of potential readers in the UK. Keith Blackmore strongly supported this idea, but Thomson felt that a "distilled version" was not appropriate – *The Times* had to be *The Times*. He asked Brock to look at "longer term development of a smaller version of the paper more friendly to time-poor urban youngsters crammed in Tubes and trains". Thus Project Sputnik gave birth to Project Hancock, the transformation of *The Times* to a tabloid or "compact" format with a strong emphasis on commuter convenience.

It was not the first time a tabloid had been considered. Few traditional readers would have credited William Rees-Mogg, the seemingly conservative editor of *The Times* from 1967 to 1981, with advocating a tabloid, but, in fact, an experimental dummy was produced while he was in the chair. According to Brock, a dummy compact had also been printed under the editorship of Thomson's predecessor, Peter Stothard, when *The Times* had held back for fear of being accused of being "tabloid". It would turn out that that fear had been exaggerated and unfounded – the paper had failed to appreciate that attitudes had changed and that younger readers were unfazed by the smaller format.

The design budget for 2003 was heavily overspent as work on the compact/tabloid forged ahead that summer under a triumvirate that was to assume an unprecedented importance in the design development of *The Times*. David Driver, the design editor, and the ebullient David Wadmore, his deputy and associate design editor, complemented each other perfectly: it was fairly said and not disparagingly meant, that Driver would give you a Savile Row suit and "Waddie" a Hong Kong tailor's overnight garment. Tomaso Capuano, who had proved his tabloid skills on The Game, was described by Thomson as "too volatile" to work on deadline-driven daily news pages, but his creativity and temperament were well suited to conceptual ventures. Led by Anne Spackman, another of Thomson's recruits from the FT, the team produced dummies of two concepts – a compact version of *The Times* and a *Times Lite* aimed at younger readers. They worked from a secret room in the main News International building. "We had no tables, no chairs, no rulers, no pens, we actually did the first dummy on the floor and then we rummaged around and found some stuff," Spackman said.

The leap from concept to the real thing was almost immediate, spurred on by evidence that *The Independent*, which went compact in Greater London on September 30, was enjoying an immediate jump in circulation. Brock said later:

> I was in a car one day with Robert [Thomson] and he was clearly talking on the phone to Les Hinton [executive chairman of News International]. He put his hand over the phone and said, 'If I asked you to produce a compact version, could you do it in 13 days or a fortnight?' And the only thing you can ever say when you're asked that kind

of question is yes. Of course I didn't have the first idea how you could possibly complete something that big. And Robert says: 'Yes, I think we can do that – I have just the man here.' So we go into a meeting . . . and I think it's Les who says: 'Could you do it in a week?' And at that point I say I really don't think I can – it's too complicated, it's too much."

It was, Brock said, one of those "marginal projects that idiots like Brock and Blackmore come up with, and suddenly once they've decided they want it, they want it straight away."

Simon Pearson, the night editor, was on paternity leave when Brock rang him at home and called him in for a meeting. Brock asked him to put together a small team of sub-editors drawn from all areas of the paper to make a tabloid version. Pearson asked: "How long have we got?" Brock replied: "A week. When can you start?" This was a dream project for a sub-editor; it involved no interface with reporters at that stage – all the copy would be taken from the broadsheet edition and all the credit (or blame) given to the subs. He was told to choose younger subs in order not to weaken the broadsheet and his key colleagues were Juanita Greville, Kathleen Wyatt and Barney Thompson from home subs and Mark Giles from sport. Greville did most of the layout with Pearson directing. Wendy Showell, a feisty production editor obsessed with deadlines, also had a crucial role imposing the necessary discipline. Thomson was confident that the project had the necessary range of skills, personalities and passion. The team worked in a secure, windowless room. By the end of the first afternoon, Pearson decided they would have to move much faster. "Talking about it that evening I said to George, 'We'll go for it tomorrow and start pouring the broadsheet into tabloid pages.' I was given a free hand in production terms . . . We gave it all we could and a very young and inexperienced team pulled together and worked extraordinarily hard, very long hours. The week in the bunker was like being in a Battle of Britain control centre.".

Spackman recalled: "We dummied it flat out back and forth, back and forth. We got better and better. We practised and practised." She spent hours patiently negotiating every day's flat plan with the advertising department and trying to fit advertisements into the different page shapes. By the time the project broke cover it was a smoothly running machine. The structure, the framework, could be largely put in place in splendid isolation, the editor considered, but the real challenge would be to make it work day after day. "That," Thomson said, "is a much more demanding moment in the history of a paper." Focus groups showed that women liked the tabloid and that 25- to 45-year-old men would be "the hardest nut to crack". The compact *Times* was launched in London and the southeast of England on Wednesday, November 26, 2003, with a cover price of 50p, the same as the broadsheet, which was for sale alongside it. A picture of Jonny Wilkinson relaxing after winning the rugby World Cup for England against Australia with a drop-kick in extra time adorned the front page. The launch edition sold 47,000 compact copies. Much of this could be attributed to the novelty of the new format, but England's dramatic victory against Australia was a factor. So could an advertising campaign for the compact that trumpeted: "It's not big but it is clever."

The launch came with a reassuring message from the editor: "*The Times* is one of the oldest and most respected newspapers in the world and we are making newspaper history again as we embark on a significant change of format. The compact *Times* will be the same size as a tabloid, but it will be very, very different to the average tabloid, as it will bring the values and the content of the broadsheet to its new shape. The compact *Times* will offer readers a dynamic and compelling read in a format that fits their lives, whether for those commuting on the Underground or for those who will sometimes want another format other than the wonderful expanse of a broadsheet. Outstanding editorial quality forms the basis of everything we do, whatever the shape, and the compact, like the broadsheet, will be informed by expertise, wit and passion." Thomson was pithier when he gave a lecture four years later in Australia. "It took an Australian to shrink [*The Times*] into a tabloid, or a compact. We used the 'c' word so it was more socially acceptable," he said (RMIT lecture, Tim Arago, *New York Times*, April 28, 2008).

Two days after the compact's launch, the Paper Round column was written by Charles Wilson, a former editor of *The Times* who had held senior positions across Fleet Street. Rupert Murdoch, he said, had been teasing his editors with suggestions of a tabloid *Times* ever since he bought the paper in 1981. Wilson concluded that three days on, the portents were highly encouraging. It had been well received by the industry and "reader feedback had been positive". *The Telegraph* seemed unable to respond and *The Daily*

Mail, a mid-market tabloid since 1971, might also be vulnerable – indeed early indications were that *The Times* had taken most of its new readers from the *Mail*. Paul Dacre, its editor, "may feel *The Times*'s tanks are a little too close to his lawn".

Wilson, with his extensive tabloid and broadsheet experience, pointed out that producing the compact was not simply a matter of decanting broadsheet pages into tabloid format. The most common broadsheet advertisement was the "25 by 4" – the 25cm by four-column shape that left ample scope for a broadsheet designer to deploy pictures, panels and different typefaces. That same size on a tabloid page was a designer's nightmare. For *The Times*, this was an expensive operation, involving doubling up of production journalists. In the sub-editors' area, the broadsheet edition was made up and sent to press first and viewed as the gold standard by many of those who worked on it. It was then "poured" into the compact format by Pearson under the supervision of Brock, who was still doing his day job as managing editor.

In an online question-and-answer session with *Times* readers a week after launch, Thomson was clear:

> In answer to the various questions about the quality and content of what we like to call our compact edition of *The Times*, readers should be confident that while the format has changed, the values of the newspaper remain very much the same. Our intention is that the stories will be constant in the two editions, even if, occasionally, a little tweaking or trimming may be necessary due to oddly shaped pages. For example, the letters to the editor are precisely the same every day, as are the leading articles and the columnists. And for those worried about whether we are going to evolve into a conventional tabloid, please be assured that we are not planning to use racier headlines to 'liven up' the compact edition.

He also raised his pet concern about the awkwardness of trying to read a broadsheet in a confined space: "I am a naturally clumsy person and do have difficulty coping with the larger pages on the bus or in a train, so I do appreciate the more convenient format. There is no doubt that commuters will find it easier to handle and that people sitting next to readers on a bus will be less inconvenienced by flapping pages and rustling noises." That was something he had been trying to ram home to his own senior executives. There was such a large car park at Wapping that many staff came in by car, so the editor wanted them to understand how tricky it could be to read a broadsheet on a packed train. Thomson reassured broadsheet enthusiasts that "we intend to keep the two editions, the broadsheet and the compact, running in tandem on weekdays, so that readers will have a choice of newspaper (as long as it is *The Times*) and there are no serious plans at the moment to change the Saturday edition". The Saturday edition was a much more complex, multisectioned paper, but the success of the weekday edition inevitably prompted a compact on Saturday and the "no serious plans" became a reality.

From Clive Milner's point of view, configuring the two versions of the paper was "an immense bit of editorial discipline". Editionising had to be simplified and a big late-breaking story could never have been properly covered. Milner gave credit to Wendy Showell for enforcing the necessary regimentation of page flow to get both formats out. Editorial may heave a sigh of relief when they send lots of pages at the last minute but press halls dread page bunching, which can be fatal for platemaking schedules. So effective was Showell's discipline on *The Times* that she was eventually promoted to work across all the titles, some of which had never felt much constrained by deadlines. With her deep technical expertise, Showell was perfectly capable of whisking a late page off screen and sending it to press unilaterally, but her no-nonsense demeanour masked a fierce pride in the quality of the finished product. The nightly production reports were her lodestar.

As Milner pointed out, however, the decisive test of the broadsheet's survival lay not in editorial discipline but in "the whole chain of putting the paper out, distributing it, looking at the numbers nightly, daily and assessing what the compact was doing versus the broadsheet. Making decisions to switch off [the broadsheet], logistics around that became huge and in the end one thing became very clear, which is where you put the compact in we sold more." It was never a question of throwing a switch and turning off the broadsheet – as the numbers came through it was a case of "here is a region massively skewed towards compact, switch off the broadsheet. Here's one that is 50:50, leave it for another week and see which way the numbers drift. Yes, it's happening: well we know what will happen next, it'll just keep growing so we'll switch it off. So it was not a binary decision, it was a chain of events." On

THE HISTORY OF THE TIMES | 49

Monday, November 1, 2004, the broadsheet was dropped entirely "in response to clear reader demand".

Readers' complaints about the compact fill three sizeable boxes in *The Times* archive. Telephone and anecdotal protests also came in. Many readers were disappointed when the decision was made to drop the broadsheet: some had been driving to neighbouring towns where the broadsheet was still available. The vituperative reactions to the compact mined a rich seam: "Beastly little tabloid", "undignified", "flashy rubbish", "meretricious", "gutter press", "horrible rag", "too many pages", "hard to handle at breakfast", "dreadful idea", "grotty comic", "a populist comic cut". "Ignore us boring old farts at your peril," said Bill Gray from Perth.

Thomson tried to answer as many reader letters as possible, because "if you truly care about *The Times* you need to address their concerns". Emollient letters and vouchers for a month were sent to the disgruntled. One reader simply photocopied the editor's letter and returned it with a note at the bottom: "Thank you, but no. Goodbye."

For some diehard broadsheet readers the compact was simply not *The Times*. For others, the editor thought, "it wasn't that it wasn't *The Times*, it was just a different experience. It's like switching from a Samsung to an iPhone or an iPhone to a Samsung. Just getting used to the new format is of itself potentially alienating and I had no doubt that once people were accustomed to the format that the substance would resonate with them. When you look at those sales figures from that period, it's extraordinary what happened to *The Times*. The increase in women, younger people, the increase generally in circulation was unprecedented. And we weren't discounting.".

The compact transformed the fortunes of *The Times*. Core sales (excluding discounted bulk and foreign copies) had declined from a daily average of 633,133 in November 2000 to 556,330 sales in November 2003, when the tabloid was gradually launched. That same month, *The Daily Telegraph* sold an average of 865,714, a gap of over 309,000. All papers were in sectoral decline as the shift away from print had become pronounced. But in November 2004, *The Times* core sale was 615,441 and in November 2005, it was 625,432. That same month *The Telegraph* sold 803,541, so the gap between the papers had narrowed dramatically to just over 178,000. Over the same period of two years, *The Times* increased its sales lead over *The Guardian* from 223,019 copies to 287,256.

And in full-price newsstand sales, the ultimate measure of reader choice, *The Times* overtook *The Telegraph*. In November 2003, the audited average daily newsstand sale of *The Times* was 450,946 and *The Telegraph* 557,301, but by November 2005, *The Times* was selling 528,918 copies daily and *The Telegraph* 497,194, while *The Guardian* was a distant third among the traditional broadsheets at 338,176 copies (Audit Bureau of Circulations). The compact had brought in new readers, not because of its size alone, but because the change in format had attracted a new audience, particularly women and younger readers, to *Times* journalism. And that profound change, combined with the emerging digital strategy, put a chronically loss-making masthead on the path to profitability.

It was not just the readers who had to get used to the new product; the production team at Wapping had to absorb a new culture. Improvisation and fast learning against implacable deadlines had been vital for the launch: very few *Times* sub-editors had any previous experience of tabloid formats and the main focus had simply been getting the paper away on time. Now, edition changes were forcing brutal decisions: broadsheet subs could take a story off page 1 and rejig it into page 2 while a page 2 story could move deeper into the paper and so on in a gentle diminuendo. The compact's tighter pages called for sharper news values and more decisive remakes based on clear decisions and priorities. A number of older staff could look back to the Rees-Mogg era when the pace was less hectic, pagination was lower and there were proportionately more sub-editors. Rees-Mogg's chief home sub, Leon Pilpel, told his team that "when you send copy to the composing room you should be able to put your hand on your heart and say you have checked everything". That was now often impractical. Readers of *The Times* were always eagle-eyed and provided a reality check for all on the paper. The collective efforts and professionalism of *Times* journalists during this exacting period had created a new reality for a paper whose fortunes had previously hung in the balance but which was now ready to confront the digital age.

Tradition remained important within the pages of the compact, but there was also innovation, and one particular feature changed the daily habits of hundreds of millions around the world. *The Times* crossword had been the global gold standard since it was first published on February 1, 1930. More than 70 years later, turning to the crossword page was still for many readers the ideal way to start the day. On November 12, 2004, the puzzles page featured a newcomer consisting of numerals, not letters, and an intriguing Japanese name: sudoku. Within weeks it gripped the country and, thanks to the international renown of *The Times*, spread exponentially overseas. But where had it originated? The person who brought it to *The Times* was Wayne Gould, a Hong Kong high court judge, who would seemingly have been happy cracking codes at Bletchley Park. He had spotted sudoku in a puzzle book in Tokyo that inspired him to spend six years devising a computer program to create an endless supply of the puzzles. When he first turned up unannounced in the reception area of *The Times* he was carrying a mocked-up back page of Times 2 with a sudoku next to the crossword. Thomson was intrigued. "I liked the symmetry," he said, "and the fact that in this ill-defined, never-ending world we cherish acts of completion." He took a few examples home for his wife, Ping, because he was worried that it might be just a male statistical obsession. She enthusiastically approved and sudoku was launched.

Within months, the word "sudoku" was almost universally known; within a year it had entered the Oxford English Dictionary, *The Times* had sold more than 900,000 sudoku books through HarperCollins, and sudoku was published in virtually every newspaper in virtually every country. In October 2005, the craze hit Japan at last after the London correspondent of *Yomiuri Shimbun* reported on the phenomenon triggered by *The Times*. *Yomiuri* has a circulation of 14 million: the website for Nikoli, a Japanese publisher of the puzzles since 1984, promptly crashed.

Sudoku kept flourishing after Thomson's departure for New York. *The Times* introduced a championship, and Tom Collyer, a Warwick University maths PhD who went on to specialise in credit risk modelling in the banking industry, won it four times, in 2007, 2009, 2015 and 2017. In the course of a masterclass he echoed Thomson: "Solving a puzzle gives me the opportunity to dip out of the real world and face a problem that can be solved completely and with a true sense of closure." A bond trader from London, George Danker, won his third title and £1,000 in 2016, completing four puzzles in 24 minutes.

The prototype spawned several descendants suggested by Thomson, including Shogun sudoku and Samurai sudoku (alliteration again!) with five interconnected grids, tredoku (a "3D" version invented by an Israeli architect) and Mini (a 6x6 version). KenKen and futoshiki diverged a little more from standard sudoku, and kakuro was a little farther away still. None of these variants was necessarily more difficult than sudoku; they just demanded different techniques. Sudoku and crosswords remained the most popular puzzles in *The Times* after they were adapted for online publishing. Each received a similar number of digital visitors, although sudoku was the more successful. The global adoption of sudoku prompted much research into its positive impact on mental acuity and cognitive development. A small corner of *The Times* newspaper had become the platform for an international phenomenon.

CHAPTER FIVE

Many *Times* journalists could remember receiving a call asking them to "pop over for a word with Sir Edward". In past years that had meant a walk across the bridge connecting the *Times* building on The Highway to the main News International offices inside the Wapping site. There they would be received courteously by the tall, elderly figure of Sir Edward Pickering, who might ask mildly about a paragraph on the Court page or the misuse of the royal coat of arms. His modesty could be deceptive, however. Pick, or Ted, as he was usually known, was the executive vice-chairman of Times Newspapers, a revered Fleet Street veteran who had been a friend and mentor for most of Rupert Murdoch's adult life. When Pickering celebrated his 90th birthday he declared that he was too old to retire, and he was working from his bed on the afternoon he died, aged 91, in August 2003. Up to the end of his working life, he would speak every Monday with Robert Thomson, who sought his impressions of *The Times* newspaper's performance and his advice on dealing with corporate politics. "He told me that I should always have a list of relevant topics to discuss with Rupert because of his insatiable curiosity," Thomson explained.

His death touched Murdoch personally. In a moving eulogy at the memorial service in St Bride's, Fleet Street, Murdoch explained why:

> "I knew Ted Pickering for 50 years. After my father he was my great mentor. He was a truly great friend to all of us here today. And to the end, he was a man in whom we all placed unfaltering trust. That was the greatest testament to Pick. He walked shoulder to shoulder with the giants of old Fleet Street. He prospered like few others in this tricky and often brutal trade. But Pick never, ever yielded his sense of truth and honesty. I was foisted on Ted as a trainee sub in 1953. I was a raw Oxford graduate. He commanded the back bench of Beaverbrook's great *Daily Express*. Beaverbrook instructed Ted to take good care of me. Years later, Ted told me how the Beaver had expressed it. 'Look after him,' he said. 'You never know where he might end up.'
>
> Ted became fond of telling people that I was the only sub he ever employed who lived at the Savoy. In fact, I never

actually did live at the Savoy. This was a rare occasion when Pick refused to let the facts stand in the way of a good story. Pick loved both the work and the off-duty pleasures of the Street. At the office, through the unrelenting day-to-day mayhem of the newsroom, he was the still, rock-steady heart of it all. Taciturn, self-controlled, unwavering through the nightly emergency of getting the paper off stone.

He was a peerless craftsman who mastered, in a manner I never saw bettered by any editor, the entire detail of newspapers. He taught me the power of the 18-word intro, the art of a picture properly cropped and captioned. He could hone a 25-word news-in-brief as well as he could craft a soaring top leader. And he had another indispensable skill. He knew how to handle cantankerous press barons. He would say: 'When you find yourself trapped in a cage with a tiger, you quickly learn in which direction to stroke his fur.' Naturally, I have always assumed he was referring exclusively to their lordships Harmsworth and Beaverbrook.

Pickering's *Times* obituary referred to his unflappability, civility and quiet methods, attributes that enabled him to deflect the barrage of phone calls and memos from the irascible Lord Beaverbrook when he was at the *Express*. Keith Waterhouse, the doyen of popular journalism style, said that the *Express* at the time was "not about news, but about presentation – which was brilliant". In 1953, Pickering was running the back bench the night before the coronation when the news broke that Everest had been climbed. Waterhouse continued: "The headline that got the *Express* off the horns of a news priority dilemma 'All This – And Everest Too!' was journalistic genius." And it was Pickering's (Waterhouse, 2010, p. 25). He was elevated to editor in 1957 but after five years in the chair he was summarily replaced on Christmas Eve by Beaverbrook and put in charge of *Farming Express*. Cecil King, a rival press baron, picked him up to become editorial director of the Mirror Group. He retired in 1977 but in 1981, Murdoch asked him to join the newly acquired *Times* as an independent director. Murdoch said in his eulogy:

I make no apologies for persuading him back into the snake-pit that was Fleet Street in the early 1980s. I knew that there was no one who carried more respect within News International, and the industry, which was in turmoil, badly needed his managerial and editorial skills too. I have to admit I was surprised when I heard that Ted saw these tempestuous years as 'the sunlit uplands' of his working life. I remember going whole weeks without seeing a sliver of daylight, let alone sunshine. I'm glad someone saw the silver lining.

Pickering had lived long enough to see a great change taking place in the "entire detail of newspapers" that Murdoch referred to in that eulogy. By 2003, the press was facing a fork in the road. One path lay in print, the other online. Since the emergence of the internet in the early 1990s, newspapers in general had clung to their print business models while unenthusiastically setting up websites that carried a digital representation of the print pages rather than providing an alternative or enhanced service. At *The Times*, Thomson's experience in establishing FT.com in the US had prepared him for the inevitable digital battles over branding and provenance. He found that while many in the tech community understood distribution, they had no particular love of journalism and little understanding of editorial creation – and that was as true at *The Times* as it was globally.

Murdoch would soon show that he was fully awake to the inexorable changes being wrought by the digital revolution, but in 2003 he was also in the throes of making a massive £750 million investment in new printing presses for his British titles. It was called Project Hal. In Stanley Kubrick's seminal film *2001: A Space Odyssey*, Hal, the onboard computer, takes over Discovery One's journey to Jupiter – this new Hal presented a different kind of challenge. Representatives from all four News International titles were encouraged to feel that they were part of a thrilling journey, moving production from the Wapping press hall to a gigantic new site at Broxbourne on the far northern outskirts of London. There would also be new facilities in Merseyside, Glasgow and Ireland.

For Murdoch, the three drivers of the project were colour, where News International could lose leadership in the market because the existing presses restricted colour and other titles could use more; saving money through increased efficiency; and making money through the deployment of faster, more flexible presses.

The limited colour capacity at News International meant using expensive contract printing sites spread around the country – at one point, *The News of the World* was printing at half a dozen different sites.

A special edition of the staff newspaper, *The News*, explained that the new generation of presses would be a huge technological leap. A welter of statistics bolstered that claim: they would be double the height of the existing presses, twice as long and half as wide again. The site at Broxbourne, near Enfield, would be the size of 23 Wembley football pitches. The plan was for twelve new presses at Broxbourne, five at Knowsley on Merseyside, two at a new site near Glasgow and three at Kells in Ireland. The project was the largest that Manroland GB, which supplied the presses, had been involved in; it was "simply off the scale", according to Norman Revill, its sales director. The machinery was to be triple-width Manroland Colorman XXL press lines with computer-to-plate lines right alongside the press cylinders to make putting on and removing plates faster and easier. Press start times of 10.45pm from Sunday to Thursday would enable 100 per cent coverage of late football results (a longstanding ambition for sports editors). Full colour on every page would end differential advertising rates and editorial arguments about where colour should fall in the book, and increased pagination would allow editorial expansion. The entire weekday paper would be printed in a single pass, with up to six separate sections.

Les Hinton told the *International Journal of Newspaper Technology* that the project would ensure that the company maintained its leading position in the national newspaper industry. The four titles (*The Times*, *The Sunday Times*, *The Sun* and *The News of the World*), would be unsurpassed in the quality of their printing and the speed with which they were produced. Stirring slogans were promulgated: "NI – always first. First with the stories, first to innovate, first in the marketplace, first with new technology." Murdoch wanted the huge investment validated independently, so his eldest son Lachlan, a passionate supporter of journalism and journalists, brought in his top Australian production people to verify the thinking in Wapping. The Australians' philosophy, Clive Milner said, was to use machinery, but with a lot of manpower and overtime; the British favoured a more technological approach – "lights out, very few people and mechanise where you can.". "We were really put through the wringer," Milner said, but Hinton told him: "Don't worry, this is a good thing because if there's that level of scrutiny then whatever the answer is, we won't have any comeback on the decision and in the end it's taken to a board for validation and rubber stamp, which is what I have got to do."

This technological triumph would come at a human cost. Integral to the project was a sharp reduction in printing staff and a complete rethink of editorial practices. Production jobs were expected to fall by two thirds. Daniel Cloke, the new human resources director, emphasised the importance of communication with the affected staff. Team briefings, letters, a telephone helpline, executive walkabouts, roadshows and one-to-one discussions were all designed to allay the real fear of redundancy. Some production staff had to reapply for their own posts; they had never had a job interview and needed coaching in form-filling. There were selection panels and a right of appeal. In the event, production job losses were severe. The move from Wapping to Broxbourne led to a permanent headcount reduction of 65 to 70 per cent, or up to 900 jobs. A press in Wapping was operated by up to five people compared with two at Broxbourne. There were some voluntary redundancies and some compulsory, but the average payoff was £86,000, or £142,240 in 2023 terms (According to Bank of England inflation calculator).

With a project of such scale, with new factories and new plant, the business had to align itself with the investment. Because of the way publishing works, Milner said, people – particularly editors – were used to being autonomous. The new presses demanded different workflows and page flow disciplines. Accordingly, teams from each title examined every aspect of the business with advice from Deloitte, the consultancy. Milner said:

It's a bit like being in a Formula 1 team. You take everything apart and, when you've dismantled every bit, there will be changes for editorial, advertising, production, distribution and editorial support and then everything has to be re-engineered. When you're taking the engine apart you have the licence to say 'Do we actually need that bit? Why are we doing that in the first place?' If it had been business as usual there would have been terrible territorial issues of people saying 'You don't need to look at that, I'm happy, it's mine, go away.'

Every editorial area was used to having its own quasi-IT department to manage its clunky Atex editorial system: *The Sun* had up to 40 extra staff just in case their system fell over. Milner continued:

> Those people could go once we had a robust editorial system, and we could ask how many colour plates, how many editions, how many changes could you do? And if something at *The Sunday Times* or *The Sun* was going well we could use that good idea as a benchmark ... It was a one-off opportunity for best-practice migration and getting people thinking in a way that not only helped an individual title but helped the business in general. And we did it across three sites and we did it across four titles and we did it across the entire company for years. So it was quite an undertaking and that's why we needed a Deloitte-type operation to keep us honest about delivery, efficiency, how much money we were saving and so forth.

> There were a few moments when individuals tried to revert to type and defend their patch rather than look at it in the round. But for the most part, because of the way it was done, we certainly delivered the entire project on time and on budget. With something of this size and scale, when I stood in front of the News Corp board, asking for a billion dollars, I don't think Les or I or the team that worked underneath us were unclear that it had to be delivered and delivered well . . . I had plenty of sleepless nights. Plenty. But we had really good teams and, in the end, the product still looks fantastic and no one could doubt the step change in quality. Colour delivery was superb – once you see full colour on every page it really does sing.

Planning permission for the Broxbourne plant was granted in 2005. It took two years to build and went into full production in 2008. More than a decade later, the sites at Broxbourne, Knowsley and Eurocentral near Glasgow were still turning out 2.7 million copies a week of *The Times*; 55 to 60 per cent of their capacity was taken up by third-party contract titles, including *The Telegraph*, the *Mail* and the *Evening Standard*. In September 2021, however, the company announced that it was closing the News Press Ireland Limited business at Kells and outsourcing printing to other third-party print sites in Ireland. Plans were also being prepared for Knowsley to close as the decline in print newspaper sales accelerated.

George Brock, as managing editor, had observed Murdoch in operation long enough to see the logic in this massive investment in print despite the dawn of digital mass media. He said: "My picture of Rupert has always been that he's perfectly well aware that newspapers in the historical sense may turn out to be dinosaurs. He just wanted to make sure that they have the longest possible tails.". For Brock, the eye-wateringly expensive investment was successful, because Murdoch followed his "principal and most successful trick in business", which was to reduce costs. "He knew enough to walk into a press room and ask 'how many people have you got on shift here?' Answer 'fourteen' and he wanders round for ten minutes and comes back and says 'you could do it with nine'. And he was usually right."

While pouring a billion dollars into Brock's print "dinosaurs", Murdoch almost simultaneously signalled News Corp's embrace of the internet. Addressing the annual meeting of the American Society of Newspaper Editors in Washington in April 2005, he told the editors that they had to embrace the internet by forging closer ties with bloggers and other web users if they were to prosper in the digital era. "Digital natives" were abandoning printed papers for web-based sources of information – a shift about which many editors had been "remarkably, unaccountably complacent", he said. Newspapers had to change the way they provided news to stay in touch with readers and advertisers. He himself was a "digital immigrant", he confessed, accustomed to a world in which editors controlled what we could and should know. "I wasn't weaned on the web, nor coddled on a computer," he said with Thomsonesque alliteration, and he had not responded as he should have done after the excitement of the 1990s. "I suspect many of you . . . did the same, quietly hoping that this thing called the digital revolution would just limp along. Well it hasn't . . . it won't . . . and it's a fast-developing reality we should grasp as a huge opportunity to improve our journalism and expand our reach."

Citing a report by the Carnegie philanthropic foundation that 44 per cent of respondents between the ages of 18 and 34 visited a website for news at least once a day, he warned: "Unless we awaken to these changes ... we will be relegated to the status of also-rans." Those younger people's attitudes towards newspapers were especially alarming. "Only 9 per cent describe us as trustworthy, a scant 8 per cent find us useful, and only 4 per cent of respondents think we're entertaining. Among major news sources, our beloved newspaper is the least likely to be the preferred choice for local, national or international news going forward."

A revolution was happening in the way young people accessed news, Murdoch insisted: "They don't want to rely on the morning paper for their up-to-date information. They don't want to rely on a God-like figure from above to tell them what's important. And to carry the religion analogy a bit further, they certainly don't want news presented as gospel. Instead, they want their news on demand, when it works for them. They want control over their media, instead of being controlled by it. They want to question, to probe, to offer a different angle." Many of those needs could still be satisfied by print. News Corporation would continue to invest in printed papers so they remained an important part of readers' daily lives. "But our internet versions can do even more, especially in providing virtual communities for our readers to be linked to other sources of information, other opinions, other like-minded people," Murdoch envisioned.

The growth of high-speed internet connections had fanned demand for rich content, including video and audio. Blog sites and message boards had proliferated. "The digital native no longer sends a letter to the editor. She goes online and starts a blog. We need to be the destination for those bloggers." There was a lesson for the editors, Murdoch continued, in the switch to a compact format, which immediately reversed circulation decline. "For nearly a year, we offered readers both versions: same newspaper, same stories, just different sizes. And they overwhelmingly chose the compact version as more convenient. This is an example of us listening to what our readers want, and then upsetting a centuries-old tradition to give them exactly what they were asking for. And we did it all without compromising the quality of our product. In this spirit, we're now turning to the internet. Today, the newspaper is just a paper. Tomorrow, it can be a destination."

Murdoch's comments coincided with a boom in the market for internet "destination sites", including portals such as Yahoo! and new search sites such as Google. Three months after his speech, News Corp announced that it was going into this market by paying $580 million for Intermix, which operated the "online socialising" site MySpace.com ("a space for friends") and the gaming and entertainment site grab.com, and folding them into a newly formed Fox Interactive Media business. The company said it was planning more "strategic investments" in the internet to capture more revenue from audiences and advertisers. *The Times* reported in September that News Corp had bought IGN, which operated some of the web's most popular computer games and sport sites, for $650 million, doubling the size of its emerging internet portfolio. It also acquired Scout Media, a sports sites operator, for an undisclosed amount. A New York financial analyst said the company was "aggressively buying its way into an internet strategy from nowhere three months ago".

Murdoch returned to his theme in March 2006 in the annual lecture for the Worshipful Company of Stationers and Newspaper Makers in London. His message was that if newspapers were to survive in the digital era, they would have to adopt multimedia strategies to engage readers when information had become like fast food. "Crucially," he said, "newspapers must give readers the choice of accessing their journalism in the pages of the paper, or on websites such as Times Online or . . . on any platform that appeals to them, mobile phones, handheld devices, iPods, whatever." Power was shifting away from editors and proprietors towards a 'new media audience' who were using the internet and new technology to inform, entertain and above all, to educate themselves."

In June 2006, Tina Gaudoin, style director of the *Times Saturday* magazine, wrote about an "American college web 2.0 phenomenon called Facebook, which mushroomed into an astonishing business by harnessing American college students' obsession with putting their details and pictures online in the style of an old college yearbook, and is thought to be worth billions". James Harding, the business editor, reported that September that Yahoo! was said to have held serious discussions to buy Facebook over a deal rumoured to value it at $1 billion (£523 million). He thought the price was too high. At the time Facebook was the seventh most popular website in the US, trailing behind News Corp's MySpace, which was the fourth most popular website in the world with 100 million users. In those early days, the fast-growing, fashionable MySpace seemed certain to prevail, to the point that on January 26, 2008, Mark Zuckerberg raised the possibility of combining Facebook with MySpace at a breakfast with Murdoch and Thomson at the Chalet Walserhuus, which Murdoch rented for meetings. (Thomson had left *The Times* a few weeks earlier for Dow Jones). Zuckerberg intimated to Murdoch that he thought MySpace's audience lead and cool image would make it the pre-eminent social site and he worried that he could not catch up. Ultimately, Zuckerberg and Facebook triumphed and, in June 2011, News Corp would cut its losses in MySpace and sell to Specific Media, an online ad company, for a mere $35 million.

Another profound moment of technological change came in January 2007. Chris Ayres reported from the West Coast of America (Wednesday, January 10, 2007) about a "mobile phone that looks more like a rectangular compact mirror, with only one button, a screen that's almost invisible when switched off and a trademark chrome casing". The first generation of the Apple iPhone was born. Steve Jobs, CEO of Apple, called it a "revolutionary and magical product that is literally five years ahead of any other mobile phone". He claimed the smartphone's touchscreen technology was as intuitive as a computer mouse. It combined a "widescreen" iPod music player, a web browser and a mobile phone. By that November, O2, Apple's UK network partner, was reporting "tens of thousands" of devices sold. In 2023, Apple sold an estimated 234.6 million iPhones around the world (International Data Corp estimate, January 16, 2024).

The Times was attempting to cope with the technological, cultural and organisational challenges. Anne Spackman, veteran of the dash to the compact *Times* early in Thomson's editorship, had since taken over from Brock as managing editor, a prestigious but less frenzied role. Now she was moved by Thomson back to the frontline as editor-in-chief of Times Online. On her own admission she was not exactly digitally savvy. When she told her family that she couldn't really believe what she was being asked to do, one of her sons said: "You? You don't even know when to double-click." Thomson had chosen her for the role because he felt her emotional intelligence would be a crucial component in improving digital performance and developing a seven-day digital operation. He wanted her to cultivate what he called "renaissance reporters" able to work across print, digital, audio and video formats. She was reporting to Thomson and Witherow, and the traditional rivalry between *The Times* and *Sunday Times* had extended into the digital age. But integration of the online operation was vital, and being a journalist herself made winning the respect of the newspaper journalists easier than if she had been a purely digital expert.

Thomson created a news production hub based on the model that he had deployed at *The Financial Times* in New York and would later unveil at *The Wall Street Journal*, where he brought together the print, digital and newswires operations in a single space to end a traditional caste system that he thought corrosive. At *The Times*, Thomson was focused on two cultural concerns: the lack of engagement between print and digital, and the traditional divide between the day and evening editing operations. "The main thing about the hub is not only to break down a barrier between online and offline . . . but what I've always thought is an issue . . . the divide between the day and the night side of a newspaper," said Thomson in an interview with Roy Greenslade in 2007. "So what we have tried to do is not just bring the paper and the website together, but to deal with that issue, and you have the day news editor and the night editor within talking distance and discussing stories, why they were conceived and why they turned up in the form that they have been written."

Spackman faced significant challenges. "We were still stuck in a mindset," she said, "particularly at *The Sunday Times* and certainly *The Times* to a certain extent, whereby if you were on the newspaper you expect the website to be a digital representation of the paper and the pages." Some of the technical work was outsourced to India, and the time difference could lead to absurd delays – it took six weeks, according to Spackman, to get the word "Exclusive" to appear in red on a digital story. More and more expensive people were added to the team to join up the dots and it became like "a gold-plated daisy chain", Spackman said. "Right from the very beginning I thought we need a different generation to lead this. The difficulty was that if you were a journalist there weren't many places to work in Britain better than *The Times*, but if you were a technology whiz you weren't coming anywhere near us because you wanted to work for Apple or Google or Goldman Sachs."

In 2006 she managed to hire Tom Whitwell, whom she knew from the outset would be her successor. He was a digital native and already had a successful blog about technology and journalism with a big online following. Initially, Whitwell was communities editor for Times Online, but after Spackman moved to comment editor in October 2008, he became editorial director of digital. He was instrumental in leading *The Times* through its transition to a paid model and in developing iPhone, iPad and Android apps for subscribers to use. *The Times* and *Sunday Times* started charging for online access on July 2, 2010, initially at £1 a day (the same as the *Times* cover price) or £2 for a week's subscription to both. They were the first News International newspapers to use a paywall and the decision was influenced by the clear success in the US of the subscriber model at *The Wall Street Journal*. Immediately after the launch the two titles lost 90 per cent of their online readers, but from then on subscriptions climbed steadily, reaching 155,000 digital-only subscribers by the time Whitwell left in 2013. He told The Drum (December 4, 2013): "The industry was incredibly hostile to the launch, with pundits queuing up to explain all the ways in which the project would fail." They had been wrong. He was leaving *The Times* in "a very strong position".

"Success was partly down to the ways we changed the relationship between the paper and its readers," Whitwell said. "We made lots of small changes, from the ways journalists respond to reader comments to the way we interpret the huge amount of behavioural data we produce each day. The whole newspaper really got behind the new model. Journalists and editors seemed to instinctively understand that if you're not paying for something, you're not the customer – you're the product being sold."

By March 2015 *The Times* and *Sunday Times* would have 172,000 digital-only subscribers with a further 229,000 taking either a print subscription or a combined print and digital one. In 2018 digital subscribers outnumbered print for the first time as they rose by 20 per cent year-on-year to reach 255,000, and *The Times* marked 500,000 print and digital subscribers combined. For the 2019 financial year, Times Newspapers reported pre-tax profits of £3.75 million and turnover of £330.2 million. It said that digital subscriptions remained "key" to its ongoing success. Ten years after the paywall went up, Alan Hunter, head of digital until 2021, said that while the consensus in 2010 had been that nobody would pay for general interest news, "now more than 300,000 do, and 'paid v free' is no longer a debate" (*Press Gazette*, July 2, 2020). Less than five years later, Times digital subscriptions would outnumber print sales by more than three to one.

CHAPTER SIX

In the early summer of 2006, to the surprise of many, Robert Thomson launched an international edition of *The Times*, printed in New York. He said it would be intended for "American readers who are global in their outlook and global citizens who are in America". The print run would be close to 10,000 copies and it would be printed and distributed in the New York and Washington areas through a partnership with News Corporation's *New York Post*. It would be sold at about 2,000 sites, primarily in New York and New Jersey. A second crucial component of the project was in building the digital profile of *The Times* in the US, as Thomson's experience with the FT had shown him that print could be a pathway platform to a much larger digital audience.

According to Thomson, *The Times* hoped to capitalise on what he called an unsatisfied demand in America for coverage of "what the US newspapers insist on calling soccer, but the rest of the world calls football". The launch coincided with the World Cup in Germany and the US edition would feature soccer on the front page; the editor acknowledged that there could be divided loyalties at *The Times* but a "dream final, from our perspective, would be England against the United States" (*The New York Times*, May 27, 2006). The US failed to win a game and England went out in the quarter-finals, but George Brock, ever a keen Murdoch-watcher, concluded that the international edition was part of a much bigger game: News Corp's attempt to buy *The Wall Street Journal*. Some members of the Bancroft family, who controlled Dow Jones, owners of the *Journal*, were resisting the sale. Among the blandishments was projecting the "London *Times*" as a serious cosmopolitan paper by printing the international edition in New York.

Brock felt that Murdoch always understood the importance of the *Times* brand and legacy better than most: the international print edition was not a commercial proposition, Brock said, it was pure PR. It was known to wags in Wapping as the Bancroft edition; its codename was Project Frank, an allusion to Sinatra's song "New York, New York".

Thomson was closely involved in the negotiations for the *Journal*, shuttling clandestinely to and fro between London and New York. It was crucial that Marcus Brauchli, editor of the WSJ, and his immediate predecessor, Paul Steiger, approve the purchase. Thomson knew both of them well and so it was incumbent on him to ensure that they were positively disposed. He and Brauchli had spent years as reporters in Asia together, though working for rival papers; Steiger had been a newspaper competitor of the FT's in the US as well as a challenger on the softball field – matches that the *Journal* tended to win comfortably. The negotiations went on well into 2007. After an offer of $5 billion had been rejected, Murdoch told Fox News: "There's plenty of time, and we just take it calmly and hope they will take it calmly," adding emolliently, "It's a generous offer and we are the sort of people with the same traditions that I think would prove great guardians for the paper."

By June 2007 the controlling shareholders had agreed to meet Murdoch; the sticking point seemed to be guaranteeing the *Journal*'s editorial independence. At this point, almost surreally, Thomson was summoned to appear before a parliamentary committee in London and questioned at great length about his editorial independence at *The Times*. The House of Lords select committee on communications was conducting a wide-ranging inquiry into the impact of online media on the traditional media. Its interest in Thomson, however, when he appeared before it on July 18, seemed to lie mostly on his relationship with Murdoch. Throughout the grilling Thomson was emphatic that *The Times* was a self-standing entity and that he had autonomy.

The committee's chairman, Lord Fowler, was himself a *Times* veteran. As Norman Fowler he had been a home affairs reporter and leader from 1961 to 1970 before entering politics and serving in Margaret Thatcher's cabinet. He asked Thomson how he had been recruited. He replied that Murdoch had proposed him to the independent directors, who would have been able to veto his appointment: "I was somewhat of an unknown quantity having been the managing editor of *The Financial Times*. Most of my journalistic career has been spent as a foreign correspondent and as a business journalist and so, for mainstream British journalism, the so-called white papers, I was not really traditionally of that stock and I was quite rightly grilled about my background and about my intentions and the directors had to be satisfied that my intentions were both serious and honourable."

The directors had asked about his views on transatlantic relations, British politics, global trends, the conduct of journalism and journalistic independence, he said. They had also asked about his views on Europe. Fowler observed that he considered *The Times* to be fairly Eurosceptic. Thomson replied that it was more euro-wary; the paper had not suggested that Britain withdraw from the European Union. Fowler then suggested that a euro-enthusiast would be unlikely to be appointed editor. "That is a very hypothetical question," Thomson replied. "I do not think that there would be one issue that solely defines the character of the editor of *The Times*. If you are looking for a Eurosceptic . . . you would find various people with far stronger views than me on the subject."

Fowler then changed tack: "It is often thought/alleged that Rupert Murdoch or a member of the Murdoch family is constantly on the phone to you; is that the case?" Thomson replied: "If they were constantly on the phone to me I would not be able to do my job. I have regular contact with Rupert Murdoch. We have discussions about world affairs. He is a very curious person. What we do not do is discuss what is in the next day's paper in any way, shape or form. There is a line there and he is very clear where that line is." Fowler asked if that was because Murdoch knew he was a safe pair of hands: "He knows exactly where you stand on these issues and he does not really have to check." "I have seen it referred to as an osmotic relationship," the editor replied wryly. "He certainly does not see the leaders before they are published."

Lord King of Bridgwater took up the questioning. Thomson affirmed that his name was on a shortlist of one that Murdoch had put to the independent directors. He and Murdoch might not have discussed the same questions as the directors did, but Murdoch had come to his own conclusions "about me as a person and as a journalist". Asked if Murdoch read *The Times* every day, he said: "I presume that he looks at [it] most days but . . . there is a lot going on in News Corporation." In answer to a question from Lord Corbett of Castle Vale, Thomson reiterated that the leader line was defined by him. "At the last election [2005], to put it crudely, *The Times* voted Labour and *The Sunday Times* Conservative. At the last Scottish election, *The Times* voted Labour and *The Sunday Times* voted Scottish National Party, for some reason." There is diversity within the group and we have that diversity because, in the end, it is the editor's decision . . . Ahead of the last election I did not discuss the *Times* leader line with Rupert Murdoch."

Baroness McIntosh of Hudnall wondered where *The Times* sat in Murdoch's personal pantheon of importance? The editor replied: "I think that *The Times* is *The Times*. He recognises its importance . . . and has supported it with investment over many, many years." The paper was a not-for-profit historically: "I read in *The Wall Street Journal* a couple of weeks ago that we lost £89 million three years ago, and if it was in *The Wall Street Journal*, it must be correct! We are now at the point . . . where, next year, there is a very reasonable chance that we will turn into sustained profit really for the first time in our recent history." Later Thomson provided more financial context: "I cannot speak for the 1920s and 1930s, but, in the modern history of *The Times*, we have been habitually loss-making. When I became editor, it was a priority for me to make sure that we were in a position of being able to sustain *Times* journalism for, hopefully, another 200 years and, frankly, with the investment that Rupert Murdoch authorised, we are now in a position where *Times* journalism will extend far beyond that."

He added: "I am often asked if *The Times* has been dumbed down. In fact *The Times* has been brained up. We have invested in foreign correspondents and in business coverage – not easy subjects but we have a social responsibility to cover them well . . . There is clearly a lot of very serious content in *The Times*." He pointed out that high-quality journalism was expensive: "I worry about whether we can employ specialists to look at politics, America, China and India, because although you can get citizen journalism from those places, it will not be of a professional standard . . . profit is a meaningful contribution to the debate about specialist journalism. Specialists at *The Times* are national living treasures."

Asked how he boosted sales, Thomson said the most important part of the relationship with the audience was trust. A tradition of objectivity was very much what the founding fathers had in mind: "I am not only the editor but a custodian of tradition." Lord Inglewood asked if he insisted on clear lines of demarcation about when news stops and comment starts? "I do, and I hope that all of our reporters do, because there has to be the objective of being objective." It was a theme raised by Roy Greenslade in an interview with Thomson at the Frontline Club in London on November 7 of the same year:

The objective of being objective is an easy mantra to chant . . . we all have beliefs, views, opinions. I think you have to have enough faith in your beliefs and perhaps even your philosophy that the facts on the ground will ultimately reflect what you believe to be true . . . I think you see it a lot in a paper like *The New York Times*, for example, of people being caught up in the emotion of an issue. And the second journalistic sin is being self-regarding. Writing stories because it's socially acceptable to give a certain twist – I find that anathema . . . that the social acceptability of the journalist influences the journalism. That's a fundamental breach, I think, of the role of the journalist.

Turning to the internet, Thomson went on to the front foot, concerned that there was a lack of understanding that the dominant digital platforms, Google and later Facebook, were potentially undermining both journalism and provenance. This would be a theme to which Thomson would return repeatedly in subsequent years and ultimately led to the first payments for journalism by these platforms in October 2019: "I think the role of Google is something, if I may be so bold, that the committee should look at both in terms of privacy issues and in terms of content issues. They aggregate a lot of our content, generate large amounts of revenue from our content and that of *The Telegraph*, *The Guardian*, the *Mail* and other newspapers, but do not contribute in any way to the cost of obtaining the content, and there is a slight contradiction which may become a large contradiction over time." He continued, forecasting the rise of both the web and the dominance of the mobile phone as a canvas: "Habits are changing and it is not only the internet that will affect reading habits but also digital delivery through mobile devices, which, for some young people, is already part of their daily lives." Even though the British market was a "cauldron of competition", newspaper readership had stayed strong and *Times* circulation was particularly high by historical standards. "Print readership is about 1.7 million and online 10 million or so." But "in various other countries, there has been a dramatic decline".

Two weeks after Thomson's examination in the Lords, the Dow Jones deal was finally clinched, with some members of the Bancroft family accepting News Corporation's $5 billion offer, at $60 a share, through gritted teeth. Given how involved the editor had been in winning the deal, few at *The Times* doubted that he would be leaving Wapping and heading to New York for good. Thomson did not confirm this until Friday, December 7, when he told a packed newsroom that he would be vacating the editor's chair the following Tuesday. He said it had been a privilege to be a custodian of *The Times* in its various forms and to share in the achievements of its journalists. "The parting is always a complicated moment for hardened journalists, who work with words and are acutely conscious that the profound and the prosaic are but a few syllables apart." That alliteration again (page 4, Saturday, December 8, 2007).

Thomson was appointed editor-in-chief of Dow Jones & Company and managing editor of *The Wall Street Journal* in May 2008 after being approved by a special committee created to ensure the paper's editorial integrity. In January 2013, he became chief executive officer of News Corp, overseeing global operations across a range of media, including news and information services, digital real estate services, book publishing, sports programming and pay-TV distribution. In comments for this volume of *The History of The Times*, Rupert Murdoch said Thomson had become his "closest friend, executor, everything".

In just under six years at *The Times*, Thomson redesigned the paper, took it from a broadsheet to a compact format, laid the groundwork for a revolution in online operations, overtook *The Daily Telegraph* in full-price newsstand sales, and paved the way for sustainable profitability after decades of losses. Editing *The Times* aside, his greatest influence in the world of journalism was to launch a global debate about the impact of the digital platforms, and the sudden shift in power from the creators of content (the journalists) to the distributors of content (Google, Facebook and Apple).

The prestige of *The Times* and its international renown meant that Thomson was able to elevate issues about the integrity of content and the impact on communities of increasingly extreme digital perspectives that were turning angst into anger.

Thomson told the House of Lords committee: "With digital readership, what you find is that people are seeking specific subjects of interest to them . . . there are two social consequences: one is that you are increasing [the audience] for people with a somewhat narrow interest; but you could argue that the broader community, which itself defines shared values in society, is being undermined by digital specificity." And, in 2007, he raised the issue of provenance, which became a global crisis more than a decade later, with an intense debate over misinformation and disinformation. He explained to the Lords committee: "For some internet content, facts are incidental if not accidental, and the problem we have as a society is that there is a significant number of people who have grown up in a different information environment ... what you have is a lot of young people who are growing up surrounded by much more information whose provenance is not clear." Thomson feared that "in the longer term, critical judgment will not be as it should be; rumours will be believed, fiction will be thought of fact, and political agendas, among other agendas, will be influenced by interest groups who are coming from some quite strange trajectory to issues based on a collective understanding that is founded on falsity."

SECTION TWO

JAMES HARDING

2007 to 2012

CHAPTER SEVEN

James Harding's last daily column as business and city editor of *The Times* was published on Friday, December 7, 2007. In the next day's paper his elevation to editor was announced in a modestly displayed story at the foot of page 4. He was 38, a few months younger than William Rees-Mogg had been on his appointment in 1967.

The following Monday, Rees-Mogg, by then 79 and still writing a weekly column for *The Times*, gave Harding a taste of things to come. When he had become editor, he wrote, "there were undoubtedly English offices with a certain romantic dignity, including the Warden of All Souls, the Master of the Rolls, the Lord Chancellor, the Archbishop of Canterbury, the Provost of Eton, the President of the Royal Society and, one has to admit it, the editor of *The Times*. It could give one a heady feeling. There is still an element of romance about the position even in a more prosaic age. It is not quite the same as any British editorship if only because in global terms, it is much better known."

They could in many ways have been hardly more different, but Rees-Mogg was an early influence on Harding, who admired and liked him. Harding recalled in the 2018 Hugh Cudlipp Lecture:

> When I took over as editor of *The Times*, I went to see the great William Rees-Mogg and we had a conversation, like two children in a playground, about which is your favourite page in the paper. William loved the Letters page, carrying, as it does, all the expertise, enthusiasms and eccentricities of *Times* readers. I loved the leader page, as it was the experience of leader conference every day that forced me to recognise what we knew and what we didn't, to come to a clear point of view that became the lens through which we saw everything else. (*The Guardian*, March 22, 2018)

Harding said in an interview for this volume that Rees-Mogg's advice about the responsibility and the opportunity of being editor of *The Times* made a deep impression. As they talked about the way Rees-Mogg had run the paper, the most striking point was that Geoffrey Dawson, editor 1912–19 and 1923–41, had got too close to government and for decades afterwards *The Times* was still paying the price of its coverage of prewar appeasement. "It was probably one of the most defining conversations I've had," Harding said. "Never find yourself in a position of going into Downing Street wanting something, asking something. It was a very formative conversation about how you make sure of that, given the place of *The Times* in British life . . . Above all [the paper] should not be too close to the established government."

As with many *Times* appointments, Harding's first joining *The Times* had been a little serendipitous. He was on leave from *The Financial Times* when he ran into Robert Thomson at a book launch. Harding recalled: "Robert said, 'By the way, what are you doing now,' in that rather 'you've fallen off the grid and you're useless' kind of way, which always gets your attention. And he added: 'Come and talk to me. I've got an idea.' So we had a few meetings about the business editor job and I arrived in 2006." During Harding's second year as business editor it was clear that News Corp was buying *The Wall Street Journal* and that once the deal was done, Thomson would be going to the United States. Candidates to replace him as *Times* editor were narrowed down to Harding and Gerard Baker, another Thomson recruit from the FT, who had become the US editor of *The Times*. Then one Saturday lunchtime Harding and Rupert Murdoch were eating burgers and fries at the Stafford Hotel in St James's Place, opposite Murdoch's London flat, and talking about the culture and nature of *The Times*. "It wasn't really a formal interview," Harding said, "but it was definitely a sounding out." Afterwards he stepped out into St James's wondering how it had gone and realised his sleeves were covered in ketchup. No matter, the following week he heard that he was going to be appointed editor.

Harding's background was markedly different from Thomson's, although there was a common thread in Japan and China. He was born on September 15, 1969, and grew up in northwest London. He was educated at two independent boys' schools: The Hall in Hampstead and St Paul's School in Barnes. He took a first in history at Trinity College, Cambridge, and won a Daiwa Scholarship, a 19-month programme of language study, work placement and homestay in Japan. The scholarship's prospectus offers "young and talented UK citizens with strong leadership potential the opportunity to acquire Japanese language skills and to access expertise and knowledge relevant to their career goals". Harding worked as a speechwriter (in

English) for Koichi Kato, chief secretary to the Japanese cabinet, and in the Japan unit of the European Commission 1993–94. He is generally credited with speaking Japanese, Chinese, French and German. Although he studied Japanese on the Daiwa scheme he says that his command of it is that of a six-year-old and in general he feels about his languages "that it's like hearing people speaking through ice".

Addressing a religion and media festival in a Jewish community centre in north London in 2018, Harding revealed that at the start of his career as a journalist he had considered reverting to his family's original name, Hirschowitz, according to *The Jewish Chronicle*. It had been changed by his grandparents after they moved from Berlin to London in 1936. When he asked his grandmother whether he should use James Hirschowitz as his byline she recommended he stick to Harding. Harding also told the audience that he had once [when at the BBC, after leaving *The Times*] been asked whether his Jewish background disqualified him from leading a large news organisation. He added that he had received "inane and insulting" abuse on Twitter (*The Jewish Chronicle*, March 29, 2018).

He joined *The Financial Times* in 1994, moving around as very junior reporters did there, covering companies and markets, then Westminster, agriculture and corporate affairs, before becoming China correspondent. He opened the paper's Shanghai bureau and covered the expansion of the Chinese financial markets until 1999, when he returned to London as media editor. Three years later he went to Washington as bureau chief and moved to *The Times* in August 2006.

Looking back to his first *Times* morning news conference as business editor, he said: "I was thinking this is really exactly like the FT. They were sitting around, the first item was about unemployment figures and they were talking about what was happening in the labour market. And then someone said, 'Oh, I've got a story. There was a couple that went away on holiday for a week, and they'd left a window open, and a family of squirrels came in and ate their house.' And suddenly the whole room came alive with, 'Really? How did that happen? What do you mean?' And there were pictures and we were going to do a recreation of what the sitting room looked like before the squirrels ate it and then what they destroyed. And I suddenly thought, 'Yes, there's a sort of spirit of life here in this paper'." Harding said it opened him to a journalism that was trying to be in touch with all parts of life. "You could have Mike Atherton telling you about cricket one day and Caitlin Moran defining a new feminism the next day, and both of them being hilarious and me thinking I can't believe how lucky I am." He continued: "The truth is, the thing I really loved about it, and still hugely admire about *The Times*, is it's an amazing group of people. So you're suddenly in this group. The FT is kind of intellectual muscle, *The Times* is that too, but it's also got this range." (*Media Masters* podcast, November 7, 2019).

Squirrels apart, Harding's first months as editor were dominated by two threatening presences: financial armageddon and Gordon Brown. Brown's takeover of 10 Downing Street in June 2007, after years of frustration at Tony Blair's reluctance to make way for him, turned out to have signified the high-water mark of the relationship of *The Times* with the Labour administration that had held power since 1997. While keeping close to Blair under his premiership, the political editor Phil Webster had also cultivated excellent relations with the new prime minister's team, especially Ed Balls, Brown's closest political ally. Once Brown had at last seized the reins of power, however, a bust-up between *The Times* and No 10 soon followed. Harding had a walk-on role in this before he even became editor. In his final months as business editor, he was invited into 10 Downing Street some weeks before Brown's first party conference as prime minister that September in Bournemouth. While there he spotted Bob Shrum, a US political consultant, who cheerfully admitted to helping Brown with his big speech. When the speech was delivered at the conference, Daniel Finkelstein, who was head of comment at *The Times*, detected phrases such as "moral compass" in it that were similar to those used in speeches by top American politicians whom Shrum had also advised. Two and two were put together at Wapping. *The Times* published a front-page story questioning the originality, and by implication the authenticity, of Brown's claims to be a politician driven by a well-functioning moral sense. Finkelstein wrote in a conciliatory Comment article that for decades Shrum had been "putting phrases in the mouths of politicians. And brilliant phrases they have been too. Who can blame Gordon Brown for wanting to lay his hands on a writer of Shrum's quality?" Brown exploded. The ashen faces of senior *Times* executives the morning after publication spoke to what one described as a "full force 10" blown by the prime minister across the Atlantic to *The Times* corporate HQ in New York overnight. Nonetheless, when Brown's allies dismissed the story as garbage, *The Times* doubled-down with a new analysis pointing out similarities between other speeches he had made and those of US politicians as far back as Jimmy Carter in 1988. In a leader *The Times* added: "That Mr Brown's minions, having been caught out, should try to smear *The Times* and its journalists was . . . far from the behaviour of the statesman that he clearly aspires to be." For Webster the story was uncomfortable, made all the more awkward since his name had been put on a splash he had not written and without his knowledge. Once the political team had returned from seaside Bournemouth to London it was obvious to all that things would never be the same. In his memoirs Brown wrote that he had "spent far more time on what now seems a trivial issue than I should" but also bracketed the piece with another in *The Sun* launching a campaign for a referendum on the EU's Lisbon Treaty as the moment it became apparent to him that the "Murdoch press would be my adversary" (Brown, 2018).

His anger was stoked by another story in *The Times* that would not go away. Francis Elliott had reported in August that Brown was considering calling an early general election because of Labour's good ratings in the polls. Despite official denials, the story had gained traction as Brown apparently dithered. At the Conservative Party conference in Blackpool a week after Labour's, David Cameron, the Tory leader, challenged Brown to dissolve parliament and to go to the country. Finally, Brown announced he would serve out Labour's full term to 2010 and insisted, to much mockery, that his decision had nothing to do with polls that showed a diminishing Labour lead. Cameron's barely disguised jubilation revealed just how badly Brown had miscalculated.

The change of editor at *The Times* in December was an opportunity to try to reset relations with the prime minister. On his first day Harding plunged straight in by joining Webster and Peter Riddell in Downing Street for an exclusive interview with Brown and Alan Greenspan, former chair of the US Federal Reserve. They had much to discuss. As business editor, Harding's pages had been dominated in 2007 by the faltering UK economy and the gathering financial storm clouds in the United States. In September the subprime mortgage crisis in America, caused when its housing price bubble collapsed, had triggered a run on the

British bank Northern Rock, a former building society, prompting the UK government to step in with a controversial £25 billion rescue plan to avoid Northern Rock's nationalisation. The Downing Street interview ranged widely: an injection of £50 billion by the Bank of England and four other central banks into global money markets to fend off recession; the signing of the new European reform treaty in Lisbon; and advice for Fabio Capello, the favourite to become England football manager. Asked if he enjoyed being prime minister at last, Brown responded: "Did I ever think it was going to be fun? Sometimes you feel that every day there's a new challenge, so you can never get bored in this job. I hope people will look back [over the past few months] and whether it was floods, foot-and-mouth, avian flu or the financial turbulence, feel that we dealt with them in the right way."

The bonhomie was short-lived, and "financial turbulence" was barely adequate to describe what was about to hit. Greenspan got closer to it when he talked in the joint interview about economies hitting stall speed. World stock markets plunged on Monday, January 21, 2008. Some £77 billion was wiped off the value of Britain's stock market in its biggest one-day percentage loss since the terror attacks in America on September 11, 2001. Next day, page 1 of *The Times* was dominated by a picture of a harassed trader with tickers showing markets everywhere down: London –5.48%, Germany –7.6%, India –7.4%, Hong Kong –5.5%, China –5.1%. The billionaire investor George Soros said the crash was "much more serious than any financial crisis since the end of the war". Northern Rock was in free fall. Its shares, which had peaked at more than £12 early in 2007, fell to 90p before dealings were suspended in February. More efforts were made to prop up the bank until on February 22 it passed into the public sector. Anatole Kaletsky, the *Times* economic commentator, was scathing. The Northern Rock bailout, he wrote, was Brown's Black Wednesday. The bailout "will demolish or, at best, discredit the entire economic policy framework created in 1997 [when Labour had come to power]. Since the creation of this framework was his one unquestionable achievement, it seems fair to say that Mr Brown's career as a serious politician ended yesterday".

The global financial turmoil intensified for month after month. By late summer, speculation was mounting that Lehman Brothers, the US investment bank, might collapse. When Suzy Jagger reported in August from New York that it was in talks to sell its entire $40 billion real estate portfolio to stem losses from the American property slump, its stock had fallen 69 per cent in a year. On Friday, September 12, Business News's Rumour of the Day was that Lehman had only days left to live unless it found a buyer. Two days later bankruptcy was imminent. *The Times* splash on Tuesday, September 16 was: "Lehman collapse sends shockwave round world". Six paragraphs stripped across the foot of the page hammered home the international financial crisis: "US nationalises AIG"; "Bank extends funds"; "Stocks in free fall"; "Goldman slides"; "Dollar dips, gold up"; "Jobless on the rise" (September 18, 2008). A fortnight later the Dow Jones industrial average had plunged almost 800 points in the worst one-day fall since Black Monday in 1987. Kaletsky commented: "We are now unquestionably in the worst financial crisis since the Great Depression".

Brown's authority had been badly shot by his failure to hold a snap election, but the global financial crash seemed initially to offer him a chance at redemption as he sought to coordinate an international response of counter-recessionary stimulus. For the remaining two years of his premiership, *The Times* entered a period of studied political neutrality. Outwardly at least, it appeared the paper remained sceptical about Cameron's new generation of Conservatives while relations with the Labour Party ranged from cordial to chilly. Camilla Cavendish, associate editor and columnist, writing on January 17, 2008, gave readers an early heads-up about the Brown operation's unsavoury side: "Lobby journalists have become used to receiving text messages, constructed almost entirely of expletives, from Damien McBride, Downing Street's press man. Maybe hacks sometimes deserve a hard time. But it is counter-productive for the political class to be so graceless under pressure." Just over a year later, in April 2009, McBride was forced to resign after being caught in unsavoury muckraking. He was accused of using a government computer to disseminate emails promoting a plot to smear senior members of the Conservative Party. It involved spreading unsubstantiated rumours that George Osborne, the shadow chancellor, took drugs and had sex with a prostitute; that David Cameron had an "embarrassing illness"; and that a gay Tory MP was promoting his partner's business interests in the House of Commons. Brown once again found himself facing into the howling wind of a hostile media climate.

The situation worsened almost immediately with a stunning leak from the Commons authorities that processed MPs' expenses claims. For years the political inhibition against raising their salaries had provided – within Westminster at least – a sort of unspoken understanding that MPs would receive generous allowances in lieu of higher pay; but it had long been claimed that this expenses system was being abused. MPs were entitled to claim an Additional Cost Allowance of up to £24,000 a year for running a second home. There was also £22,000 of "incidental expenses provision" for office expenses over and above salaries for staff. Rules about employing relations were virtually non-existent. A drive to flush out the details of expenses claims, using freedom of information laws, was nearing completion in early 2009 and was set for release in July. In May, however, *The Daily Telegraph* started to publish details culled from a leak of the entire expenses files. For the following two months MPs' expenses dominated the news agenda with a relentless exposé that laid bare in excruciating detail every claim, large and petty, venal and banal. *The Telegraph* did an excellent job of proving how MPs used the lax rules on expenses to make sizeable profits on their properties. It revealed claims for ride-on lawnmowers, a swimming pool boiler, a love seat, rabbit fencing, gardeners, mole extermination, moat cleaning and a £1,645 "duck house". The outrage had reached the point where it threatened the legitimacy of the political process itself, a *Times* leader said on Saturday, May 9. The firestorm claimed dozens of careers and led to a number of criminal convictions. The owner of the duck house, Sir Peter Viggars, admitted that he had made a "ridiculous and grave error of judgment" and revealed that his ducks had never liked it anyway.

For the *Times* parliamentary team it was a miserable period. *The Times* had to play catch-up every evening after *The Telegraph*'s first editions arrived. Rupert Murdoch expressed his "disappointment" that the story had not come to *The Times*. The misery was compounded by the fact that the paper had been offered some of the same material for cash and had turned it down, but there was a reason: *The Telegraph*'s source material had been stolen. *The Times* (and *The Sun*) had been approached in February by a businessman offering to sell data about all MPs' expenses for £300,000. They would have to pay blind, without knowing what the disk contained, Philip Webster explained in his book, and would have been buying stolen goods (Webster, 2016, p. 368). Harding defended the decision not to buy, reinforced by the advice of the in-house lawyers, but after two months of humiliation everyone was feeling the pressure. With hindsight, as more and more preposterous expenses claims were revealed, it became clear that there would have been a public interest defence in paying for stolen goods and publishing the disk. Harding explained:

> The legal advice was that you wouldn't pay for stolen goods and the mistake that the paper made was in not looking at what those goods were. We didn't fully appreciate what the public interest would be. So we had the very uncomfortable experience of following in the second edition stories that were appearing in the first edition of *The Telegraph* for too many days than I care to remember. I think it was an interesting experience for me because the first year I'd been editing the paper we'd had a lot of wins and then [this story] comes along and you're losing. I actually learnt a lot about the culture of the newsroom and the strength of the newsroom. I remember thinking that it's one thing when the wind is in your sails and it's another when you're pedalling against the wind. And a lot of things that we then ended up doing in the years afterwards were actually shaped by that. We got tougher about our determination in terms of campaigning journalism, investigative journalism. We were more determined as a result of it . . . I don't think Rupert Murdoch was the only person who thought it was the story that got away. I'm not sure there was anyone in the building who didn't think that.

Despite the fact that many of the most egregious offenders in the expenses scandal were Tories, Cameron adroitly seized the political initiative and positioned himself as the reforming insurgent against a sleaze-mired Brown. While the *Times* news pages continued to keep their distance from this Tory operation, the Comment section was less reserved. There were multiple personal and professional ties between a number of columnists and the Tory new guard. Michael Gove, a key architect of the Cameron takeover, had himself been with *The Times* until relatively recently. There were times when the political team at Westminster felt exposed: it was clear that their colleagues on the Comment pages knew far more about the Cameron operation. The suspicion was that information was too often flowing in the wrong direction. In 2008 Cameron had hired Andy Coulson, former editor of *The News of the World*, a News UK stablemate of *The Times*, to be his spin doctor. Coulson clearly believed that it was more important to cultivate good relations at editor level and above than to curry favour with reporters. With Labour heading for seemingly inevitable defeat in an election that had to be held in 2010 at the latest, Brown faced a series of plots to force him out. James Purnell launched the first, resigning as work and pensions secretary in June 2009. Webster, a golfing friend of Purnell, got the story but the coup flopped as Peter Mandelson, ennobled and brought back into government by Brown, prevented it from triggering a wider insurrection. In January 2010 Geoff Hoon and Patricia Hewitt launched a last effort to drive out Brown. This time it was Francis Elliott, Webster's deputy, who got the key interview. It again failed to lead to a wider revolt.

Alastair Darling, the chancellor, had known about the plotting but concluded along with most other Labour MPs that with just months to go before the election the time for regicide had passed. Tellingly, he had failed to tip off Brown: of all the fissures in that dying administration none was as serious as that which divided Brown and Darling on the correct political response to the global financial crash. Darling wanted to level with the country about the depth of the financial hole the country was in, arguing that such honesty was better than appearing to be in denial. But Brown had been furious when his chancellor said in August 2008 that the country was facing the most challenging financial situation in 60 years and the two were at loggerheads for most of the rest of their period in government. The dramatic deterioration of public finances had helped Cameron and George Osborne, the shadow chancellor, to make inroads into Labour's reputation for economic competence. Brown, however, refused to acknowledge that the crash had changed the terms of debate. The eventual endorsement of the Conservative Party at the 2010 election by *The Times* was a surprise to nobody. By now Harding had decided to replace Webster with Roland Watson. The pair had worked as rival correspondents in Washington previously. Watson, who had also spent time in the parliamentary office under Webster, had been at Eton at the same time as Cameron, but although friends at school, they had since forged very different paths and did not socialise.

Harding saw Watson as "relentlessly hard-working, trustworthy, with insightful political judgment, level-headed, not easy to push about". Scrupulous and understated, the new political editor shared little of Cameron's swagger.

The would-be prime minister's self-belief was tested as Brown started to make ground in the polls as the general election on May 6 drew closer. Election night itself, the last in *The Times* offices on The Highway at Wapping, was a tense affair. Watson and his team holed up in one of the glass-sided offices that fringed the main newsroom to get on with the job of reporting the results, while various corporate executives sat around Finkelstein who delivered a running commentary. As the night wore on, blithe predictions of a Tory landslide foundered on the reality of something much more messy. The Conservatives had won 306 seats, Labour 258 and the Liberal Democrats 57. It was the first hung parliament since 1974.

In a leader on Saturday, May 8, *The Times* said Cameron had the moral right to govern, even if he lacked the constitutional right, and Brown should get out of the way rather than seek to shore up his position by trying to do a deal with the Liberal Democrats. Over the next few days all possible permutations for a government were aired. For *The Times*, it was a story that demanded good contacts with all the parties as well as a good grip of the policy issues at stake in the complex set of negotiations. It also required stamina: a political team that had already been working flat out for more than a month reporting the election now had another week of 18 hours days.

On Monday, May 10, a *Times* leader urged Cameron and Nick Clegg, the Liberal Democrat leader, to forge an agreement that would transform their parties and British government for good. The next day Brown resigned. The splash on Wednesday, May 12, was headlined "Embracing change". A new political era opened with Cameron as prime minister and Clegg as his deputy in Britain's first coalition government since the Second World War. Both sides committed to a full five-year term.

CHAPTER EIGHT

Harding in his first year as editor made a radical change to the position in *The Times* of its most sacrosanct feature: on Monday, June 2, 2008, readers opened the paper to find that the leaders had been moved to page 2 from the centre of the book. The third leader, headlined "Modern Times: The latest chapter in our long history of reinvention", explained that the rationale was a belief that the modern newspaper was about information and the ideas that made sense of it. Looking back, Harding would explain that the decision was influenced by *The Economist*, which placed leaders at the front of the book and so in his words, "you knew what *The Economist* stood for".

Given that commoditised news was so readily available on the internet and that one of the great strengths of *The Times* was that it would give an informed, incisive point of view, he felt that a paper calling itself the Thunderer should not bury its opinions in the middle of the paper. A countervailing view was that readers were being presented with an opinion before they had had a chance to read the relevant news report. "That argument never really stood up for me," Harding said, "because [previously] some stories came before the leaders and some after them." Bringing the leaders forward to page 2 "focused the thinking of the paper around how it saw the world on economic and business policy, on social issues and politics and international affairs. And it made you think what you cared about. And that was really important to me."

The leaders moved as part of a bigger redesign triggered by new presses coming onstream as the £760 million Project Hal begun under Robert Thomson in 2005 came to fruition. The new Broxbourne press hall in Hertfordshire had opened in February. The last copies of *The Times* printed in Wapping had rolled out of the old press hall there on April 19, and ten days later the "New Knowsley" press hall on Merseyside had opened. High-quality colour printing on the new presses gave *Times* designers fresh opportunities in news presentation. A central point of his redesign, Harding explained, was making a compact newspaper a more intelligent paper in what was historically a tabloid format.

The in-house redesign manual told designers and sub-editors that editorial display "should exude calmness, authority and confidence . . . *The Times* aims each day to inform, entertain, delight and surprise our readers". The redesign was "contemporary, restrained and elegant. Sections are colour-coded to help navigation. Readers should be able to distinguish immediately between news, commentary and analysis. Display choices indicate story styles (hard news, human interest, humour, news features and so on)." Page 3, opposite the new leader page, was to become an alternative front page with the second strongest hard news story of the day. That was another key change by Harding. Traditionally, page 3 had offered a change of pace with a softer, human interest story; that would now appear less prominently on page 4.

More space was to be given to opinion, and letters received increased prominence. A revamped Times 2, "a daily magazine covering life, style and the arts", included more games, puzzles and a *Young Times* section for children. On June 2 it led on Stefanie Marsh's exclusive interview with Natascha Kampusch, who was kidnapped at the age of ten and held in a cellar for more than eight years until she escaped in 2006. A new motoring column by Giles Smith revealed "the truth about SUVs and marriage". The Daily Register section now included a "modern miscellany for readers wondering about things to do, where to go and what's happening away from the headlines" and a daily photograph from the enormous *Times* archive of pictures going back to the early days of newspaper photography.

The leader on June 2 invited comments on the changes, saying: "The success of *The Times* is underwritten by the intelligence of our readers." Predictably, Sally Baker's Feedback column the following Saturday carried a mixed bag of responses. Complaints about the layout of the crossword vied with a general acceptance of the Register section; leaders on page 2 were acceptable although difficult to read in bed with the light behind them. Derek Harris summed up: "I'm a thoroughly miserable b***ard, so when I heard on *Today* that you'd mucked around with the paper, I swore. So well done on the revised layout. It's only right that leaders and opinion have more prominence, and from what I can ascertain, you've improved the paper immeasurably – signed, your suspicious and generally offensive loyal reader."

Complainants received letters from the editor explaining that the adjustments to format, design and presentation "were intended to reinforce the paper's traditional strengths, namely balanced and thoughtful reporting, courageous coverage of world events, intelligent opinion, vivid photography and the very best writing". Harding added personalised footnotes answering specific comments to many of his replies. Two former editors approved: Simon Jenkins said the new look was a "triumph", and Charles Wilson said *The Times* had improved since Harding's appointment and "looks in very good shape editorially". He added that his only doubt was about page 2, a problem that nobody had ever solved. If a reader survey showed that more people were reading the leaders in their new position "you would have won by a knockout".

While the look of the paper changed, there were also other significant moves within the *Times* offices in Harding's first year as he reshaped his editorial top team. One of his earliest appointments, in January 2008, was the promotion of Keith Blackmore from executive editor to deputy editor. Blackmore had joined *The Times* in 1988 after five years in Bermuda, where he had been a reporter for *The Royal Gazette* daily paper and the weekly *Mid-Ocean News* and then editor of the weekly *Bermuda Sun*. He was to play a central role at the paper in the next five years as Harding's confidant. Drawing on his long experience of rising from deputy sports editor to senior management, he told the new editor light-heartedly that "*The Times* is a ship that runs. Your job is to stand at the front of the ship and just wave."

David Driver, design director, retired on August 8, 2008, four days after his 66th birthday and two months after the big redesign had been launched. He had been recruited to *The Times* by Harry Evans in 1981. While laying a lawn at home and grovelling in the mud, he remembered, he had heard his wife call through a window that Evans was on the phone. Evans explained that he was moving from editing *The Sunday Times* to *The Times*, and would Driver like to go with him? Driver had been for 12 years the highly innovative and respected art director of the *Radio Times* in what was seen as the golden age of British magazines. He was slightly puzzled by Evans's call as he was also in negotiation at the time with Tina Brown, Evans's wife, to be art director of *Tatler*, which she was editing. Neither seemed to know what the other was up to. Driver had never met Evans but went in the next day for a meeting with him. Perplexingly, Evans seemed to be mainly concerned about the livery on the *Times* delivery vans. Asked for his thoughts about the paper, Driver said he would reintroduce the royal coat of arms to the masthead immediately. He accepted the job, and the coat of arms reappeared on July 30, 1981, the day after Charles and Diana's wedding.

In his 27 years at *The Times*, Driver went from drawing his meticulous page plans on paper in noisy, smoke-filled newsrooms to designing on-screen in air conditioned, carefully lit and comparatively tranquil open-plan offices. He had a profound influence on the look and feel of *The Times* over a quarter of a century, always striving to push forward typography, layout and the very format of the paper. He could be an exacting colleague. Those who had known him earlier in his career said he had mellowed somewhat by the time he arrived at *The Times*, but he was never satisfied with less than the best and his pages were always greater than the sum of their parts. In the days when passports listed occupations, he gave his as journalist, not designer; his approach was always based on a deep understanding of the written word, as he made clear ten years after retirement, in an interview with *Eye*, the graphic design magazine: "Going to *The Times*, I assumed I'd be impressed by the standard of handling words and sub-editing. But they were nowhere up to the standard we had at *Radio Times*."

Information graphics were one of the innovations that Driver was most proud of. He had developed the skill at school, where he would turn his geography books into graphic stories and his essays would have a pullout graphic with complementary information. In 1982, after just a year at *The Times*, he presented readers with a full broadsheet page devoted to a graphic with specifications and silhouettes of all the British fighting ships heading to the Falklands war. "That really opened people's eyes to what you could do," he told *Eye*.

Driver transformed the graphics department from a provider of single-column black and white maps into one of the paper's most creative layers of journalism, with young graphic artists adding value and interest to reports in all areas of the paper. The exception to that youthful talent was the delightful veteran Richard Leadbetter, who had retired in 2005 aged 82. The bearded, checked-shirted master of the page 1 puff, universally known as Dick, would respond to Driver's desperate call on deadline of "Where's my Dick?" with a cheery cry of "Just a minute!", often followed by "Something's wrong with my machine". Tim Hames, chief leader writer, left *The Times* in July 2008. Having flourished under the editorships of Peter Stothard and Robert Thomson, he thought that Harding would want to move the leader line "in a much more sympathetic Cameronite direction". Hames was offered what he saw as a "half-baked" post as public policy editor, which he declined.

Hames's views had fluctuated over time. But he was not wanted as a columnist and the gap between his opinions and the editor's was widening. A year later he became special adviser to John Bercow, who, having formerly been a right-wing Tory, had just been installed with Labour support as the Speaker of the House of Commons. Daniel Finkelstein replaced Hames as chief leader writer and made wholesale changes to the team, bringing in Oliver Kamm, Phil Collins, Hugo Rifkind and Joe Joseph to write leaders. Camilla Cavendish remained with the team and he also enlisted Rachel Sylvester and Alice Thomson. As Finkelstein described it, "We developed a more consistent liberal/conservative centre-right position".

It was under Harding, in 2010, that *The Times* made what remains in many ways its defining digital decision, when it began to charge for digital subscriptions and introduced what became known as the paywall. Commercially and strategically, the decision was driven by James Murdoch. It was a bold move, defying received industry wisdom at the time, but *The Times* implemented it with conviction. Thanks to Rupert Murdoch's relationship with Steve Jobs, the paper was sent four iPads before the Apple tablet device was launched in the UK in the summer of 2010. It meant that *The Times* could be downloaded by iPad users from day one. It also meant there were just under four weeks to design a new digital version of a newspaper, one that gave readers the sensation of turning the page, that had the architecture and hierarchy of the paper, and yet all the interactivity and functionality of the screen. It also informed the redesign of the website, which adopted the visual language of the paper, something that was at odds with most newspaper websites at the time. It was an approach that stood the test of time and shaped the editorial digital thinking of *The Times* for more than a decade. It also drove the introduction of Times+, the membership model that was key to subscription growth. And it reset the economics of the paper, as print sales entered a long period of structural decline, digital sales – despite the many, many sceptics at the time – were to grow and grow. On the day the iPad was launched, Harding wrote a note to Steve Jobs to thank him, noting that this was the first day since 1785 that people could buy a copy of *The Times* on anything other than paper.

Anne Spackman, a key figure in the modernisation of *The Times* under Thomson and Harding, had been in the frontline of change at *The Times* for several years, first in the switch to the compact format and then in developing Times Online. When she moved to the calmer pastures of comment editor in October 2008, Harding said: "Anne Spackman has done an extraordinary job at Times Online bringing our journalism to more people than at any time in our history. She has expanded the nature of what we do as a news organisation, introducing a 24/7 newsroom, launching *The Times* archive and developing our podcasts, video and reader comments online. Since the relaunch of Times Online in February 2007 we have increased traffic from 9 million to 20 million unique monthly users."

Just as she had been uncertain about becoming online editor, Spackman had some misgivings about her suitability for the role of comment editor; but she found that it was the best job she had ever had, working with a team of talented copy editors who included Robbie Millen (later literary editor), Paul Dunn and Tim Rice. She wanted the pages to be like university tutorials and seminars where readers could get rich and varied intellectual stimulation from interesting bylines. While longstanding regulars such as Libby Purves, Matthew Parris, David Aaronovitch and William Rees-Mogg retained their weekly slots, she was keen to mix them with topical pieces commissioned each morning from outside experts in relevant fields. She was gratified to find that "nobody ever puts the phone down on you when you say you are comment editor of *The Times*".

More staff moves followed as Harding put his stamp on the paper. Richard Beeston became foreign editor, David Wighton business and city editor and Anoushka Healy assistant editor, strategy and development. In May 2009, at the start of the cricket season, Christopher Martin-Jenkins, chief cricket correspondent for 20 years, was replaced by the former England captain Mike Atherton. Harding also hired the marine scientist and archaeologist Frank Pope in a unique new role that Pope himself later explained in lyrical terms: "I was the ocean correspondent for *The Times*: the world's only national newspaper with a reporter dedicated to covering the 71 per cent of the planet that is covered by water. The beat is as wide as the horizon and as deep as the Mariana Trench, covering everything from offshore energy to environment, piracy to science, shipwrecks and exploration." The biggest weekly feast for *Times* readers was the Saturday paper, an enormous multisection edition with sales significantly above those of the weekday *Times*. Here, too, Harding was not afraid of change.

A cull of Saturday supplements closed down Body & Soul (covering health and well-being) and The Knowledge (the listings magazine) in 2009. Gone, too, was a stand-alone books section introduced by Thomson. To some extent these changes were driven by a perennial need to find savings. What stopped them being mere cost-cutting measures was the arrival of Nicola Jeal, a features editor of something like genius, whom Harding had been trying to poach from *The Observer* for more than a year. For Harding her arrival was "the most important appointment in the redesign of the Saturday paper – and for *The Times*'s features and magazine writing in the 15 years since". She remade the *Times Saturday* magazine along with much of the rest of the paper and, Harding feels "in every way, it was all the better for it".

Some of the apparent culling was in any case deceptive. Books coverage was cut back to four pages in a new Saturday Review arts and culture section, but how much of substance was lost in that move is open to debate. The stand-alone books section was (or often seemed) largely given over to features, interviews and first-person pieces by literary-minded celebrities. There were regular columns by Jeanette Winterson, David Baddiel and the literary editor Erica Wagner, all sharing their passion for literature and urging readers not to be afraid of books. Actual coverage of books was relatively sparse, as if book reviews were thought rather old hat.

As literary editor Wagner – charming, shaven-headed, tattooed, wearing Doc Martens – had long cut her own dash, whizzing to book events by motorbike. Manhattan-born and Cambridge-educated, she was a literary insider: she had studied for an MA in creative writing at the University of East Anglia, where she was taught by Malcolm Bradbury and Rose Tremain. Her first writing experience had been forging the signatures of Kermit the Frog, Fozzie Bear and Miss Piggy; her parents ran the official Muppet Show fan club and she helped out with replying to letters from the viewing public.

Wagner had been appointed literary editor in 1996 under Peter Stothard who, while editing *The Times*, also directed which books should be reviewed. She was the author of *Gravity*, a collection of short stories about "the loneliness of the human condition", and *Ariel's Gift*, exploring the relationship between Ted Hughes and Sylvia Plath. She served as a judge for the Booker Prize on two occasions, as well as for the Women's Fiction prize and the Goldsmiths Prize. She shares responsibility for awarding the Goldsmiths Prize to *Ducks, Newburyport*, a thousand-page, single-sentence stream-of-consciousness novel.

Harding had no fear of being thought highbrow. While he loved the way *The Times* could find interest and entertainment in placcs where *The Financial Times*, his previous employer, would never have thought to look, he also relished intellectual seriousness, and he was confident that *Times* readers relished it too, in books pages, arts coverage, opinion columns and elsewhere. Eureka, a science magazine, was launched in October 2009. The 64-page supplement, beautifully designed by Matt Curtis, came free with the paper on the first Thursday of every month. It was the first monthly science magazine distributed in a national newspaper and covered topics from life sciences to earth sciences. *The Times* had the biggest and most authoritative science team of any national newspaper, and Eureka gave them a unique showcase. At the time of its launch, News International said that the title reinforced the company's "commitment to invest in quality journalism and to expand the award-winning team of science, health and environment writers at *The Times*". Advertisers in the first issue had included BAE Systems, Shell and BMW. By the time it closed three years later, after 37 issues, Eureka had a readership of 552,000, of which the vast majority were in the ABC1 social category. At the Chelsea Flower Show in 2011, the *Times* Eureka Garden in association with the Royal Botanic Gardens, Kew, designed by Marcus Barnett, won a silver flora award.

Almost unnoticed in the transformative whirl, Harding made a big change in his personal life, too, as the Media Monkey column of *The Guardian* noted on July 9, 2009:

If you edit a national newspaper, you might as well use it to announce your engagement. And so it is in today's *Times*, with an item Monkey spotted tucked away in the Register on page 52 under Forthcoming Marriages: 'Mr JP Harding and Miss K Weinberg – The engagement is announced between James, son of Dr and Mrs Michael Harding, of London, and Kate, youngest daughter of Sir Mark Weinberg and the late Sandra Weinberg, and step-daughter of Lady Weinberg, of London.' Aw, bless. Congratulations to them both.

When they married in 2010, Harding became son-in-law to two prominent figures in London society. Sir Mark Weinberg was a financier and Lady Weinberg, better known as Anouska Hempel, was a creator of luxury hotels.

On the corporate side, Rebekah Brooks, editor of *The Sun*, became chief executive officer of News International in 2009. Chris Longcroft joined the business and the following year succeeded Clive Milner as finance director of operations, covering print sites across the UK, Ireland and Europe. He became chief financial officer in 2012, with a portfolio including operations, human resources, facilities, security and licensing, and he would later become News UK's chief financial officer and publisher of *The Times* and *Sunday Times*. Longcroft's immediate challenge was to plug the losses at Times Newspapers Ltd (comprising *The Times* and *Sunday Times*), which reached £87.7 million in 2009. Project Walter involved Longcroft, Harding, Emma Tucker and Anoushka Healy looking at *The Times* "line by line" with a view to reversing the losses.

An update provided for Brooks in December 2009 mentioned a Monday–Friday relaunch accompanied by a cover price increase; potential savings by closing T2 (£4 million) and The Game (£0.8 million); and editorial savings of between £5 million and £10 million. Further savings were made in 2010 when all the News International titles moved to Thomas More Square, the large office block between St Katharine Docks and the Wapping site, which was bought for £150 million by St George, part of the Berkeley Group, in May 2012. Project Walter would bring immediate benefits. By April 2012 Times Newspapers Ltd was reported to have cut annual pre-tax losses to £11.6 million for the year to July 3, 2011 – a quarter of the £45 million pre-tax loss for the same period in 2010. It did so despite the resurrection of Times 2, which had been discontinued early in March 2010 as part of Project Walter but was restored as a pullout section on Wednesday, October 13, 2010. Its resurrection came in response to a chorus of reader complaints, some from men who said they gave the section to their wives over breakfast while they read the news or did the crossword in the main paper, others from wives who claimed to be content with this arrangement. "It's back," trumpeted the page 1 puff, "bigger, brighter and still the best." Next day Emma Tucker, the editor of Times 2, wrote that hundreds of readers had already expressed their delight. Domestic harmony was restored. "Everyone has second thoughts," a leader said. "It's second nature. And what tastier dish is there to any diner than seconds? We hope you enjoy the feast."

Along with the rest of News International, the carbon footprint of *The Times* was shrinking too. James Murdoch, executive chairman of News International from 2007, was an early adopter of non-polluting cars with his Tesla electric roadster, which had a dedicated power socket in the executive car park at Wapping. In January 2008, News International became the first major newspaper group in the UK to go carbon neutral. Among simple energy-saving initiatives, shorter delays before monitors went into sleep mode had cut the PC and Mac carbon footprint by 668 tonnes a year; printing emails was discouraged; the staff canteen emphasised British sourcing for ingredients and sustainable fish, and offered vegetarian and vegan options; and Green Tomato's hybrid vehicles were the preferred London taxis for staff use. The main UK supplier of newsprint used 100 per cent recycled content. For every tree felled in sustainably managed forests, three were planted. The inks had no heavy metals and could be removed during the "de-inking" process and the Broxbourne presses were 20 per cent more efficient than the Wapping ones. From 2008, electricity for all News International's UK-owned properties came from 100 per cent renewable sources. Videoconferencing facilities were increasingly being used as a practical alternative to air travel. For Wapping staff, one big change after the move from the print site was the loss of the large car park they had used since 1986; they were encouraged to travel by bike instead.

CHAPTER NINE

The Times was often chary of describing an investigation as a campaign, to avoid any suspicion of an agenda beyond normal news values, and the very idea of a campaign might have made its Leeds-based reporter Andrew Norfolk uncomfortable. Yet the social and political impact of Norfolk's groundbreaking investigation of child sex abuse by organised grooming gangs in the north of England could hardly be described as anything but a campaign. Encouraged by James Harding, he overcame his own unease about the dangers of racial stereotyping and wrote a sustained series of many articles over several years that were recognised by his peers with the Paul Foot Award in 2012, the Orwell Prize in 2013 and journalist of the year at the British Journalism Awards in 2014.

Norfolk was revered by colleagues as an investigative news reporter of the old school: in an interview with *The Guardian* (September 28, 2014) he said: "My job is to write news stories. I think the best way I can help is to carry on working as a journalist." After Durham University, Norfolk joined the *Scarborough Evening News* in 1989, *The Yorkshire Post* in 1995 and *The Times* in 2000. His happiest times were on his first paper, he said: "I didn't have an ambitious bone in my body in terms of making it to a national newspaper." Although he admired some recruits to the trade, he worried about more and more aspiring journalists initiating political careers – private school, Oxbridge, policy wonk, power – without ever being junior reporters, away from London. "It's very old-fashioned but I also think it's important to have a few years where, if you screw up, people can walk into your office and let you know about it."

In a rare first-person piece (August 28, 2014) Norfolk explained the background to the sex abuse story that had occupied him since he had moved from London back to Leeds in 2002 as the northeast correspondent for *The Times* to write about "people who are not typical *Times* readers". It began in 2003 when Ann Cryer, the Labour MP from Keighley, West Yorkshire, revealed her concerns about the targeting of girls aged between 12 and 14 by "Asian men" outside the gates of two local schools. Their parents said they had been lured into a world of flashy cars, alcohol, drugs and sex but the police and social services seemed to be uninterested. When a

Muslim councillor came to meet the five mothers who had helped Cryer to compile a list of 66 men suspected of grooming he was upset and took the list to the community elders. They looked at the names and then said it was nothing to do with them. A senior West Yorkshire police officer suggested that the girls might have "made a lifestyle choice"; Cryer said that young girls in short skirts and skimpy tops were seen as easy meat by some Asian men. They did not understand that a girl dressed like that simply because it was the fashion: "They think it's a come-on and that white girls are easy." At the time, Norfolk felt deeply uncomfortable about his report: "Innocent white victims, evil dark-skinned abusers. Liberal angst kicked instinctively into top gear." He covered it briefly before moving to other topics. As years passed, however, he had a nagging feeling that he hadn't done his job properly. Occasional stories and court cases came across his desk of girls sleeping with a "boyfriend" and then being asked to prove their love by sleeping with another young man and then with more friends. The men in court invariably had Muslim names and there was always more than one man in the dock. The trigger for Norfolk's investigation came seven years after his original 2003 story. In August 2010, he heard a radio news report that nine men in Greater Manchester had been convicted of offences against a 14-year-old girl. They were not identified, but Norfolk's hunch that they had Muslim names was correct. Trawling for three months through court records and local library newspaper archives, he unearthed some startling figures. It took two more months of digging to get the full picture. Police forces, social services, the Home Office and Barnardo's refused to discuss the issue. Eventually staff at two small independent children's charities introduced him to parents of some of the victims. On January 5, 2011, *The Times* splashed his explosive story. It was headlined "Revealed: conspiracy of silence on child sex gangs", with a subhead: "Most convicted offenders of Pakistani heritage. Young girls abused across North and Midlands." Norfolk's exposure revealed a pattern of sex crimes committed by men who had befriended and then abused girls as young as eleven. Most of the girls were white and, of the 56 men convicted in 17 prosecutions since 1997, 50 were from Muslim backgrounds and most were of Pakistani heritage. Police forces, charities and agencies working to help girls who had in some cases endured years of abuse, had denied publicly that ethnicity had any relevance to that pattern of on-street grooming. A decade of silence had made it easier for predators to groom girls. Children had been moved around the country in cars and used for sex by older men, leading to abortions for girls as young as 12. A 13-year-old victim from South Yorkshire examined by a nurse had, it seemed, been raped more than 50 times. Mohammed Shafiq, chief executive of the Ramadhan Foundation, an anti-extremism charity, wrote in *The Times* that day that the sexual exploitation of young teenagers was a crime against humanity and one that Islam totally forbade. White girls were being groomed because the men thought they had fewer morals and were less valuable than Muslim girls. They also believed that there would be no reprisals within their own communities. That form of racism, Shafiq said, was abhorrent in a society priding itself on equality and justice. "I would like to see imams and mosques addressing these crimes in their Friday sermons," he wrote, "explaining the Islamic ruling on such evil acts and that an attack on a white girl is as forbidden as an attack on our own daughters and sisters. I know there are some imams who have done this with great bravery." That day's leader on the scandal was long and nuanced:

> There is a case for saying that relations between different ethnic groups are as good in Britain as they are in any developed nation. For that to remain the case, it must be possible to conduct a frank conversation when problems surface. Today, *The Times* exposes a pattern of sex offending by groups of older men who have been befriending girls aged between 11 and 16 on the streets of towns in the North of England and the Midlands and then subjecting them to appalling, degrading sexual crimes. Most of the girls are white and, of the 56 people convicted in 17 court prosecutions since 1997, 50 were from Muslim backgrounds and most were of Pakistani heritage. Police sources have indicated to *The Times* that the prosecutions may well be an indication of a much deeper problem than is known. Yet a senior detective from the West Mercia force has conceded that the police and child protection workers are frightened to raise the issue for fear of being branded racist.
>
> It is common for the quite different forms of identity that are contained in race, ethnicity, nation and religion to become confused. It would be absurd, as well as insulting,

to say that the abuse of minors, or even a greater propensity to commit this crime, were somehow encoded in either the ethnicity or the religion of men of Pakistani origin. The obvious point bears repetition: more than 80 per cent of sex offenders in Britain are white men and the overwhelming majority of men of Pakistani origin are quite capable of living within the law. So, to that extent, the reluctance of the police and the relevant charities and agencies to draw ethnic conclusions is justified. That said, the pattern of crime exhibited in this case is so unusual that it is irresponsible not to attempt to understand why gangs procuring girls from the streets should be so prevalent within one community. The important point to remember is that sex crime is as much about power as it is about sex.

It continued:

There is one category that helps to explain the abuse of young girls. The dominion of men over women is a depressingly common species of injustice. Few societies can plead their entire innocence on that score. In these cases, the idea took the form of cultural superiority in the noxious belief that young white girls are lesser beings. The purity of Muslim girls was defended stoutly while white girls were castigated as being routinely sexually available. Within this self-contained world of delusion, behaviour is easily reinforced. Networks of people can gather in which the participants act according to the sanctioned rules of the group, with barely any thought to the laws that govern the world outside. These cases are a sharp reminder that closed communities have a dark side. Knowledge of the abuse is likely to have been widespread yet there is a tyranny of custom in some communities that suggests betraying members of that community is itself a sin. It is easy, in these circumstances, for good men to do nothing.

That is why this story needs the disinfectant of sunlight. The blunt fact is that procuring girls for sexual purposes is a crime. To that extent, the background of the criminals is beside the point. The internal trafficking of young girls who are drugged and then raped by older men is a disgraceful abuse. Already, voices have been raised in the community to express the outrage that is felt by its majority of law-abiding members. The law is also blind to background, as it should be, and when the truth emerges justice must follow.

Norfolk's revelations brought an immediate government response. Nick Clegg, the deputy prime minister and MP for a Sheffield constituency, denounced the actions of criminal pimping gangs as "grotesque". Keith Vaz, chairman of the Commons home affairs select committee and MP for a Leicester constituency with a large Asian-heritage population, said the Serious Organised Crime Agency should lead an inquiry into on-street grooming because of Norfolk's reports. He insisted that racial and cultural sensitivities should not hinder any investigation. Once a national inquiry had been ordered, Norfolk thought his work was done. But Harding told him that the story would be his full-time job until every agency in Britain with a responsibility to safeguard children had measures in place to ensure they were protected and their abusers held to account. Week by week Norfolk's revelations continued. Over the next three years he spent months at trials where he was often the only reporter present. A prosecution at Liverpool Crown Court in 2012 led to multiple convictions for nine men, all but one of Pakistani origin, for horrendous offences against girls from Rochdale, one of whom, aged 15, was put in a bedroom blind drunk and used for sex by 25 men in one night. Norfolk's reports triggered allegations of Islamophobia and racism, and two death threats. Support came from forward-thinking Muslim clerics and from Trevor Phillips, chairman of the Equality and Human Rights Commission. And in 2013 the Commons home affairs select committee issued a scathing report on agencies' failings. The scale of the scandal was reflected in the remorseless flow of *Times* headlines:

January 11, 2011: "Botched inquiry left sex gang free to abuse for years"

January 15, 2011: "He took my little girl and sold her for sex. How do you expect us to feel?": The story of Anna, who was an innocent, sunny-faced girl of 11 and two years later had been used so many times for sex that she had forgotten what childhood was.

January 21, 2011: "Anger as grooming film is withheld": An acclaimed film supposed to be shown in schools to warn girls about the dangers of on-street grooming was still being withheld three years after being commissioned by a government crime agency.

January 22, 2011: "Men used girls in exchange for drinks and phone credit": Shrewsbury Crown Court case.

February 12, 2011: "Hate and violence taught at Muslim schools"

April 7, 2011: "Police hid sex-grooming scandal in seaside town": Splash on exploitation in Blackpool and supportive responses to Norfolk's reporting from David Cameron, David Blunkett, Jack Straw, Martin Narey (Barnardo's) and Trevor Phillips.

April 8, 2011: "Six police units in one county to trap sex predator gangs": Lancashire, where 796 children had been identified as at risk.

June 15, 2011: "Young girls lured with drink were 'sold for sex'", "She thought these men valued her. They did, but only as a commodity": Nine men at Stafford Crown Court as first trial for trafficking British child begins.

June 16, 2011: "Suspects befriended 13-year-old girl then raped her"

June 21, 2011: "Restaurant and chip shop workers would queue up for sex when I was 16, says girl"

June 25, 2011: "'No hiding place' call over child-sex gangs": Tim Loughton, minister for children and families says some cases went under the radar because of racial sensitivities.

June 30, 2011: "Quarter of predators who groom young girls are Asian, says report": Child Exploitation and Online Protection Centre (Ceop) research shows 90 per cent of abuse victims were white girls in their early teens

July 15, 2011: "I was scared – they had so much control, says teenager at centre of child-sex trial"

August 4, 2011: "Witness in sex-grooming trial in tears as she is forced to read out details of abuse": Cross-examination by counsel for the defence.

November 4, 2011: "Imams say abuse 'disgraces Islam' as child agencies deny race link"

November 21: "Action on the gangs who groom girls for sex": Splash on government action plan to be published

November 21, 2011: "Raped, pimped and driven to despair: the girl, 16, who was failed at every turn": Victim's suicide bid while authorities, school and police stood back.

November 22, 2011: "The fear of causing offence has allowed sex abuse to spread for years unchecked"

February 22, 2012: "Grooming gang forced girls to swap sex for vodka, cash and pizza, court is told"

May 9, 2012: "Asians pick me up. They get me drunk, they give me drugs and have sex with me. I want to move"

May 10, 2012: "How children's home failed to protect its only resident from sex by 25 men": A privately run care home in Rochdale charged the authorities £252,000 to provide round-the-clock "intense and individual protection" for one teenage girl but did not stop her going missing 19 times in three months and having sex with numerous men.

May 15, 2012: "Kebab shop owner ran teenage brothel"

June 18, 2012: "The 'carers' who permit child sex": Report by joint parliamentary inquiry on children who go missing from care.

September 25, 2012: "Amy's parents thought she was happy and safe. They were wrong."

September 26, 2012: "Police chief faces wrath of MPs over grooming": Chief constable of South Yorkshire to appear before Commons home affairs select committee.

September 28, 2012: "Action on child sex gangs": Splash on new national forum to tackle child sex exploitation.

November 21, 2012: "Role of Asian gangs is played down by report on thousands of child sex victims": Report by deputy children's commissioner Sue Berelowitz.

November 22, 2012: "Stop dodging the truth about Asian gangs, says father of raped girl, 13"

December 5, 2012: "MPs commend *Times* reporter for exposing child grooming gangs": Norfolk and *The Times* thanked by Keith Vaz, chairman of the home affairs select committee, for the "diligence and dedication in exposing a series of most shocking events".

January 16, 2013: "Men 'groomed girls with drugs before horrific abuse'": Old Bailey trial of nine men.

February 23, 2013: "I was beaten and branded by sex abuser, woman tells jury": Man branded her with hot metal so that everyone would know he owned her.

March 6, 2013: "Prosecutors ordered to crack down on sex abuse": Keir Starmer, the Director of Public Prosecutions, pays tribute to Norfolk for "shining a light".

March 26, 2013: "Girl, 14, was congratulated on pregnancy by child sex leader"

May 15, 2013: "Betrayed: the child victims of sex gang"

May 18, 2013: "They told me that I should put Nicola back into care and forget about her": Mother of a victim of Oxford grooming scandal tells why she never gave up on her.

June 6, 2013: "Minorities told: your culture is no defence": Damian Green, police and criminal justice minister, reports on a grooming task force.

August 6, 2013: "Girl, 17, tried to kill herself after ordeal at sex trial"

August 7, 2013: "Child abuse victims get handpicked trial judges": Lord Chief Justice's response to growing concerns about cross-examination of child victims.

August 23, 2013: "He bought me chicken and chips from a place just up from the petrol station. He stroked my face": How a good-natured 13-year-old became a broken twice-pregnant abuse victim who drank, lied and picked fights with the world.

There had been many days, Norfolk wrote in August 2014, when he secretly longed for it all to end. "It was just too bleak, the details of the crimes too grotesque, too calculated to make one utterly despair of human nature. In those dark days, it was always the girls and their families who kept me going ... The victims who decided to trust *The Times* with their stories are the closest this tale will ever come to having heroes or heroines." *The Times* had changed the way Britain tackled such crimes, Norfolk added. "Our stories prompted two government-ordered inquiries, a parliamentary inquiry and a new national action plan on child sexual exploitation. Police forces, the Crown Prosecution Service and local authorities have been forced to transform their approach to street-grooming offences, leading to extra resources, improved training for frontline staff and an explosion in the number of investigations and prosecutions." The government had also ordered a sweeping review of protection for young residents of children's homes.

Norfolk's story was not yet over, however. An independent report for Rotherham council by Professor Alexis Jay, published in 2014, identified at least 1,400 victims there. Jay was then appointed to chair the Independent Inquiry into Child Sexual Abuse, which in October 2020, after sitting for five years, finally started a two-week public hearing of evidence on abuse by "organised networks". On October 24, Norfolk revealed that, although it was ostensibly seeking to establish "what went wrong and why" in relation to past "institutional failure to protect children", the inquiry had refused to take evidence about the most notorious sex-grooming scandals. Norfolk wrote: "Henrietta Hill, QC, lead counsel to the inquiry, told the hearing on its opening day that the inquiry 'carefully considered the extent to which, if at all, it should focus on areas such as Rochdale, Rotherham and Oxford, all of which have attracted public attention'. The inquiry decided, she explained, that it was 'more appropriate' to focus instead on 'different areas, not least because it was intended that this was a forward-looking investigation building on analysis that's already been done'." As Norfolk pointed out, none of the six areas the inquiry did focus on – St Helens, Tower Hamlets in east London, Swansea, Durham, Bristol and Warwickshire – "has witnessed a major prosecution of a south Asian sex-grooming gang. In all six areas, according to the 2011 national census, the proportion of the population that is of Pakistani origin is lower than the national average." A senior officer from South Wales police had told the inquiry that there was "no data" to support the suggestion that there were any incidents of child sexual exploitation related to gangs in the Swansea area. Norfolk wrote: "Victims and experts blamed the decision on a 'cowardly' reluctance to look at a pattern of group crimes in which men of Pakistani heritage had been over-represented." Nazir Afzal, a former chief crown prosecutor who brought to justice the Rochdale sex-grooming gang, had described the inquiry's conduct of the investigation as "a nonsense". He told Norfolk: "With the other strands of this inquiry it's been about looking back at what went wrong to see what we can learn from those mistakes. This section decided it was going to look forward, but you can't move forward without looking back at the failures." Maggie Oliver, a former Greater Manchester police officer who exposed the alleged cover-up of sex-grooming crimes in the region, accused the inquiry of being "too frightened to open the hornets' nest". Sammy Woodhouse, a Rotherham victim, told Norfolk: "They are trying to bury what happened in places like Rotherham and Rochdale because they're scared of being called racist." A *Times* leader said that justifying this omission by saying the investigation wanted to look to the future, not the past, would not wash. Such timidity failed the victims and raised the possibility of missing important lessons. Harding considered the Rotherham investigation to be his most important experience in terms of learning that the best reporting takes an extraordinary commitment of time and needs courageous editors to support it. The paper faced reputational issues in telling the story, but "the fundamental point is that that's really what a paper is there for, to look deeply into some things that it happens to bring to light. That's what I thought Andrew did and I learnt a lot from him, from the team on the news desk that drove the story and from the chief lawyer team that made sure it got into print despite the government's best efforts.".

Matthew Parris had put similar points less diplomatically after attending Norfolk's Orwell prize ceremony in 2013. He wrote:

> The prizegiving had been preceded by a speech from the former Labour MP Chris Mullin. I greatly admire Mr Mullin but almost choked on my popcorn as he spoke about fine journalism achieved 'despite' the proprietors of newspapers. What sneery, snivelling, ignorant leftie rubbish. Who does he think pays for Andrew Norfolk's investigations or for my columns? Does he know nothing about the losses being clocked up by quality newspapers all over the world? Does he think that a proprietor concerned only about profits, or an editor interested only in how today's work will sell tomorrow's edition, would fund a long, expensive, lonely and uncertain journalistic project such as Andrew's? Does he not understand how many proprietors down the ages have loved newspapers, cared about their survival, believed in their journalism and knowingly acted as patrons to talented journalists and tremendously important investigation, reporting and scrutiny, whose commercial usefulness is often a complete unknown? Does he realise how precarious now is the whole future of daily newspapers in Britain? Apart from historic buildings and football clubs I know no other sector where owners and investors appear so willing to pay for the privilege of losing money in the public interest. Andrew, at least, when he spoke, gave credit for his achievement to the pockets and the patience of his bosses at *The Times*. Somebody needs to.

Norfolk was not the only campaigning journalist given space to fight for justice for children during Harding's editorship. Camilla

Cavendish fired her first shot in Times 2 on Monday, July 7, 2008. Her target was the family courts, which she believed should be opened up to scrutiny because of miscarriages of justice. Under the headline "The secret state that steals our children", she wrote:

Two weeks ago I got a phone call from a woman I hadn't seen for four years. She was calling to tell me that she was moving abroad, unable to bear the pain of living in the same country as the daughter she is no longer allowed to see. "I wanted to thank you," she said, "for being the only person who ever gave me a fair hearing." I was seized with guilt. This woman had asked for my help, and I had utterly failed her.

Cavendish went on to explain that this "rather pretty and utterly normal young woman" had first contacted her in 2004 seeking assistance after being trapped in a custody battle with her former partner over their daughter. "The mother had started to worry about her ex-partner's behaviour during his visits to their daughter," Cavendish wrote. "She approached social services to ask if they could supervise his visits. When the child then told a teacher that her father had touched her in bad places, the police were called. They filmed the child repeating the allegations. The upshot? A psychologist who watched the film but never met the mother, father or daughter wrote a report alleging that the mother had coached the daughter to lie. He never appeared in court, and was never cross examined. Yet the court, encouraged by social workers, accepted his view. The judge ordered that the daughter should go to live with her father – a man the mother was convinced was an abuser.

My bitter regret, now, is that I did so little about that case. At the time I couldn't help wondering if there was not more to it than the mother had let on. And there may well have been. But today, I'm not so sure. Because so many elements of her story fit patterns that I have since heard again and again. The reliance on experts who have never met the accused. The stormtrooper behaviour of some social workers. The legal aid solicitors acting for parents who are always in a rush. This mother was plunged into a world of acronyms and organisations that she knew nothing about. She was always on the back foot. Having been the person who reached for help from the system, she became its victim. The tale niggled away at me. I started asking questions.

Cavendish discovered a world in which every year thousands of children were taken from their parents in a secret and sometimes unjust process, "a world where courts need no criminal conviction to remove your child, only the word of a psychiatrist or doctor, and can deny you the chance to call any expert in your defence. A world that uses the 'welfare of the child' to gag you from discussing your case. Where even if you prove yourself innocent on appeal, your children may already have been adopted: in which case you will never be allowed to contact them again." Once Cavendish had begun investigating, "the stories began to pour in. People left messages on my answering machine saying that the system was rotten but that they dared not speak out, because they had managed to get their children back. Some had taken a sick child to hospital, only to be accused of physical abuse. Some had been accused of 'emotional abuse', a category that has no definition in British law but which has jumped 50 per cent in the past ten years as a reason for taking children into care." She faced formidable bureaucratic and legal obstacles in trying to evaluate what she was being told:

Since local authorities generally would not talk to me, citing confidentiality, I still had only part of the picture. Was there really a problem, or were these people all lying? I looked for figures. Were particular local authorities taking above-average numbers of children into care, for example? How many of these proceedings were contested? How many mothers were being accused of having Munchausen syndrome by proxy, a psychiatric disorder that is supposed to be rare but seemed to be cropping up too often in my conversations? I would call the Home Office, which would refer me to the Lord Chancellor's department, which would refer me to the various incarnations of the education department, which would usually refer me back to the Home Office. Many of my questions were met with the answer that the data was 'not held centrally'.

This whole area started to look more and more like a hole inside government that ministers were simply not interested in.

Telling the stories was fiendishly difficult. First there was the legal requirement to avoid publishing anything that might even indirectly lead to the identification of the child involved. This is understandable, but it means that what journalists can write is sometimes so thin, so patchy that it is hard to ask anyone to believe us – because the most pertinent facts are often very distinctive. It also means that we can never humanise stories with photos, of the kind that helped to secure the freedom of Angela Cannings and Sally Clark. This is despite the fact that children can be pictured and named in adoption magazines, even while their frantic parents are trying to mount an appeal to get them back. Secondly, there were often additional reporting restrictions. Some of these were sought by local authorities as soon as I called them to try to get their sides of the stories. Some of these orders were so badly drafted that our lawyers simply could not tell what we could say. Some bore no relation to the draft that we had been sent before the hearing. It costs money to fight such orders, money that local media may not have and nationals are reluctant to commit. The more often my articles were spiked or denuded of interesting detail, the more incensed I became. I began to feel that we, the liberal press, were part of a conspiracy of silence against people who had no voice. Worse, their children had no voice.

Cavendish wrote:

It is impossible to describe the shock, the isolation, that parents feel once their child is gone. Even educated people who can afford a good lawyer struggle to think straight. They feel alone against the system. Judges rely on reports by experts, social workers and guardians, many of whom are used to working together. This can produce a fatal lack of objectivity. I have spoken to some exemplary social workers and judges in the past few years. It is not my intention to demonise them all. But we must be able to spot whether the same individuals are reaching erroneous conclusions over and over again. At the moment any expert, social worker or judge who makes mistakes, goes beyond their brief or is on a crusade against parents is virtually immune from scrutiny. They do not expect that their evidence or their judgments will ever be made public.

She concluded with an appeal to *Times* readers to write to their MPs in support of the campaign, "because to sever a child from its family without due cause is licensed state oppression of the worst kind. It is, in fact, child abuse." Unsurprisingly, after such a powerful article – and more that followed – victory was not long in coming. All levels of family courts were opened to accredited media from April 27, 2009. Jack Straw, the justice secretary, said that the changes would help to increase public faith in the court system. "People need to trust the justice system," he added. "One important way is creating a more open, transparent and accountable system while protecting children and families during a difficult and traumatic time in their lives." Cavendish was awarded the 2008 Paul Foot Award for campaigning journalism and in 2009 won "campaigning journalist of the year" at the British Press Awards, when the judges said: "A good newspaper campaign should be about an issue of serious injustice and strong public interest. A great one will be unexpected, one in which the outcome is not a done deal and which will in the end effect serious change. This campaign does that." *The Times* was named Newspaper of the Year. For *Times* staff, their most heartfelt campaign, Cities Fit For Cycling, was triggered by a tragedy on their own doorstep. It is best explained in the words of the leader that Harding published on November 5, 2012:

Mary Bowers is a reporter at *The Times* and, among her colleagues, a popular one. For the past year, however, while many of them have spoken to her, she has not spoken to them. For, a year ago yesterday, Mary was knocked from her bike at a junction in front of the offices in which she worked. Crushed and horrifically injured, she has not yet regained full consciousness.

This newspaper makes no apology for having begun a campaign on such a personal basis, only an apology for not having begun one earlier. Since Mary's accident, more than 100 cyclists have died on Britain's roads. The youngest was eight years old; the oldest was 80. So far in 2012, eleven have died in London, three in Edinburgh, and two on the same stretch of the A1 outside Nottingham. Those who survived injury in 2011 – of whom Mary was one – number a startling 19,108, with more than 3,000 seriously injured. To point out that roughly twice as many Britons die on bicycles each year as die serving in Afghanistan is not, of course, to compare like with like. But they do.

This time last year, *The Times* began to advocate cities fit for cycling. The response has been overwhelming. Thirty-six thousand members of the public have pledged their support, as have all three major political parties. Winning Best Media Campaign award at the National Transport Awards, this newspaper's campaign was described as 'relentless, informed and passionate'. Government, parliament and the mayor of London all deserve praise for the seriousness with which they have responded. The House of Commons Transport Select Committee has endorsed our campaign. News International, which publishes *The Times*, is to fund a report by the All Party Parliamentary Cycling Group into why more people do not cycle, and how they might do so.

The campaign has also prompted behavioural changes, encouraging drivers of heavy vehicles to fit suitable mirrors and turning alarms. While cyclists too can always benefit from taking greater care, statistics show clearly that the vast majority of incidents between motor vehicles and bikes are caused by driver, rather than cyclist, error. But the stated aim of this campaign has never been to change drivers or cyclists. Rather, it has been to change the cities in which they cycle and drive. It can be done. In Copenhagen, where 90 per cent of people own a bicycle and over a third of them ride weekly, the introduction of separated cycle lanes has seen fatalities plummet. It is not enough to daub a few roads with streaks of blue. The change must be structural and geographical.

Many articles followed, but the surest measure of the campaign's success was that over the following decade, propelled by Boris Johnson, as Conservative mayor of London, and by his Labour successor, Sadiq Khan – and given further impetus by a surge in the popularity of cycling during the Covid-19 pandemic – a network of segregated bicycle lanes was constructed across central London.

CHAPTER TEN

Election nights – particularly US presidential nights – had long been a sub-editor's joy at *The Times* and the pressure was always intense. Alternative headlines and intros for different results were written ready for pages to be rejigged and slipped as fast and as frequently as possible, although at some point early in the morning a harassed press hall manager would say that the logistics of distribution made it pointless to continue sending him new pages. On the night of Tuesday, November 4, 2008, the subs – and the press hall crews – excelled themselves. In what seemed then to be the most extraordinary election in modern times, Barack Obama surged way past the 270 electoral college votes needed for victory. "This is our time," the man who would become the first Black US president told tens of thousands of jubilant supporters in Chicago. Change had come to America, "where all things are possible". Obama told the crowd that "the road ahead will be long, our climb will be steep [but] ... I promise you, we as a people will get there." At Wapping, page 2 of Wednesday's *Times* was slipped in the early hours for a short pre-prepared leader headlined "Obama Fulfils the Dream". "The election of Barack Obama, the son of a Kenyan goatherd, as the 44th President of the United States of America is a moment to savour, proof that the promise of a better day, expressed in prose that rises like poetry, can still carry an electorate," it declared. He faced difficult questions on energy independence, health care, poverty and Iraq. But those questions, the what-ifs, the fear of disappointment "are not for today and, perhaps, not ever ... The essential point about President Barack Obama is the privilege of being able to write this sentence. A Black man has been elected to the highest office of the most powerful country of the world and, to borrow one of his own phrases, a righteous wind is at his back." A slip was not enough for such an occasion. A special 6am edition was being prepared as copy surged in from America. Martin Fletcher and James Bone were in Grant Park, Chicago. The celebration that began at 10pm Chicago time, they wrote, was ecstatic and unstoppable. Daniel Finkelstein commented that the old politics had been swept away. Michelle Obama, Sarah Vine wrote, seemed to be the personification of sanity – a clever, independently minded lawyer, attractive in a normal, accessible way and with a sassy and self-deprecating demeanour. In Georgia, Suzy Jagger talked to Ora Wlliams, 92, who had been moved to vote for the first time after watching Barack Obama on television. Born to Black farm labourers, she had picked cotton as a child. Ben Macintyre mapped the long road from 1870 when Thomas Mundy Peterson, the son of slaves, became the first African American to vote, via Rosa Parks's Alabama bus protest and Ruby Bridges, the first Black pupil at an all-white school in New Orleans, to Martin Luther King and his "I have a dream" speech and Colin Powell, the first African American to be head of the US armed forces and then secretary of state.

The 6am edition would have been too late to reach many readers, so Thursday's issue did it all over again – but more so with a 24-page souvenir pullout. A leader said that nowhere more than in America was the competition for power more open, inspiring or capable of real change. John McCain, the defeated Republican candidate, had made a concession speech of enormous grace and humility, conveying his respect for the democratic process and his understanding that in the manner of his losing he was helping to make history. George W Bush, the outgoing president, had called the result "a triumph of the American story". *The Times* agreed. "America may have faltered in its efforts to export democracy, but this time, at home, it has delivered a masterclass in the real thing." Derek Walcott, the St Lucian Nobel Literature laureate, wrote a poem exclusively for *The Times*, entitled *Forty Acres (to Barack Obama)*. The allusion was to "a young Negro at dawn in straw hat and overalls" ploughing a forty-acre cotton field "till the land lies open like a flag as dawn's sure/light streaks the field and furrows wait for the sower". The original title was to be *Forty Acres and Fifty States*, after the Civil War freed slaves were promised 40 acres and a mule to plough them with. Walcott explained: "The country did not give the Black man the 40 acres and a mule as promised. But tonight, instead, they gave the Black man 50 states and the White House."

James Bone focused on Michelle Obama's ancestors. They had suffered slavery, segregation and humiliation, Bone wrote, and her heritage embodied a dark past that many Americans would prefer to forget. Jim Robinson, a hard-working, god-fearing slave and great-great-grandfather of the new First Lady, had lived in a cabin in Slave Street on the Friendfield Plantation in Georgetown, South

Carolina. Those cabins were still standing, bereft of glass, heating and indoor plumbing; the last one was vacated in the 1960s. Bone painted a picture based on detailed genealogical research of a family that had moved from the south to the industrial north after the Great Depression of the 1930s. Michelle Obama's grandparents lived in Chicago, where her father, Fraser Robinson III, worked for the city as a maintenance man. She came of age in the post-civil rights era and thrived, studying at Princeton and Harvard Law School. Lisa Armstrong, fashion editor, considered the new First Lady's crimson and black Narciso Rodriguez dress, which drew "a hail of poisoned arrows" on the internet. Taste is subjective, she wrote, and the agenda behind the dress was more interesting. Every detail of the picture was scripted, from the red (a gracious olive branch to the defeated Republicans) to the choice of a Cuban American designer and the dash of black for a cool, modern look. The matchy-matchy family look – the Obamas' daughters were in red, too – was probably a nod too far to girl-band styling and control freakery. "But these are early days. Heck, they were early minutes."

Damian Whitworth tackled presidential dogs. Obama had promised his daughters a new puppy, and Whitworth saw more in that than met the eye. Harry Truman had said: "If you want a friend in Washington, get a dog." Despite his sweeping victory, Obama needed to uphold one of the White House's most cherished traditions, that of the First Dog. George Washington owned ten hounds. Theodore Roosevelt's pitbull tore the seat out of the French Ambassador's trousers. Franklin D Roosevelt's scottie received sacks of fanmail and was buried alongside his master. Lyndon Johnson picked his beagles up by their ears. Gerald Ford used to whistle for his golden retriever to break up boring meetings. George Bush Sr's springer spaniel wrote a book. The Clintons arrived at the White House with a cat, Sox, and then acquired a labrador, Buddy. During the Monica Lewinsky scandal, Whitworth said, Buddy appeared to be the only member of the president's family who was pleased to see him. "You will hear a great deal more about the First Dog," he predicted. The First Dog turned out to be a hypoallergenic Portuguese Water Dog named Bo, from Bo Diddley and the president's initials. With the advantages of hindsight, the hype about Obama may seem to have been naive; but when journalists call their work "first drafts of history" they know that time will reveal their misjudgments sooner or later.

In Obama's case, while he would remain an iconic figure throughout his presidency and beyond, the task ahead of him quickly outweighed the euphoria. The victory celebrations were still echoing when the Dow Jones index fell 486 points, reflecting the growing economic crisis and two unfinished wars, in Iraq and Afghanistan. James Harding ensured that *Times* readers were reminded of this uncomfortable truth. Anthony Loyd and the *Times* photographer Jack Hill spent election night watching the celebrations on "a huge widescreen television" in the officers' mess at a remote Pakistani army fortress at Khar in the tribal area of Bajaur, near the frontier with Afghanistan. The broadcast was punctuated not by cheering crowds but by heavy artillery blasting from gun positions at the gates, exchanging fire with Taliban raiding parties. Loyd wrote that the gunfire was a reminder of America's ill-conceived and muddled strategy in Pakistan, which had failed to secure a single security objective there since 2001. While Obama was saying on-screen in a CNN interview that "the biggest threat to Pakistan right now is not India, which has been their historical enemy, it is actually the militants within their own borders", the officers in the mess "did not look overly convinced". One, a "multilingual, charming and erudite" senior intelligence officer, made clear their doubts about their role in America's war on terror and the hunt for Osama bin Laden. "The trouble is I don't think bin Laden exists," this officer told Loyd, "I think he is a myth. A creation." Two-and-a-half years later, in May 2011, Obama announced that bin Laden had been killed by US special forces in a Pakistani garrison town, Abbottabad, which is barely four hours' drive from Khar; but when Obama's vice-president, Joe Biden, pulled US troops out of Afghanistan in 2021 and let the Taliban take over again, Loyd's scepticism was vindicated.

Loyd's presence in distant Khar on Obama's election night was an example of Harding's understanding of the long-term significance of foreign news and his commitment to the expensive, difficult business of reporting it. Early in his tenure, he promoted Richard Beeston to be foreign editor, coordinating the network of reporters around the world, planning and supervising the response of *The Times* to significant events and adding his own pungent and succinct commentaries and analysis to the main foreign news stories of the day. Beeston, who had reported from the Middle East during an outstanding career as a foreign correspondent, was in his element organising *Times* coverage of the Arab Spring, an upheaval that proved to be Obama's first big foreign policy test.

It was triggered by the self-immolation of Mohamed Bouazizi, a Tunisian street vendor, on December 17, 2010, after his stall had been confiscated by police. Violent protests forced President Ben Ali of Tunisia to flee to Saudi Arabia in mid-January 2011 after 24 years in power. A *Times* leader on January 20, the day of Obama's inauguration, said that the uprising in Tunis would embolden cowering rebels elsewhere. It was an accurate prediction. By the end of January, Egypt was in turmoil with almost 900 people arrested in anti-government demonstrations. The new Obama administration urged President Hosni Mubarak, a longstanding US ally, to implement reforms. The chaos and violence increased. Martin Fletcher wrote from Tahrir Square, the hub of the protests in central Cairo, that he was witnessing a people losing their fear and finding their voices after 30 years of suppression. On February 3, a page 1 picture by Peter Nichols of a Mubarak supporter on a camel lashing protesters in Tahrir Square was a reminder that the old regime was trying to fight back; three people were killed and 1,500 injured.

On Saturday, February 12, however, under the headline "History unfolds", Fletcher and James Hider told how Cairo erupted in joy at the news that Mubarak had resigned after an 18-day rebellion that would, a *Times* leader said, change politics throughout the Arab world. Fletcher wrote a week later that the Arab Spring was advancing across north Africa and the Middle East like water pouring from a broken dam. A "Friday of Rage" saw protesters fired on in Bahrain, and there were disturbances in Yemen, Jordan, Kuwait and Syria. Demonstrations were also planned in Iraq, Iran and Algeria. A *Times* leader said western states "should act boldly to demonstrate to Arab reformers that their risks would garner swift rewards". Developed economies should follow the postwar Marshall Plan to provide assistance financially and in improving governance. Well-judged and generous intervention could prove decisive in helping democracy to emerge. In Libya's capital, Tripoli, and its key eastern city, Benghazi, Colonel Muammar Gaddafi faced the most significant challenges of his 41-year reign. While the Tunisian and Egyptian presidents had rolled over quickly in the face of street protests, Gaddafi declared in a defiant broadcast on February 22: "We will cleanse Libya inch by inch, house by house, home by home, alley by alley, person by person, until the country is cleansed of dirt and scum." The death toll in Benghazi climbed into hundreds as his forces attempted to crush the rebellion there.

David Cameron wrote later in his memoirs, which were serialised in *The Times*, that he feared that a massacre would take place if Benghazi fell to Gaddafi's forces. "To do nothing in these circumstances was not a neutral act," the former prime minister wrote. "It was to facilitate murder." He recalled, however, that Obama, who had been elected on a pledge to disentangle the US from foreign conflicts, was reluctant to provide the military support that would be needed for a western intervention. "I had the distinct feeling that the world's great superpower was dithering while Benghazi was about to burn." Fletcher in Tripoli and Hider in Benghazi filed repeated updates of Gaddafi's advances against the rebels and the rising civilian death toll. In a leader on March 11, *The Times* rebuked the new man in the White House: "President Obama favours a wait-and-see policy on Libya. He should understand that we have waited and we have seen. The situation in Libya is now one in which to do nothing is effectively to help a brutal dictator reassert his power." On March 17, urged on by Britain and France with the support of Lebanon, the United Nations security council passed Resolution 1973 pledging "all necessary measures", except for troops on the ground, to protect Libyan civilians. Next day, Cameron recalled: "I finally spoke to Obama on the phone. He said the US would help in the first week – one week of heavy military support to take down air defences – but then we, Britain, and France would be on our own. He was unenthusiastic and matter-of-fact, but this was at least a clear and decisive response. And then it happened. On March 20, American, British and French aircraft destroyed Gaddafi's tanks, armoured carriers and rocket-launchers, and his forces began to retreat."

The Libyan civil war was far from over, however, and continued for several months. Fletcher filed on March 31 from Benghazi after seeing rebels on the retreat again from Gadaffi's advancing troops, who had changed tactics by abandoning heavy armour for four-wheel drive vehicles that would not be so easily identified by

French and British warplanes. Times Online offered an interactive graphic of the coalition airstrikes and the fighting flowing from Tripoli to Sirte and Benghazi. Anthony Loyd was in the thick of it with the rebels, reporting on July 1 that a fighter on the frontline between Brega and Ajdabiya had shown him his grandfather's Lee Enfield rifle with bullets stamped GB1940. It had first seen action against Rommel's Afrika Korps and was, the rebel said, "200 per cent better than a Kalashnikov". The most sophisticated air power in the world was backing the revolution but on the ground the fighting recalled the Desert Rats, Loyd wrote. With his soldier's eye (he had served with the Royal Green Jackets), he commented that the state of the rebel frontline would not impress a British sergeant major. There were no bunkers or shell-scrapes to protect them from incoming artillery. They sheltered in huts built of old wooden ammo boxes, with tank shells and mortar rounds parked haphazardly in the sand. But they did at least now have US uniforms and Qatari desert boots. By October Gaddafi was cornered. His end was unheroic. Rebel forces dragged him from a storm drain in Sirte, his home town, on October 20 after his convoy had been attacked by a French Mirage jet. Badly injured but conscious, he was bundled onto the bonnet of a pick-up truck. A picture on page 1 of *The Times* the next day showed him with a bloodied face moments before his death. Cameron welcomed a day to remember for all Gadaffi's victims. His commitment of British forces had been brave and right, a *Times* leader said. "The prospect of genocide was recognised in time and a terrible future averted. This was a good deed in a weary world."

CHAPTER ELEVEN

The first ripples of the tsunami that was to engulf News International, owner of *The Times*, and lead to the closure of *The News of the World* (NoW), its sister newspaper, had reached Wapping in January 2007, when Clive Goodman, the NoW's royal editor, and Glenn Mulcaire, a private investigator, were convicted of illegally intercepting phone messages belonging to Prince William and Prince Harry. The NoW said this was an isolated incident, but in July 2009 *The Guardian* claimed that the practice was more widespread and that News International had made secret settlements of more than £1 million to hacking victims. By January 2011, after the actress Sienna Miller was paid £100,000 in damages, the ripples were becoming waves. The Metropolitan Police set up Operation Weeting to investigate phone hacking. Andy Coulson, who had resigned as editor of the NoW when Goodman and Mulcaire were convicted, now resigned as David Cameron's director of communications, and in April, Neville Thurlbeck, the NoW's chief reporter, and Ian Edmonson, a former assistant editor, were arrested on suspicion of phone hacking.

The Times reported on the unfolding story without any comment in its leader columns. Soon, however, Harding felt impelled to condemn the NoW and, by implication, News International, whatever the consequences for him personally. The breaking point came on July 4 when *The Guardian* reported that Mulcaire had hacked the voicemails of Milly Dowler, a murdered 13-year-old schoolgirl, after she went missing on her way home from school in 2002 and had deleted some of the messages. This was sensational, as the Dowler case was a cause célèbre in the summer of 2011: her killer, Levi Bellfield, had only just been convicted on June 23 of her abduction and murder in a widely publicised trial. The allegation was that by deleting voicemails on her phone, which could have indicated that she had listened to them and deleted them herself, the NoW had misled the police and given her parents false hope that she was alive. In fact, Bellfield had killed her shortly after abducting her, but her body had not been found for six months. The *Guardian* report was inaccurate: the NoW had hacked Milly's phone but had not deliberately deleted the messages. This was unknown at the time, however, and would not be clarified until June 2014 when Mr Justice Saunders told the Old Bailey phone-hacking trial that claims that someone from the NoW had deliberately deleted Milly's voicemail messages were "not true". He said that the act of hacking a voicemail account could mean messages were deleted automatically by the mobile phone provider.

The Guardian would eventually publish a grudging correction stating that the NoW was "unlikely to have been responsible for the deletion of a set of voicemails from the phone that caused her parents to have false hopes that she was alive". But in the summer of 2011 the allegation went virtually unchallenged. What made it all the more incendiary was that the editor of the NoW in 2002, when Milly Dowler was missing, was Rebekah Brooks, who in 2011 was chief executive of News International, owner of Rupert Murdoch's UK newspapers including the NoW and *The Times*. The News International offices in Thomas More Square were promptly besieged by a scrum of reporters as the UK's prime media company became itself the biggest news story. On July 5, unaware that *The Guardian*'s story the previous day had got it wrong, *The Times* carried reports on pages 1 and 3 by Sean O'Neill, crime editor, recounting the hacking and deleting allegations. That evening, Harding signed off the paper's first editorial comment about the affair, to be published next day, and then walked round the block with Keith Blackmore, his deputy, whose view was that the paper had no choice but to publish the leader and keep faith with the readers. Although it was mild in its references to News International, compared with what future leaders would say, they both expected to be sacked. "We'll start looking for work tomorrow," Blackmore said , but Harding suspected that, although there would be a strong reaction that night, things would then quieten down and he would be pushed out six to eighteen months later.

> There is no doubt but that journalists are now in their version of the MPs' expenses scandal. If there is proven to be truth in the allegations that journalists on *The News of the World* hacked into the voicemail of the murdered schoolgirl Milly Dowler, there will not be a journalist in the country who, after the warranted anger, will not feel shamed and depressed. There is a lot that is not yet known about this case but this much we do know: this is beyond reprehensible.

> Before today, *The Times*, which, like *The News of the World*, is owned by News International, has taken the view

that it ought not to comment on the issue of phone hacking. We have sought to report the story straight, in good faith, without taking any editorial view. A supportive line invites the accusation of speaking from the party script. A critical line is easily written off as a deliberate, insincere attempt to create distance from the story. But anyone who has serious faith in the public purpose of journalism has to record his or her dissent from the behaviour that has now been alleged. Anyone who believes in the nobility of the trade of reporting the truth, the better to inform the readers, and anyone who believes in the contribution of vibrant comment to a raucous and well-informed democracy, has to be clear when a line has been crossed. Over and above the internal inquiry that will be conducted at News International, this matter now requires the most rigorous possible police inquiry, which must be carried out, in David Cameron's words, 'without fear or favour'. It is also welcome that the Speaker has allowed an emergency debate in parliament today.

For it is clear that, at this stage, these are all only allegations. There is much that we still need to know. Were journalists at *The News of the World* involved or just their consultant Glenn Mulcaire? Was Milly Dowler's phone actually hacked or is it simply the case that Mulcaire had obtained her number? Did *The News of the World* and Mulcaire do the same in the case of the Soham victims [two girls killed in a notorious double-murder] and, if so, when? And given the reports of phone hacking by other national newspapers, how much of this was exception and how much, across the industry, the rule?

It must become clear, in time, whether allegations harden into facts and whether the criminal law has been broken. It will also become clear whether the investigation into Milly Dowler's death was in any way hampered, something Surrey Police say was not the case. But, even before the intervention of the law, journalism has a responsibility and an ethic. Its claim to public credibility rests on conducting its work in a way that is defensible to a reasonable person, known in the trade as a reader. We will, no doubt, learn more, and none of it is likely to be edifying. Whatever else emerges, this is a watershed moment for British journalism. What happened needs to be investigated and, in the public interest and the interests of journalism itself, brought to light. It ought to go without saying that nothing of this nature can ever happen again. But then it ought to have gone without saying that nothing of this nature could ever have happened in the first place. This is why it is so important that the truth be known.

These questions, about journalistic integrity, will now occupy public attention for some time to come. But the anguish of the Dowler family is happening now. Much has been written and said about the pain that the Dowlers had to endure in court as their lifestyle was impugned in the (vain) defence of the man who killed their daughter. It was, surely, the least they deserved that, after the tragedy of losing a daughter and the strain of the witness box, the Dowler family might have been left as free of this awful case as they can ever be. Unfortunately they have been denied even that small mercy.

Harding later recalled:

The night that we wrote that leader I had some confidential calls and it was very tense and I remember in the months after that there was real tension between people at the top of the company and people on the newsroom floor and I took the view that we were either going to get sacked by our readers or sacked by our proprietor. You either reported the story as you saw it, which we set out to do, or you were not going to do it – you were going to try if you like all the way through to temper your reporting, try and angle your coverage to accommodate the facts of the story and the interests of the company.

Harding gathered half a dozen of the most senior staff to discuss tactics.

In the end we said let's just report this like any other story. And, actually, great credit to the newsroom at *The Times*, they got on with it. I had one person in that time come to me and say, 'Are you sure that we're doing this right? You know I have a mortgage.' They were worried about some kind of retribution against *The Times*. My thinking at the time was in the end, it would be to the credit of *The Times* and News Corp's ownership that the independence of it in the reporting of this story was clear, but it caused a great deal of anger.

On Thursday, July 7, the closure was announced of *The News of the World*. The next day, Andy Coulson, the former NoW editor and Cameron's former spin doctor, was arrested for questioning over allegations of phone hacking and the corrupting of police officers. That morning, Cameron called a press conference at Downing Street and announced a "full, public inquiry" with a judge in charge to find out among other things "what exactly was going on at *The News of the World*" and "what was going on at other newspapers". He branded phone hacking as "disgusting" and the hacking of Milly Dowler's phone as "truly despicable".

On Sunday, July 10, the last issue of *The News of the World* was published. Rupert Murdoch landed at Luton airport that morning in his Boeing 737 corporate jet. In the evening he left his flat in St James's Place with Rebekah Brooks in an orchestrated demonstration of loyalty for the media crowd outside. Asked what his top priority was, he gestured to her with a smile and said: "This one." Four days later, in a leader, *The Times* accused News International of failing to answer its critics and allowing "suspicions to grow into shock, disgust into fury".

The next day, Brooks resigned and Murdoch met the Dowler family behind closed doors in a central London hotel. Mark Lewis, their lawyer, said: "He was humbled, shaken and sincere. This was something that had hit him on a personal level. He apologised many times and held his head in his hands." At the end of that tumultuous week, in a leader headlined "Power and Responsibility" on July 16, *The Times* said that News International had "finally begun to show that it understood the gravity of what it had permitted to happen". The right things had now been said and done: the company had issued an unequivocal apology to the country; Murdoch's act of personal contrition towards the Dowler family and the decision by Brooks to take responsibility "finally give genuine legitimacy to News International's response"; the company had started out on the long road back to credibility. "Above all," the leader concluded, "institutions of all kinds who wield influence and lay claim to authority have to live by the standards they demand of others."

The same day a full-page advertisement ran in *The Times* headlined: "We are sorry." In the form of a nine-sentence letter signed "Sincerely, Rupert Murdoch", it apologised for serious wrongdoing at *The News of the World* and promised that "in the coming days, as we take further concrete steps to resolve these issues and make amends for the damage they have caused, you will hear more from us". News International subsequently paid the family £2 million and Murdoch made a further personal donation of £1 million to charities chosen by them.

Brooks was arrested that weekend. *The Times* reported on Monday, July 18, that she had been questioned at a police station in London for more than 12 hours about allegations of phone hacking and corruption. She was released on police bail until late October. On July 19, Murdoch appeared before the Commons culture, media and sport select committee, telling MPs that his appearance was "the most humble day of my life" and laying bare his regret about the scandal. Flanked by his son James, executive chairman of News International, and with his wife Wendi sitting behind them, Murdoch mixed contrition with defiance, blaming people he had trusted for mistakes and admitting that he had perhaps lost sight of *The News of the World* "because it was so small in the frame of our company".

In the final moments of the session a man suddenly rushed at the seated, 80-year-old Murdoch and pushed a paper plate of white foam into his face, calling him a "greedy billionaire". He was promptly flattened by Wendi Murdoch, who was heard to say "I got him". Within minutes, as the attack had been caught live on the television cameras, she became a Twitter heroine. One select committee member, the Labour MP Tom Watson, normally an energetic critic of Murdoch, told him: "Your wife has a very good left hook". The *Times* boxing correspondent, Ron Lewis, corrected him in the next day's paper – it was more of a right slap. The attacker, Jonathan May-Bowles, 26, a comedian, was jailed for six weeks, reduced to four weeks on appeal. At the end of that eventful July, Lord Justice Leveson, an appeal court judge, was formally appointed to lead the public inquiry into the culture, practices and ethics of the press. Its remit would also include contacts between the press and politicians and the press and the police; the extent

Robert Thomson reads a copy of the compact edition of *The Times*, which he introduced in 2003.

Philip Howard joined *The Times* as a home news reporter in 1964, retired as a senior leader writer in 1998, but remained a regular contributor until his death in 2014.

Features supremo
Nicola Jeal.

Chief news photographer Jack
Hill. In 2014 he and Anthony
Loyd were kidnapped by a
rebel gang in Syria.

Writer Melanie Reid near her home in Scotland. Her weekly Spinal Column in *The Times Magazine* has chronicled living with disability since she broke her neck and back in a riding accident in 2010.

Richard Beeston, *Times* foreign editor until his death from cancer aged 50 in 2013.

Peter Brookes on Europe's migrant crisis, September 4, 2015.

Peter Brookes on Tory rivals Boris Johnson and Michael Gove,
July 8, 2016.

James Harding arrives to give evidence to the Leveson Inquiry, February 2012.

Social distancing: *The Times* office at London Bridge during Covid, July 2020.

The then Duchess of Cornwall attends an editorial conference in Thomas More Square, October 2013.

Pia Sarma, *Times* editorial legal director and deputy corporate counsel of News UK.

From the Balkans to the Middle East, and Afghanistan to Africa, Anthony Loyd has covered wars, conflicts and humanitarian crises around the world for more than thirty years.

Emma Tucker became the first female deputy editor of *The Times* in 2013. She would later serve as editor of *The Sunday Times* and *The Wall Street Journal*.

Christopher Martin-Jenkins, chief cricket correspondent from 1999 to 2008.

John Witherow in the editor's office at London Bridge.

to which the current regulatory regime had failed; and whether warnings about media misconduct had been ignored. Although the judge had a grand judicial title, he was a knight, Sir Brian Leveson, not a peer; but he quickly became known as "Lord Leveson", to the annoyance of sticklers for accuracy, particularly when the misnomer appeared in *The Times*.

CHAPTER TWELVE

Robert Jay QC, counsel to the Leveson inquiry, said on its opening day at the Royal Courts of Justice in November 2011 that it needed to cover more than wrongdoing at *The News of the World*. What was not immediately apparent was that *The Times*, despite its editorials on the integrity and responsibilities of the press, had a murky episode of its own for Leveson to unravel.

James Harding's turn to give oral evidence came on Tuesday, January 17, 2012. That morning he published a long leader that said it seemed "the appropriate moment to make clear to our readers the newspaper's view on the future of the press". The leader, which filled the whole of the leader space on page two, set out at considerable length how the Leveson inquiry could give Britain a better and freer press without statutory regulation. For some readers, however, the most arresting point came only a short way down the opening column: "The phone-hacking scandal has exposed some unpleasant truths about the press. It appears that *The News of the World* routinely used illegal means to unearth stories of questionable, if any, public interest. As the evidence of wrongdoing came to light, News International, Rupert Murdoch's company that also owns *The Times*, was unable or unwilling to police itself. This was a disgrace."

In a witness statement submitted to the inquiry in advance, Harding indicated that *The Times* did not indulge in shady practices and that he had clamped down hard on the merest hint of them. "*The Times* has never used or commissioned anyone who used computer hacking to source stories," he wrote. "There was an incident where the newsroom was concerned that a reporter had gained unauthorised access to an email account. When it was brought to my attention, the journalist faced disciplinary action. The reporter believed he was seeking to gain information in the public interest but we took the view he had fallen short of what was expected of a *Times* journalist. He was issued with a formal written warning for professional misconduct."

Harding did not disclose the reporter's identity and in his appearance before the inquiry that day he was not asked. His witness statement, however, was closely scrutinised at *The Guardian*, which appeared to have no trouble decoding it and piecing together a revelation that spelt serious trouble. That evening *The Guardian* website ran a prominent story under the heading *"Times* reporter hacked into police blogger's email". The implications of this were tumultuous.

In April 2009, a blog named NightJack – a play on police slang for an officer on night shift – had won the Orwell Prize for political writing. With a readership of up to half a million a week, it was written by an anonymous serving officer who gave a behind-the-scenes insight into frontline policing. Patrick Foster, a young *Times* reporter who had joined as a graduate trainee in 2006, thought that the blogger was using confidential police information from genuine investigations and that his activities appeared to be in breach of police regulations. He discovered the author's name, Richard Horton, a detective constable with Lancashire Constabulary, and took the view, corroborated by Alastair Brett, legal manager for *The Times*, that publication of Horton's identity would be in the public interest. When Horton won an injunction to protect his anonymity, Brett challenged it in the High Court.

During preparation for the case, Horton's legal team discovered that Foster had form as a hacker. As a PPE undergraduate at Oxford he had been suspended for six months in 2004 for "snooping" on the university's IT system and claiming in *The Oxford Student*, a student newspaper, that the institution's computer systems were open to breaches of security. This episode was no secret. The online archives of the Bradford *Telegraph and Argus*, Foster's home newspaper, carried a report of an interview with him in which he was quoted as saying that he had "wanted to alert the university to the problem they faced and, instead of saying 'thank you', they were going to punish him very severely". He had appealed and the sentence was reduced to a fine of £150. Horton's lawyers asked the *Times* legal team to confirm whether or not Foster had identified Horton using a similar method. Brett dismissed the suspicion of hacking as "baseless" (Alastair Brett v Solicitors Regulation Authority (SRA) [2014] EWHC 2974) and gave an assurance that the identification had been achieved by "self-starting journalistic endeavour" in a "largely deductive exercise".

The injunction hearing was held on June 4, 2009, before Mr Justice Eady, who issued his decision on June 16. Foster, Eady ruled, had identified Horton by a process of deduction and detective work, mainly using information on the internet. Blogging was essentially a public rather than a private activity, the judge said, and bloggers had no right to anonymity. Brett and Foster had won. Horton was identified in *The Times*; he was reprimanded by the police and his blog quickly lost its readers until he cancelled it altogether.

Now, three years later in 2012, only hours after Harding had given evidence to Leveson, *The Guardian* was asserting that Foster's story was based on material obtained by email hacking. "*Times* sources", it stated, had identified Foster as the reporter referred to in Harding's witness statement to Leveson. Foster had "openly disclosed that he guessed security questions for an anonymous email account" run by Horton in order to write his NightJack story, it said. While *The Guardian* celebrated another swipe at the Murdoch press, there was consternation in *The Times* legal department, where Brett was no longer in charge, having left the company in 2010. The in-house lawyers immediately understood that if Foster had indeed identified NightJack by hacking, then *The Times* may have duped Mr Justice Eady and misled Lord Justice Leveson, a double whammy that had to be unique in the annals of media law.

The *Times* legal team launched an emergency search of old email traffic for evidence of whether or not *The Guardian* was correct. As Foster had also left the paper – he had been dismissed over another matter, nothing to do with NightJack – this was no easy task. But as a result of the hacking scandal at *The News of the World*, News International was already engaged in a huge trawl of its email archive. The keywords NightJack, Horton, Brett and Foster were added to the search.

Within hours enough was found to trigger a statement that appeared in *The Times* on Thursday, January 19, two days after Harding's appearance before Leveson. In stilted sentences and bearing no byline, the usual clues to a lawyer's hand, it began: "*The Times* published a report exposing the identity of an anonymous police blogger after a journalist at the newspaper had hacked into his email account." It not only confirmed Foster's hacking but also revealed that he had "informed his managers before the story was published that he had, on his own initiative, hacked into Mr Horton's email account. The incident raised issues about the approval process for news gathering at the newspaper." It added, however: "The role the hacking played in Mr Foster's investigation remains unclear. Mr Foster identified Mr Horton using a legitimate process of deduction based on sources and information publicly available on the internet." In other words, this was a partial confession while the email trawl continued.

The January 19 holding statement soon carried a rider in the *Times* online archive: "Clarification: The facts in this report have been updated in a subsequent article." The rider linked to another, much longer piece published on Wednesday, February 8, under the headline "Times editor James Harding apologises for email hacking". This reported how Harding had been recalled to make a second appearance before Leveson on the previous day and had opened his evidence by saying: "In the last couple of weeks I have learnt a great deal more about what happened in this incident. As editor of the paper, I am responsible for what it does and what its journalists do. So I want to say at the outset that I sorely regret the intrusion into Richard Horton's email account by a journalist then in our newsroom. I am sure that Mr Horton and many other people expect better of *The Times*. So do I. So on behalf of the paper, I apologise." He said that he had also written to Mr Justice Eady to apologise.

Harding was given a far tougher time than in his first appearance. Robert Jay drilled down into a series of emails uncovered in the past two weeks that revealed Foster had told Brett he had hacked into Horton's account to identify him as NightJack. In one, Foster suggested delaying a story on Horton to put a "little more space between the dirty deed and publishing". As Foster had also subsequently identified Horton by legitimate means, Brett had decided not to disclose the hacking to the court on the grounds that this information was "confidential and privileged" and "would incriminate Mr Foster". Jay took Harding back to June 4, 2009, the day of the injunction hearing before Eady.

The inquiry was shown an email sent that evening from Brett to David Chappell, the managing editor of *The Times*, copied to Harding, stating that Foster "had gained access to the blogger's mail account and got his name". Harding told Jay that he did not believe he had read this email, which arrived while a big political news story was breaking: James Purnell, the work and pensions secretary, had resigned from the cabinet and had sought the resignation of Gordon Brown as prime minister. Harding said he had not even known that Brett had gone to court over NightJack that day. "The biggest shock was *The Times* had taken the case to the High Court," Harding said. "I was not aware of this fact. I've never heard of a case where the legal manager takes a case to the High Court without informing the editor, the deputy editor or managing editor."

Harding told the inquiry that he had first been informed the following day of a "concern" that Foster had hacked into Horton's email account. Jay asked why Eady was not then also informed, adding: "Had he been told that, his reaction might have been rather different. He might have exploded."

Another email unearthed for the inquiry showed that Chappell wrote to Brett on June 14, while Eady's judgment on the NightJack injunction case was still pending, asking for advice on what the consequences would be if the truth about Foster's actions were revealed. Two days later, Eady issued his ruling permitting publication of Horton's identity. *The Times* not only named him but published an article by him in which he explained the origins of his blog and took the blame for the effects of his exposure on his family and the reputation of the Lancashire police. Harding told Leveson: "We felt that having taken up the court's time we had little choice but to publish." Afterwards, Foster was given a written warning about his hacking. Harding said he had believed the disciplinary action had dealt with the problem, but "I can now see that we gave insufficient consideration to the fact of the unauthorised email access in deciding whether or not to publish." He added: "In retrospect, I regret that I did not initiate a full investigation into exactly what happened. It is easy, with the benefit of hindsight, to ask why there was not a thorough examination of who said what to whom and when back in 2009."

Harding admitted that the whole affair was "terrible", but he argued that the reason it was being discussed was because *The Times* had brought it to the inquiry's attention. Leveson interjected: "Except, except, except – and I appreciate that it's easy now to look backwards – it was made abundantly clear that had somebody joined the dots together and realised that this was an offence under the Computer Misuse Act, which did not have a public interest defence, *The Times* would have taken a different view, and yet that information was known to Mr Brett." He pointed out that Mr Justice Eady could have changed his judgment if he had been informed of "something dramatic" after the hearing. Harding said he strongly believed there had been a public interest in revealing Horton's identity but he would not have approved of the hacking. "If Mr Foster had come to me and said, 'I would like to seek unauthorised access to a person's email account to identify a police officer as an anonymous blogger', I would have said that I didn't believe that that intrusion was warranted in the public interest."

Looking back at a later date, Harding said that "when you're editor of the paper, regardless of what you're told directly and what you may or may not know directly, you are responsible for the paper and its conduct – it sits with me".

Leveson also called in Brett himself to give an account of his actions. The former house lawyer's evidence on March 15, 2012, illustrated what Harding had been grappling with. Brett was a legendary figure at Times Newspapers, where he had worked for 33 years before leaving the company. Alex Wade had reported in *The Times* in 2003 that he was "known for his impassioned commitment to press freedom – so impassioned that he has been described as 'certifiably insane' . . . he epitomises the old-school Fleet Street lawyer". At *The Sunday Times*, some executives knew him fondly as "Blubber Brett" because of the high emotional charge they associated with him. They also greatly respected, however, his relentlessness in organising the paper's defence in great libel cases, such as his long but ultimately successful battle with Thomas "Slab" Murphy, an IRA godfather, in the 1990s.

Brett's testimony at the inquiry made Leveson quite testy. Brett recalled that Foster had come to him for confidential advice and had told him that he had hacked into Horton's email account. (*Times*, March 16, 2012). Brett said that he had been furious and told the reporter that he needed to find a legitimate way to identify Horton. "I have a duty to the newspaper," he told the inquiry, "and then I have a duty not to mislead the court and I thought the journalist had put me into a crashingly difficult situation of duties and obligations and everything else. In 33 years that I was at *The Times*, this was the one and only case I had. And God, I wish I could have done without it." But he supported the view that there was a public interest in identifying a police officer who was "misusing information and putting it onto a public blog". Brett had warned Foster that the story was legally unpublishable if it was based on unlawfully obtained information. Foster had subsequently told him that he "had cracked it and could do the whole lot from publicly accessible information".

Brett told the inquiry that, when preparing to contest Horton's privacy injunction, he had been "oblique to an extent that is embarrassing" while instructing one of his own lawyers. He told Foster to submit a witness statement to the High Court that claimed he had identified Horton using entirely legitimate means. In a tense exchange, Leveson put it to Brett that the statement was not accurate. Brett replied: "It is not entirely accurate, no." He added: "My Lord, we are being fantastically precise." The judge, who appeared to be angry, said: "Oh, I am being precise because this is a statement being submitted to a court. Would you not want me to be precise?" The judge said that another claim in the witness statement was "utterly misleading". Brett conceded: "It certainly doesn't give the full story."

Brett said that he had not known that Foster had been suspended at Oxford for hacking into its computer system until Horton's lawyers had asked about it. He had advised Foster not to "engage" on hacking and to "just keep it simple, say how you did it legitimately". He conceded that he was concerned that Foster might have been prosecuted for the hacking if he told the truth. Leveson remarked that, had Mr Justice Eady "known the truth", the outcome of the NightJack case might have been different. Leveson said that the episode raised important questions about the accountability and practices of newspapers: "The reason that it, to my mind, is very important is that we have a highly reputable newspaper, a highly reputable lawyer who has been advising that newspaper for a very, very long time, and there is a real issue about the closeness of that relationship and the possibility that there is room for, if you like, a blindness about the overarching issues involved which impact on the practices of the press." He added: "The press rightly hold all of us to account. Who is holding the press to account? That's why this issue has achieved significance."

That night News International said in a statement:

Today's testimony by *The Times*'s former lawyer Alastair Brett was a painful reminder of an occasion when *The Times*'s conduct failed to meet the high standards expected of this newspaper. As has been previously stated, the handling of the NightJack case was deeply unsatisfactory.

News International has changed governance and compliance procedures, including formalised guidance to the in-house legal team, to ensure that rigorous internal processes are adhered to in future.

A month later Rupert Murdoch gave evidence to Leveson. He attacked phone hacking as "lazy" journalism – "it's going to be a blot on my reputation for the rest of my life" – and also said that he had twice been disappointed by *The Times*. First, for not buying the stolen cache of MPs' expenses when they were offered to the paper and were bought instead by *The Telegraph* (he was "jealous" of the story, which had been a "great public service") and again over NightJack. He had been "appalled" by Brett's misleading the court and was "disappointed" that the editor had published the story identifying Horton.

Leveson would write in his 2,000-page inquiry report that he had analysed the NightJack incident in some detail with Brett because it had been subject to litigation. "On the basis of this evidence," he wrote, "it would certainly be possible to draw a number of important conclusions about what happened at *The Times* and about internal governance and legal risk management. However, because the journalist who was said to be at the centre of this incident has now been arrested for offences of computer hacking and attempting to pervert the course of justice, it is not appropriate to risk prejudice to that investigation or to any possible trial by further discussing it." (The Leveson Inquiry, Chapter 2, 1.33).

The Crown Prosecution Service announced in August 2014 that Foster had accepted a caution in relation to the Computer Misuse Act and would not be prosecuted. He joined *The Telegraph* a year later and then became a director of Lexington Communications, advising clients on corporate communications, media relations and crisis management. He later set up his own consultancy. Brett's conduct was referred to the Solicitors' Regulation Authority; its disciplinary tribunal found in 2013 that he had knowingly allowed the High Court to be misled, suspended him from practising for six months and ordered him to pay costs of £30,000. At his appeal the following year before Mr Justice Wilkie, Brett said that he had realised Foster's statement to the High Court was potentially misleading only when the issues were investigated by Leveson. Wilkie found that Brett had recklessly, not knowingly, misled the court, but he agreed with the tribunal that Brett had failed to act with integrity. Horton sued *The Times* for "aggravated damages" and in October 2012 it paid him £42,500.

Although the Leveson inquiry and the NightJack episode were of such significance to *The Times* in 2012, two great national pageants that summer gave Harding, his staff and their readers some light relief. The first, the Queen's Diamond Jubilee on June 4, was planned with great precision as a parade of 1,000 boats down the Thames over a seven-mile route from Battersea to Wapping, led by the 86-year-old monarch and the Duke of Edinburgh in a royal barge. Comparisons were made with a Canaletto painting, but on the day the sky could have hardly been less Venetian – drab, grey, drizzling and windswept, with the Thames murky and brown. More than a million sightseers were undeterred; many had taken up station on the riverbank and bridges early in the morning. Apart from a short break to collect a shawl, the Queen and the duke, 90, stayed on deck throughout the event. Afterwards he was admitted to hospital with a bladder infection. Nobody could miss the point being made. "Duty, tradition, stoicism – their profoundly British behaviour matched the profoundly British weather," David Cameron wrote in his memoirs.

The second event, the 2012 London Olympics, may have been by definition international, but its opening ceremony on July 28 was a joyous national pageant with the Queen in a starring – and startling – role. The arena ceremony in the Olympic stadium, on an evening of fine summer weather, evoked a green and pleasant land, a Spirit of Britain vision of an idyllic Merrie England giving birth to the altruistic common endeavour of the National Health Service. But nothing could match the scenes shown on the giant screens in the stadium and broadcast around the world. In a remarkable vignette that had been kept completely secret, the Queen welcomed James Bond, played as in the most recent films by the actor Daniel Craig, to her drawing room in Buckingham Palace. Applause and laughter filled the stadium as they left together to fly in a helicopter . . . to the Olympic stadium. Fact and fiction fused as the audience looked up and saw a helicopter hovering overhead. As the screens showed a figure in the Queen's distinctive pink dress brush past Craig and leap out, a pink-clad parachutist emerged from the helicopter accompanied by "Bond" in his dinner suit. Union Jack parachutes opened. Seconds later, while the dare-devil impersonators landed safely, the real Queen and Prince Philip received a standing ovation as they walked into the arena.

For the athletes, it was hard act to follow, but Lynne Truss wrote at the end of the Games that London had been transformed by Olympic magic (Saturday, August 11, 2012). She had been to water polo, shooting, rowing, cycling, tennis, the Serpentine for the men's ten-kilometre swimming marathon and Horse Guards Parade for the beach volleyball, "getting increasingly choked up about how well the Games had been run". Team GB finished third in the medals table with 65 medals, including 29 golds. In her Feedback column Rose Wild gave a special "well-spotted" award to Howard Granville, of Stanmore, Middlesex. "While studying your comprehensive and otherwise excellent results service," he wrote, "I was amused to see that in the women's triathlon results, GB's Vicky Holland has been listed as V Netherlands." What a collector's item, Wild said. Granville blamed a spell-checker and hoped to see Britain's 1500m hopeful Hannah England listed as Hannah Great Britain. *The Times* outsold all its rivals during the London Olympics, thanks in no small part to the innovation of a wraparound pictorial cover each day of the Games.

Then it was back to Leveson, who published his report at the end of November. The following morning, *The Times* devoted seven pages to it. *The News of the World* and *The Sun* were specifically named and shamed with examples of their misdeeds. Even more malpractices by *The Daily Mail* and *The Daily Express* were itemised. Pictures of wronged celebrities marched across the pages JK Rowling, Sienna Miller, Prince Harry, the Duchess of Cambridge, Heather Mills, Steve Coogan and Charlotte Church.

Harding was primarily concerned about what the Leveson report had to say about press regulation. Two days before its publication he had written a signed opinion piece in *The Times* advocating a system of independent regulation with a judicial but not statutory backstop. It should be able to investigate and punish, ensure that people who had been wronged got prompt and prominent redress, and safeguard free expression. It should be run by the public, not by editors or proprietors. And it should be empowered to fine papers for wrongdoing.

He also took a swipe at *The News of the World*, as an example of a newsroom not only whose methods were wrong, but which had also lost its moral bearings. "The failure of News International to get to grips with what had happened at one of its newspapers suggested that the company had succumbed to that most dangerous illusion of the powerful, namely that it could play by its own set of rules." He concluded: "It is time for Fleet Street to own the mistakes of its past . . . Time to change the way newspapers are regulated. But . . . we must do it in a way that keeps parliament and press apart." When Leveson then recommended "a genuinely independent and effective system of self-regulation" underpinned by legislation, Harding moved quickly to coordinate a response by national newspapers. On December 4, 19 editors and top executives went to Downing Street and were warned by David Cameron that, while he was declining to enact legislation for statutory regulation, "the clock is ticking" for the industry to agree a system "that absolutely meets the requirements of the Leveson report". Next day, Harding sent the 19 an agenda for an 8.30am breakfast meeting in a private room at the Delaunay brasserie in Aldwych. The minutes show that they agreed unanimously to accept the Leveson principles for establishing a new independent regulator, with the important exception of statutory underpinning. It was a blueprint for the Independent Press Standards Organisation (IPSO), which was established in 2014.

But more serious events were about to unfold for Harding at *The Times*. In fact there were signs that all was far from well with his relationship with Rupert and James Murdoch. James Murdoch had been angry about the *Times* coverage of phone hacking and had stopped speaking to him. Harding says company executives had told him the Murdochs wanted to get rid of him. The editor was convinced he was being sacked because of the commentary on phone hacking, and it undoubtedly led the company to feel he was being disloyal.

Certainly News Corporation was taking relentless fire from all directions and to have one of their most respected publications criticising them angered the Murdochs and senior management. Most newspapers caught up in their own company crises tend to steer clear of commenting on them, for obvious reasons. They let their rivals lead the way and report what is necessary for a paper of record. Readers tend to understand this. In criticising his own company Harding was certainly acting independently, but much of Fleet Street thought he was being naive. They described it as a "Yes, Minister" moment in which Nigel Hawthorne would say to Paul Eddington that a proposal he was considering enacting was "very brave, minister" before it was promptly dropped.

The criticism of phone hacking was not the only reason the Murdochs and Robert Thomson wanted change. It was thought by them that *The Times* was not as sharp as it should have been and was somewhat adrift. The combination of this with phone hacking was combustible and was to lead to Harding's departure.

In the week following the Delaunay summit, Keith Blackmore was on holiday in Berlin. After several telephone calls from Harding he returned early to London. Over dinner at La Famiglia in Chelsea, Harding said he thought he was going to resign the next day. He felt he had been pushed into it. "I decided to 'resign' at the instigation of the company," he says.

Harding would have liked to continue. He was aware that, under the terms of the legal undertakings Rupert Murdoch had agreed with parliament on acquiring *The Times* and *Sunday Times* in 1981, the hiring or firing of the editor had to be approved by the *Times* board of independent directors. He could have sought the protection of the independent directors; some of them thought he should have done. It was clear to him, however, that the company wanted a change.

No editor can expect to continue without corporate support, not least because the company controls the editorial budget. Nor is it possible, in the medium or long term, for an editor to run a newspaper that had ambitions for difficult investigations and campaigns without the support of the proprietor and management. The stand-off that must ensue if he refused to go would have risked damaging the paper. The title had already been through several rounds of cost-cutting and redundancies. Further cuts were likely to be required so that, in effect, he would be protecting his own job at the expense of others.

"I didn't want him to [resign], " Blackmore said. "I thought he should stick it out.". Harding reluctantly went ahead, however, telling staff in the newsroom (*The Guardian*, December 13 2012): "It has been made clear to me that News Corporation would like to appoint a new editor of The *Times*. I have, therefore, agreed to stand down. I called Rupert this morning to offer my resignation and he accepted it." He had expected on the night of his first editorial about the hacking scandal at *The News of the World* that he would survive for no more than 18 months. "It didn't go exactly as I'd thought," Harding later said, "because it was a little longer than 18 months so it was just at the point when we thought actually things had really changed. We'd got to the other side of 2012 with *The Times* having had a better Olympics than any other newspaper on Fleet Street by far; we'd just won another Newspaper of the Year; we'd done [Andrew Norfolk's] Rotherham investigations; we'd had a series of big scoops and just as the paper got to the end of Leveson that's when that happened.".

The news of his resignation was met in the *Times* office with consternation and not a little anger. Twitter lit up with tributes to Harding by reporters, among them Fay Schlesinger and Alexi Mostrous who, jointly, had just won Investigation of the Year at the British Journalism Awards for an undercover exposé on tax avoidance by high-profile figures including the comedian Jimmy Carr, one of the entertainers at the Queen's Diamond Jubilee celebrations. Schlesinger wrote: "James Harding's departure is a massive loss for us. Office quietest I've ever known it." Monstrous echoed her: "Newsroom shocked into silence by James Harding's resignation. He was a fantastic editor." Blackmore was close to tears. Harding in turn paid tribute to his deputy, saying in his farewell speech that "most of the good things that we've done as a paper in the past few years have been Keith's idea. More than that, he is a man of decency, judgment, taste and an extraordinary appreciation for all types of talent, except his own." It was a measure of the bond between them that, after a brief stint as acting editor, Blackmore would eventually follow Harding to the BBC and then to Tortoise Media.

Matthew Parris wrote in the Comment section of *The Times* website:

> James Harding is the fourth *Times* editor under whom I've written for the paper. What has been so tremendously encouraging and confidence-building about his editorship to *Times* writers like me has been to have an editor so fresh and open-minded in his daily approach to the news; so full of enthusiasm for what his reporters and columnists were attempting; and so brimming with ideas for what more we might attempt. Never jaded, never cynical, never demoralising, always optimistic and full of belief in what we were all doing . . . It should not be assumed that every

editor tears open his newspaper every morning, engaged with everything it's saying and discovering, and racking his and his colleagues' brains for proposals for doing it better. It should not be assumed that with every Fleet Street editor the remark that 'this might sell newspapers but it would be beneath a paper like ours to do it' could clinch the argument but with James it always would. James Harding has been an inspirational, an energising and a moral force for us. I don't know where else to say this so I'll say it here.

Some people speculated that Harding had gone because of his criticism of the way News International had handled the hacking dispute, or even for supporting Barack Obama's bid for the presidency. Others cited falling circulation. *The Times*'s ABC figures had fallen year by year from 633,718 in 2008 to 397,549 in 2012, although that took no account of the rise in online traffic. Les Hinton told a private lunch of journalists in 2018 that Harding left because the paper "wasn't doing well". A former editor said that he had been unable to control budgets, an accusation not supported by the large drop in Times Newspapers Ltd's pre-tax losses under the Project Walter cost-cutting programme. Looking back, Robert Thomson emphasised that Harding was a brilliant journalist and ambassador for *The Times* and said that when he was appointed he had been the candidate best suited to building the paper's digital personality, which was a priority. That side of the paper did evolve positively but the overall content mix was not as compelling as it could be, and lack of editorial empathy with the readers had started to be reflected in sales.

Murdoch confirmed none of the speculation when asked about Harding's departure in an interview for this volume. He said: "You know, the editor of *The Times* is quite a public position, perhaps more then than now. You can go to some embassy every night to dine, be the oracle. And I think, I don't know whether it was ego, but something went wrong. A bit offside. With Robert [Thomson] as well as me. So he resigned and went to the BBC.". Harding joked in a speech six months after leaving that if a "proprietor has a different view of things from the editor, I understand that the proprietor is not leaving" (Speech at Journalists' Charity lunch, *The Guardian*, July 5, 2013). Long afterwards, however, he confessed that leaving *The Times* was the most painful experience of his working life. The pressure on him had been mounting, he said, with accusations of disloyalty and the conflict of interest between the NewsCorp management and the staff and what they perceived to be the readers' rights. He did not want to make his departure into a public fight that would undermine the perception of *The Times* and its independence, and he had insisted that he wanted to speak to Murdoch personally before going. When he rang Murdoch for the last time they had a "very courteous conversation".

Harding was reflective on the role of Murdoch as proprietor. He said he broadly shared Matthew Parris's view, "which is that Rupert Murdoch's ownership, with the awkward exception of my sacking, has enabled decades of incredible journalism and extraordinary work. Challenging, courageous, creative, funny, inventive, inspiring, enjoyable. Some of the very best in the world".

There was another blow for Harding before he went. His farewell issue was set for December 31, though he was no longer in the office by then. William Rees-Mogg, with whom he had formed such a strong bond on becoming editor in 2009, dictated a column for it to Anne Spackman, comment editor, on December 14. In the event, Harding's farewell issue, overseen by Blackmore, carried both the column and the columnist's obituary. Rees-Mogg died on December 29, aged 84. The obituary profiled a man who had been unquestionably one of *The Times*'s most influential editors. Like Harding and Thomson, he had first made his name as a journalist at *The Financial Times*, becoming chief leader writer at the age of 27 and assistant editor at 29. In his early thirties, he moved to *The Sunday Times*, serving as city editor, political and economic editor and deputy editor before taking the chair at *The Times* in 1967 aged 38 and staying in it for 14 years. Rees-Mogg maintained that no writing – including his own – could not be improved, but as editor he took scant interest in the production of the night's paper. He usually left at about 6.30pm after a brief chat with the night editors. From Friday evening to Monday morning he was in the country. He barely knew any sub-editors: when he gave a lunch in the office for "rank-and-file" subs they queued at the door to shake hands and to be introduced to him.

Although he was not a natural newsman, he loved a scoop. In his final year as editor, he scooped the rest of Fleet Street. Page 1 of *The Times* on February 24, 1981, carried a picture of Lady Diana Spencer and, under a "staff reporter" byline, the news that "The engagement of the Prince of Wales and Lady Diana Spencer is expected to be announced today". The staff reporter was John Witherow, future editor of *The Sunday Times* and *The Times*, and his source was Rees-Mogg, who in turn had been told by William Whitelaw, the home secretary and Margaret Thatcher's deputy.

On leaving *The Times*, Rees-Mogg had become one of the "Great and Good" – vice-chairman of the BBC's board of governors, chairman of the Arts Council and of the Broadcasting Standards Council, accepting a knighthood and then a life peerage. But he returned to *The Times* as a regular columnist in 1992 – "coming home" as he put it – and was continuing to file fortnightly when he died. As a supremely fluent writer he could still turn round a polished piece in the shortest time in his eighties. In a tribute to him Spackman wrote that, after Barack Obama had addressed both Houses of Parliament during a state visit to Britain in May 2011, she had taken a phone call at 5pm from Harding. Who, Harding asked, had heard Obama's speech live and could assess it for that night's issue as a piece of oratory, preferably comparing it with previous speakers in Westminster Hall? Spackman rang Rees-Mogg's London home. He was out (naturally he had no mobile phone). At 6.15pm he rang the office. What did he think of the speech, Spackman asked – very good. Could he give it perspective – yes, he had heard the Pope and Nelson Mandela live. Could he write 1,000 words – yes, that would take 100 minutes. At 8pm Spackman put on headphones and took the 1,000 words of lucid copy which ranged over Cicero, Elizabeth I and Gladstone. In a fitting tribute to Harding's mentor, the Rees-Mogg obituary ran over three pages in what was the last edition of *The Times* for both of them.

SECTION THREE
JOHN WITHEROW
2013 to 2022

CHAPTER THIRTEEN

John Witherow did not hang about. As soon as he was named as the acting editor of *The Times*, on Friday, January 18, 2013, he went upstairs from the *Sunday Times* floor to *The Times* and addressed the newsroom, telling anxious journalists not to be alarmed and that he was not "wearing a horned helmet". Next day, he did his usual 14-hour Saturday shift getting *The Sunday Times* away but on the Sunday, which was his 61st birthday, he left his home in Putney to visit the *Times* offices again and chatted encouragingly with the skeleton staff putting together Monday's paper. He knew that many at *The Times* felt they had lost a widely liked young editor and gained a grizzled Murdoch veteran who had survived for nearly 20 years as editor of *The Sunday Times*.

Had they talked to his closest lieutenants on the Sunday paper, they would have been told that Witherow was not the rough-tongued "alpha" editor some feared he was, but a complex figure with a range of managerial styles from wily, manipulative and menacing to mischievous and funny, and that he was driven not just by an ambition to be the best but above all by a love of news and investigations. He had also come home at last to the newspaper he had first joined as a 28-year-old and which he had long been keen to lead.

The road to the editor's chair at *The Times* had been far from straightforward. John Witherow was born in Johannesburg on January 20, 1952, the youngest child of a South African civil engineer and his English-born wife. They became disillusioned with the National Party government, which had come to power in 1949 bringing in its policy of apartheid, and decided to emigrate to Britain when John was four. They found 1950s Britain hard going, however, thanks to postwar austerity and the bleak climate. That prompted them again to leave to forge a new life in Australia. But they failed to settle in Melbourne and returned to the UK when John was eight. He went on to be educated at Bedford School and, at the age of 19 before going to university, went on a gap year that gave him his first taste of journalism.

Through family contacts in South Africa, Witherow got voluntary work in South West Africa, the neighbouring former German colony now know as Namibia. He found himself in a territory that, although remote, was in the frontline of the armed struggles that scarred southern Africa in the latter decades of the 20th century. South Africa had governed it since the First World War under an old League of Nations mandate and had continued to do so in defiance of international law after the mandate was repealed by the United Nations. If anything, apartheid was enforced with even greater zeal in South West Africa than in South Africa itself. An armed independence movement, SWAPO, was fighting the South African military in Ovamboland on the territory's border with Angola, where the Portuguese colonial army was also facing an armed independence struggle.

Witherow was meant to go to Ovamboland to teach at an Anglican school, but the authorities refused to give him a permit. He was stuck kicking his heels in Windhoek, South West Africa's capital, when he had the idea of starting a library for Africans from the townships who had almost no access to books. With the help of a contact in Johannesburg, John Kane-Berman, a former Rhodes scholar who would go on to become chief executive of the Institute for Race Relations, he raised thousands of pounds from donors in Britain and the United States to start the library. The most generous by far was Paul Hamlyn of Octopus Books in London.

Through his contacts, Witherow was in touch with the local Anglican church, which was led by a "raw-boned, dynamic" Anglo-Irish bishop called Colin Winter, an effective opponent of apartheid and of the repressive activities of the local administrators in South West Africa. Winter and his aides were continually hounded by the Special Branch, "who bugged our offices and blatantly followed us around Windhoek in an effort to intimidate", Witherow recalled. Ultimately, after a campaign against Winter in the local Afrikaans press, Bishop Winter was deported to Britain. His diocesan secretary, Dave de Beer, a South African, was placed under a banning order, effectively a form of house arrest, and sent back to South Africa. De Beer was also the local stringer for the BBC World and Africa services, which took great interest in the territory and needed a replacement for him. With a cheery "good luck", de Beer handed the BBC string to Witherow. "I knew next to nothing about journalism but did my inadequate best to report on the political developments with the generous patience of the BBC editors," Witherow said. After returning to Britain at the end of his gap year and studying history at York and then journalism at

Cardiff, Witherow was taken on as a trainee by Reuters, which sent him to Madrid for 12 months. Many years later, in his retirement speech as editor of *The Times* in 2022, he remembered how his traineeship came to a sticky end:

> I had returned from Madrid and was promptly invited into the office of the head of news. He was an intimidating Scotsman with a shock of white hair and a solemn manner. 'I want you to go to Buenos Aires,' he said. 'It'll be a three year posting.' 'Marvellous,' I said. 'When?' 'Next week,' he said. 'Ah,' said I. 'That's tricky. My mother is really ill and I'm in the process of buying a flat. Can we postpone it for a while? I'd love to go?' 'No,' he said. 'It's next week or nothing.' 'Well I'm afraid I simply can't go next week,' I said. This man then leant across his desk and said in a menacing manner: 'I've never had a trainee turn down a posting before.' So I left his office realising my brief life at Reuters was about to end and there would be no galloping across the pampas and flirting with beautiful Argentine senoritas.
>
> That is when I decided I wanted to join *The Times*. No other title would do. So I wrote to the paper and was called in for an interview. A week or two later I got a letter saying there was no vacancy. This was a blow. So I wrote again, asking them to reconsider. A polite letter came back saying they had reconsidered and no, there was still no vacancy. Desperate times called for desperate measures. So I wrote to Fred Emery, a senior honcho at *The Times*, and said I was prepared to work for six months for not a penny of payment. If after that time they thought I was capable they could offer me a job and if not, I would meekly depart. I heard nothing for several weeks. In the meantime I had been put on the graveyard shift at Reuters working from ten at night to eight in the morning. The *Times* were indeed desperate. I then got a letter inviting me back to the office in Grays Inn Road. I was told that *The Times* could not possibly employ someone unpaid but, seeing I was so bloody keen (brackets desperate) for a job, they might as well give me one.

He quickly discovered the difference between working for an international news agency and Britain's oldest national daily newspaper:

> On my first day, the deputy news editor invited me over the road at lunchtime to the Blue Lion pub to meet other journalists. He proceeded to sink seven pints of beer while I nervously sipped halves. He then went back to news editing, seemingly reading PA copy off the printer. I slunk back to my desk and tried to sober up. Fleet Street then ran on a river of alcohol and I suspect much of the content of newspapers was written by people who were half cut or frankly pissed. The office, too, was nothing like our ones here. It was a rabbit warren, with typewriters clattering, five pieces of carbon for seven paper sheets and cigarettes hanging out of mouths as hacks typed away. The noise and the smoke somehow gave it an edge and the sense of news being urgent and revelatory.

Within the first few weeks Witherow was covering the siege of the Iranian embassy, lying flat in the road as gunfire echoed around Knightsbridge and the SAS stormed the building on May 5, 1980. Drama of a different kind was brewing in the *Times* office itself: Roy Thomson, proprietor since 1966, was selling his newspaper titles to Rupert Murdoch. William Rees-Mogg's long tenure as editor of *The Times* came to an end and Harry Evans moved over from *The Sunday Times*, only to be sacked by Murdoch a year later in March 1982. For several days Evans refused to go. *Times* staff were vocally divided between his supporters and those of his deputy, Charles Douglas-Home, who stepped up to editor after Evans finally agreed to resign.

Almost immediately, *The Times* was handling its biggest story for decades: the Argentinian invasion of the Falkland Islands. Witherow was dispatched as part of the press pack on board HMS Invincible in the British armada heading for the South Atlantic. He later remembered self-deprecatingly that everyone involved in that conflict discovered something new about themselves: in his case it was that he was not cut out to be a war reporter.

> I was the William Boot of *The Times*. I think they ideally would have liked [Robert] Fisk to have gone but he was

stuck in the Middle East and they sent me because I was single and they didn't want worried wives on the phone all the time. They thought it wasn't going to be a war anyway but they had to cover themselves. It was long periods of boredom getting down there. We were very constrained in what we could report and heavily censored and low in the pecking order of communications. It all went through the Ministry of Defence and sat around in dusty offices for days.

On his return, Witherow was sent to work for six months at *The Boston Globe* on an exchange deal that introduced him to American journalism with its greater freedom of action and higher self-regard than its British counterpart. Restless, the following year Witherow moved "across the bridge", the walkway that divided the two buildings in Gray's Inn Road housing *The Times* and *The Sunday Times*, and went to work for the Sunday paper's hard-driving new editor, Andrew Neil. He took the turmoil of the Murdoch operation's move to Wapping in 1986 in his stride and, after several years as defence and then diplomatic correspondent, he was promoted to foreign editor in 1990. Saddam Hussein's invasion of Kuwait that year and the subsequent Gulf War were an opportunity to get himself noticed. He distinguished himself with his handling of coverage, bonded with Neil on a trip to the war zone together and soon emerged as the obvious heir-apparent, becoming the powerful head of news and, in 1994, acting editor after Neil resigned.

Neil bequeathed a ten-section *Sunday Times* that weighed in at 2lb 8oz and was selling more than 1.3 million copies each week. It was highly profitable, making £1 million a week and thus, in Murdoch's eyes, partly propping up the loss-making *Times*. No rival broadsheet had such reach, with a circulation equal to that of *The Sunday Telegraph*, *The Observer* and *The Independent on Sunday* combined. Witherow recalled in his retirement speech:

When I took over from Andrew I knew I was inheriting a strong, robust beast of a paper. After Wapping it had become a huge multisection behemoth with jokes about paperboys getting dislocated arms from lugging weighty copies to doorsteps. Not only had Andrew made it multisectional after the defeat of the print unions at

Wapping, but he had made it controversial, Thatcherite, anti-union and firmly in favour of the free market. While it alienated some of the *bien-pensants* who had adopted the paper under Harry Evans, it retained a good record on investigations and Andrew had happily waded into royal controversies over Diana's faltering marriage and Thatcher's tense relationship with the Queen. The paper boomed in the late 1980s and early 1990s, taking in huge amounts of advertising and continued to sell well. And when Thatcher fell, Andrew had gone on to support Michael Heseltine for the leadership, a move not approved of by Rupert Murdoch who saw Heseltine as too statist and interventionist.

Neil also bequeathed to his successor a framed quotation from the historian AJP Taylor, a prolific newspaper contributor, which stated: "The editor is always right. He has to bring out the paper; he knows what will interest or satisfy the readers. If a journalist does not like the editor he must go elsewhere and not complain."

In Neil's case, however, it was the editor who had had to go. His pugnacity and flair for self-promotion had made him a household name but had also irked his proprietor to the point where their ways had to part. By contrast, as editor, Witherow kept a public profile as low as Neil's had been high. While Neil was still known as the former editor of *The Sunday Times* for several years after his departure, the actual editor was getting on with the job in comparative obscurity. Les Hinton, who arrived as executive chairman of News International in 1985, wrote in his memoir that Witherow was the "most in-the-office, heads-down editor" (Hinton, 2018, p. 325). Or, as Hinton once put it in awe to an interviewer: "You can't get him to go out for lunch after Wednesday. He is a very, very involved editor."

Witherow recalled Hinton's arrival with gratitude:

> Les, an exiled Liverpudlian who had lived both in Australia and America, had worked for Murdoch since he was 16 and was close to the proprietor and a subtle reader of his mind and intentions. Thus I was able to continue to improve and expand the title, introducing a Technology section, greatly improving the quality of the Culture section and converting the newsprint Style section into a proper glossy woman's magazine.

On the other hand, "Les forced me to close the much-loved *Funday Times* against my wishes, saying that if I didn't the cuts would fall elsewhere in more painful places."

One big contrast with the Neil years was that the editor's "bollockings" were no longer delivered in public. Those who had worked in senior positions under Neil felt almost unanimously that he had been a brilliant and inspiring editor but that his humiliation of his executives in front of each other if they failed to reach his exacting standards had turned editorial conferences into a blood sport. Unlike Neil, Witherow relied on a small inner group of loyal senior executives who mostly stayed with him throughout his editorship, and he remained loyal to them. He had only two heads of news, Mark Skipworth and Charles Hymas, and one managing editor, Richard Caseby, for much of his 19-year term at *The Sunday Times*.

If Witherow's editorial conferences were low-key and business-like, he was tough and relentlessly demanding when his office door was closed. He once asked another of his key lieutenants, the sports editor, Alex Butler: "What do they think of me out there?" The exchange, Butler recalled, "took place when I walked into his office on one of those long Friday evenings at *The Sunday Times* when John usually took great delight in tearing up the sports pages I had been crafting all week. I replied:

> 'They think you're a c***, John. Actually, they think you're a complete c***.' A huge grin spread across his face. 'That's fantastic.' He laughed out loud. For several seconds. Before the smile disappeared. He leant forward. And asked: 'Who thinks I'm a complete c***?' That question hung in the air for an uncomfortably long few seconds before the smile returned.

Butler added that it was meant as a compliment. "Yes, he was tough. Unbelievably tough. But you had to respect his talent and his drive for the highest standards."

Butler was from the same mould. Though generous-hearted, he was also "unbelievably tough" on his sports staff when the occasion required and the editor was on his back. He remembered a historic night for English football, Saturday, September 1, 2001, when the England team were playing Germany in a World Cup qualifying match in Munich. The three pages that he had planned for their expected defeat seemed more than enough. Just before kick-off

Witherow was taken ill and had to leave the office for medical treatment, which was unprecedented for a Saturday evening.

> Germany scored first. England equalised and scored again and again to 5–1. I had to rip up all my plans. There was pandemonium in the office. People shouting. Pages being scrapped and redrawn. Then my phone rang. It was John, obviously still unwell. His voice the merest whisper. It sounded as if he was gasping for breath. 'What are you doing with the England game? . . . go to five pages . . . more if you can . . . and don't make the paper late.'

Will Lewis, a former *Sunday Times* business editor and later publisher of *The Wall Street Journal*, said that Witherow was the most formidable person he had worked with. "He demands so much of his people. He lives for the job. His rigour and obsession with detail is something I was genuinely shocked by when I first got [to *The Sunday Times*]. His energy levels are staggering – nothing is ever good enough, which is great, for an editor."

Lewis had joined The *Sunday Times* from *The Financial Times* thinking that he knew everything. "John put me right on that. He's a brilliant but brutal editor. Nothing is ever good enough for him, so he ripped me up and put me back together again." (*Press Gazette*, September 4, 2017).

If Witherow's relentless, determined, never-ending enthusiasm, as Butler put it, was one key to his success at *The Sunday Times*, the other was to keep his team on their toes by his unpredictable ability to switch in a moment between stony-faced editor and the genial figure that Jane Martinson of *The Guardian* was surprised to encounter in a rare interview (July 28, 2008). Despite a reputation as a tough perfectionist, Martinson wrote, Witherow was relaxed, thoughtful and funny, even doing impressions of rival newspaper executives. His public image seemed to be largely derived from his failure to grant many interviews – "are they a useful thing to do with your time?" – and from the contrast with Andrew Neil.

By then, after 14 years in the job, Witherow had already cast his eyes at *The Times* as a fresh challenge. In 2007, when Robert Thomson was clearly heading for New York, Witherow wrote to Murdoch making the case for himself to succeed Thomson as editor of *The Times*. Murdoch took him out to lunch and gently told him he wanted James Harding to take over while Witherow continued at The *Sunday Times*. By 2013, Murdoch had changed his mind. He concluded that *The Times* needed someone with Witherow's huge experience. Andrew Knight, chairman of Times Newspapers Holdings at that time, summed up the difference in editing style between Harding and Witherow. It was the difference, he said, between soft and hard journalism. "James saw the catholicity of the paper, the width of the paper, the soft culture and features side. He knew a lot more about those aspects than John did, they were what lit his fire. But he wasn't the editor John is. At core, James's passion wasn't news. Whereas John's is." It was no coincidence that Witherow once said much the same about Murdoch, describing him as "a brilliant proprietor. He has invested in journalism and lets you get on with it. He loves journalism. He's just curious, a journalistic trait." (Interview with Newsworks, January 29, 2015). Before Witherow could move to *The Times*, however, there was an obstacle to overcome. The independent national directors (INDs) of Times Newspapers Holdings did not immediately accept the proposal that the editor of *The Sunday Times* should simply switch saddles to *The Times* and that Martin Ivens, Witherow's deputy at the Sunday paper, should step up to the editorship there. They wanted to explore the undertakings given by Murdoch in 1981 to preserve the separate identities of the two titles. They also thought they had been insufficiently consulted, and they had a strong affection for Harding.

The independent directors at the time were Rupert Pennant-Rea, chairman of the Economist Group and former deputy governor of the Bank of England; Veronica Wadley, London Arts Council chairwoman and former editor of the London *Evening Standard*; Sarah Bagnall, a director of the PR agency Pelham Bell Pottinger and a former *Times* financial journalist; Baroness Eccles of Moulton, a UK delegate to the Council of Europe and a director of Opera North; Lord Marlesford (formerly Mark Schreiber), adviser to financial institutions and one-time *Economist* journalist; and Stephen Grabiner, former *Daily Telegraph* executive and chairman of the management and standards committee established by News International in the wake of the hacking scandal.

Knight had the task of liaising between Murdoch and this formidable group. At the time, Knight was staying as a guest in a relative's house. The man of the household was a well-known TV historian with a lively journalistic streak who had to be kept in the dark. Knight became a recluse in a quiet room in the house for a stream of secret phone calls with Murdoch and his long-time mentor, Sir Edward Pickering. He recalled:

> 'Under the arrangements,' I said to Rupert and Pick, as loud as I dared, 'you have to consult the directors first. Just set up a meeting with them. Explain why James isn't the right editor and I will support you. John has long wanted to edit *The Times* and I reckon bringing him over from *The Sunday Times* is great.'
>
> With a trowel, I laid on to Rupert the INDs' irritation over Harding going. But here's a classic example of the clarity of Murdoch's mind. He listened to me and, particularly, to Pick who agreed with me. Murdoch had read all the internal papers which he never ignores. But his mind is clear water. 'Ah,' he said, probably with an expletive, 'we'll just make them acting editors. The Independents may not want to approve them now – but they will after a while when they've seen John and Martin at work. They'll both be so good, within a year the directors will fall into line.' I thought, 'My God, why didn't I think of that?' Had Murdoch thought of the 'acting editor' gambit before we talked? I don't think so, it had more likely just occurred to him during the conversation.

Witherow had been acting editor for a while when first put in charge of *The Sunday Times* so, like Murdoch, he was confident the process would work its way through. He was right. After an eight-month wait, a down-page paragraph on page 4 of *The Times* (September 28, 2013) announced that both Witherow and Ivens had been appointed editors. News UK had assured the directors that the titles would remain separate in accordance with the 1981 undertakings. At 61, Witherow was the oldest new editor of *The Times* since 64-year-old William Casey in 1948.

CHAPTER FOURTEEN

The new editor adapted easily to the different rhythms of daily paper journalism. He explained that Sunday papers were more stressful because you get only 50 shots a year; everything is focused on one day and if it goes well it's great and if it goes badly you suffer for several days afterwards because you know you missed things and didn't do it properly.

> The joy of coming to a daily newspaper was that if you got it right, great, and you move on to the next day. But if you got it wrong, dammit, I'll sort it out tomorrow. You don't have to wait a week to rectify things if you get the balance wrong or the weight of stories or you just miss them. So that is a delight and I like the pace of it.

Two months into his editorship, *The Times* won Newspaper of the Year at the Press Awards dinner in London. The judges praised its "impressive quality combined with superb scoops, columnists that are among the most well-known in the industry and increasingly innovative digital offerings". Witherow, as acting editor, accepted the award and admitted that he felt like an imposter. Gesturing to the tables of *Times* award-winners and executives, he said: "It is due to the wonderful people here and all the other people at *The Times* who have produced this newspaper . . . every day of the last year. They are fantastic staff, as I have discovered in the last couple of months and I'd particularly like to thank James Harding, the former editor . . . He should be accepting this award."

Despite this accolade, Witherow was determined to make changes to Harding's *Times*. Although acting editor, he did not feel constrained and he had clear objectives. With his managing editor, Craig Tregurtha, a straight-talking individual who had risen through the sport pages, he set about trying to cut the paper's heavy expenses and expensive payroll. There were urgent reasons for doing so.

News Corporation was split into two in May 2013. The more profitable entertainment arm became 21st Century Fox while the publishing arm became the "new News Corps" under Robert Thomson as CEO. The British newspaper titles were rebundled as News UK within Thomson's publishing empire. The split meant that *The Times* could no longer be subsidised by profits from the entertainment businesses. Witherow and Tregurtha were determined to make sure it was not a drain on the new News Corp's finances. The aim was initially to bring the title to a break-even position, but they also had a clear vision to make it profitable. For that to happen editorial costs had to be reduced by millions.

Witherow, with Tregurtha at his side, spelt out the new reality to staff on June 10, 2013:

> For several years now *Times* Newspapers has been losing money. The company has tolerated this because it could use profits from elsewhere in News Corp to pay for our papers and because the proprietor has a passion for newspapers. I fear that era of being subsidised is coming to an end. The separation of the two companies means that the newspapers will form a bigger and more exposed element in the new News Corp.

He announced that 20 journalists would go, picked by himself.

The ensuing round of job losses was the third in three years and meant that 180 journalists had been culled in that time. In 2010 about 60 had left, including 20 who were given no choice. A year later James Harding had told staff that another 100 jobs would be going, with casual sub-editors at the top of the list. There was much more to come under Witherow.

As the cuts took hold, every part of the newsroom budget was examined. Each desk was told to cut costs, every item of spending was appraised – all the way down to the number of rival newspapers delivered to the office every morning. Staff were told to take the Tube instead of using taxis to get around London, expenses were sent back and receipts demanded for everything. Tregurtha, painfully, found himself having to oversee the departure of colleagues from his days on sport as the cuts took hold. But the mission was clear – to make the paper more efficient, without the reader seeing any drop in quality, and in doing so to give it a sustainable future. The balancing act between finding economies and giving the editor the resources he needed made managing editor a brutally demanding post: constantly on call to hire, fire, implement big budgets, negotiate contracts and control staffing levels, liaise with marketing and advertising, help with legal issues and employment tribunals, supervise critical under-the-radar projects and implement and devise strategic restructuring. Pastoral care was vital too. The safety of war correspondents was a constant concern, as was crisis management of emergencies. Personal problems of mental and physical health and domestic worries might need skilled help and support. Tregurtha summed it up by pointing to his office door and saying: "When you walk through this door you have a problem – which becomes my problem."

He was assisted by a strong managing editors office which looked after both *The Times* and *Sunday Times*. His longest-serving number two was Liz Harris, whom Tregurtha first brought onto the paper's staff directly from News UK's human resources department. This in itself was an unusual step – the managing editor's office was normally the domain of journalists who moved into a managerial role. But Tregurtha knew that Witherow's transformation of the paper would require HR expertise and in Harris, an uncompromising, wry Australian who had worked at Sky, he found someone equally straight-talking and determined to get the paper onto a strong financial footing. Harris's organisational skills were tested as she planned each departmental restructure to comply with strict employment law. Staff found they were required to work across print and digital – and eventually across the two titles. Those who couldn't, or wouldn't, left.

It was not just a question of cost. After 19 years at the helm of *The Sunday Times*, Witherow had clear ideas of how to run a newspaper. He understood that a daily paper brought different challenges, and if anything he seemed to relish having more to do and less time to do it in. But his views on what made a good paper – and a good editor – had been formed by long experience, and they were firm. Anyone unable to share them could move on. By the middle of his first year a number of senior and long-serving staff had left. The leader writer and associate editor Camilla Cavendish moved to *The Sunday Times* in February. In March, Anne Spackman, former managing editor, editor-in-chief of Times Online and comment editor, departed. Ian King, business and city editor, left for Sky Television. In April, Martin Fletcher, the archetypal dashing foreign fireman, long-serving war correspondent and news editor, also went.

Among those taking redundancy was Ruth Gledhill, the last full-time national newspaper reporter dedicated to covering religion. Her role was absorbed into general news coverage, which she felt was right because it was "putting the subject in its proper place, putting the power of the story, in news terms, where it belongs".

She added: "I am happy to go." A member of the *Times*'s Wapping Great Voices choir and a keen ballroom dancer at one time, she left with a farewell at Wilton's Music Hall, a much-loved relic of the old East End hidden up an alleyway near the Wapping office.

Gledhill had been on the newspaper for 27 years and for much of that time had been a well-informed thorn in the side of an often fractious established church, with a record of successfully identifying the next Archbishop of Canterbury and an unerring nose for an ecclesiastical row. James Harding told a story about Gledhill in his 2018 Hugh Cudlipp lecture:

> There are many different varieties of untruth. Propaganda, spin, partial reporting. I remember walking across the newsroom floor in *The Times* a few years back and hearing Ruth Gledhill, our extraordinary religion correspondent, getting increasingly worked up. 'You told me you'd gone to Jerusalem. You told me you were there,' she was saying, 'but then I discover you weren't. You lied to me. And you're . . . a bishop.' It's not just politicians, fishermen and people on dating websites who struggle with the truth. (*The Guardian*, March 22, 2018).

Not all those moved from their jobs by Witherow left the paper (though many did). Among staff given new challenges by the new editor (and still with *The Times* when Witherow retired in 2022) were Jeremy Griffin, promoted to head of news and then executive editor; Mike Smith, who went from head of news in 2014 to comment editor and later foreign editor of *The Times* and *Sunday Times*; Ian Brunskill, almost from the start given wide-ranging responsibilities as assistant editor and later associate editor of both *The Times* and *Sunday Times*; and Roland Watson, who moved from parliament to the foreign desk and then to comment.

Witherow was committed to both employing talent and developing it. Recruitment had to diversify beyond white, middle-class, southeast England to get away from the perception of *The Times* as the old establishment newspaper. "Time was that if you went to the right college and had the right connections, you were in," Witherow said. Those days were over. Much effort was put into recruitment and the graduate trainee scheme was broadened from reporting to subbing, pictures, data journalism, design and sport.

The new editor was also determined that *The Times* would stop pretending that it never made mistakes. He was adamant that newspapers must get things right – and that when they got them wrong, they must acknowledge and correct their errors, and learn from them. Corrections were relocated from haphazardly placed down-page paragraphs to a new Corrections and Clarifications column prominently placed on the Letters page. It served as a firm commitment to correcting mistakes, allowed readers to see what had been corrected, and became an archive that helped staff to avoid repeating errors. "If we make a mistake we must correct it swiftly because that enhances the readers' respect for a title," Witherow said. "They understand mistakes get made in hundreds and thousands of words but if you dig in and then try and argue about it over a petty point it does you no favours. If it's wrong, correct it, rapidly."

This had by no means always been a given, even at *The Times*. Ian Brunskill, whom he put in charge of maintaining and improving editorial standards, observed in an email to all staff: "Ten years ago we made hardly any mistakes. Or that's what you'd think if you looked at an old edition of the paper. Corrections were rare and mostly well concealed. It wasn't that we really got fewer things wrong. We just found more excuses for not putting them right. That's not what we do now."

This was the harbinger of a new era in newspaper journalism. As assistant editor, Brunskill became Witherow's point man for complaints-handling, compliance and dealing with the new and more powerful press regulator that was taking shape in the aftermath of the Leveson inquiry. The newspaper industry, while accepting the urgent need for reform, was determined to safeguard its independence and resist statutory regulation of the press under a parliamentary charter, as the Cameron government was proposing. This meant attempting instead to set up an effective self-regulatory body of its own with real teeth. Witherow told BBC Radio 4's *The Media Show*: "I think the press must go ahead with its own form of self-regulation and prove to the public and politicians that it's fair, robust and free."

The Times and other newspapers pressing for self-regulation backed the creation of IPSO with a remit far beyond the complaints-handling function of the former Press Complaints Commission (PCC). From its foundation in 1990 the PCC had made a reasonable job of resolving complaints against the press, but its failure to mount an effective investigation into phone hacking – a task it was never really competent to carry out – had doomed it after Leveson. It had to go. IPSO must be, and be seen to be, an altogether tougher proposition. Like the PCC, it would enforce the Editors' Code of Practice and investigate complaints into alleged breaches. It would be able, however, not just to demand corrections but also to dictate their form and prominence and, when appropriate, insist that adverse adjudications were published in full by the title concerned. It could impose fines of up to £1 million and had the power to launch a formal investigation into editorial standards at any publication where there appeared to be evidence of systemic failings. Member publishers would be required to submit detailed annual reports setting out the measures they had taken to comply with the system of self-regulation under IPSO. Sir Hayden Phillips, a retired civil servant, was chosen to chair the appointments panel of IPSO (November 6, 2013). Witherow, Lord Brown of Eaton-under-Heywood, a retired Supreme Court judge, Dame Denise Platt, a former civil servant, and Paul Horrocks, a former editor of the *Manchester Evening News*, were the first members of Phillips's panel, which would in turn appoint the regulator's board. Some 90 per cent of the industry, including *The Times*, signed up to IPSO. Three national titles, *The Financial Times*, *The Independent* and *The Guardian*, declined to join and instead chose to rely on their own internal complaints-handling systems.

The fact that IPSO's members funded it was denounced as a fatal flaw by the energetic and vocal supporters of Hacked Off, the "campaign for a free and accountable press" that had been set up in 2011 by phone-hacking victims and critics of the press. Among Hacked Off's most prominent supporters were Hugh Grant, the actor, who had made tabloid headlines in 1995 after being arrested for "lewd conduct" in Los Angeles, and Max Mosley, the former chief of world motor sport, who had won £60,000 damages from *The News of the World* in 2008 in a breach of confidence case after it had published a report on his alleged involvement in a sadomasochistic orgy.

Firmly opposed to any system of regulation that the press itself might support, Hacked Off dismissed IPSO as a sham and "the illusion of reform". Hacked Off and its allies had been influential in shaping a cross-party preference in parliament for some degree of statutory regulation. This led to the creation of the Press Recognition Panel, a statutory body that would formally recognise and approve a press regulator. IPSO refused to seek approval and the panel was instead reduced to recognising the Independent Monitor for the Press (Impress), which regulated a handful of small, obscure publications but had the support of the politicians, celebrities and academics most implacably hostile to the established press. Founded by Jonathan Heawood, a former deputy literary editor of *The Observer*, it was funded by Mosley to the tune of £3.8 million.

While policing tougher self-regulation at *The Times*, Brunskill also undertook a thorough revision of its style guide at Witherow's request, making it more permissive than some of its predecessors. "It is a guide, not a straitjacket," his introduction explained (a principle set out with admirable clarity by Simon Jenkins and Philip Howard in their 1992 style guide but rather buried by accretions of pointless pedantry in the intervening years). "Consistency is a virtue, but it should not be pursued at the expense of clarity, elegance or common sense." The new guide "avoids unnecessary prescription and prohibition. It tries to distinguish linguistic superstitions from grammatical rules. It hesitates to condemn usage that neither baffles nor offends. English is not a language fixed for all time. Speech changes and its written form should change too. *The Times* must use the language of its readers, but that language at its best, clearest and most concise." As well as setting out the paper's preferences in such matters as capitalisation, hyphenation and variant spelling, the guide contained more general entries "intended to encourage reflection about words and the way we use them". There was also guidance on such topics as attribution of stories followed up from other papers, how to write headlines and captions, and matters covered by the Editors' Code such as discrimination, reporting suicide, and intrusion into grief and shock. At Witherow's request, Brunskill reinforced those messages – and noted significant lapses – in a weekly email to all staff.

CHAPTER FIFTEEN

In parallel with overhauling *The Times* internally, John Witherow quickly began changing the appearance of the newspaper itself. This began even before he launched the cost-cutting drive. On June 3, five years to the day after James Harding had moved the leader page forward to page 2, Witherow moved it back again to the centre of the paper. In a signed message explaining his decision, printed amid the news stories now restored to page 2, he wrote that readers had been perplexed by seeing editorials on current affairs before they had read the underlying news story. He elaborated on this in conversation later: Harding had told him that having leaders on page 2 "was more like *The Economist*. I just didn't think that worked. *The Economist* is different, it's a weekly magazine but calls itself a newspaper. I don't think it works on a daily." With this came a shift in emphasis. Witherow edited leaders briskly for sense and style; endless last-minute tinkering of the kind in which some of his predecessors seemed to delight was not his way. Leader conferences were shorter and more business-like, and leaders were produced earlier in the day. He first appointed Phil Collins, the former chief speechwriter to Tony Blair, as his chief leader writer. When Collins became a columnist, he was replaced as chief leader writer by Giles Whittell, who had a background as a science journalist. Leaders now often championed driverless cars, market-orientated measures to deal with climate change and – this one a special interest of Witherow's – animal welfare. (He once told a Cheltenham Literature Festival audience that he liked rugby, ballet and hedgehogs – "they get a raw deal".)

The Eurosceptic and socially conservative Tim Montgomerie, founder of the grassroots website ConservativeHome and a *Times* columnist since 2011, was Witherow's first (and short-lived) comment editor. He was replaced by Mike Smith, previously head of news. Generally, in contrast to the approach taken under Harding, Witherow placed greater emphasis on the readers' desire for familiarity. More regular columnists were appointed. The Comment section was lacking an economics specialist – Ed Conway, economics editor at Sky News, was appointed in 2014. Similarly, there was no foreign affairs specialist: that role was filled by Roger Boyes, the paper's diplomatic editor and a former

Berlin and Warsaw correspondent. Other additions included two former *Economist* journalists, Edward Lucas, a Putin-watcher and ex-Moscow correspondent, and Emma Duncan, its former deputy editor. Jenni Russell, a former contributor at the *Evening Standard* and *Sunday Times*, joined, giving an unashamedly metropolitan liberalism, pro-Remain perspective. (Her husband, Stephen Lambert, the television producer, was Witherow's occasional ocean-sailing buddy. In the autumn of 2014 they crossed the Atlantic in Lambert's yacht with two friends from *The Sunday Times*, Matthew Campbell and David Mills.)

Matt Ridley, a "luke-warmist" sceptic of the environmentalist consensus, a free-marketeer and a Brexiteer, became a regular contributor in 2013. Melanie Phillips, a former news editor of *The Guardian* in the 1980s who had made a long journey rightwards, was a striking addition to the opinion team in 2014. Coming from a Labour-voting Jewish family, she had found at *The Guardian* that antisemitism was gaining traction on the political left and that even the most impeccably progressive male reporters were reluctant to take instructions from a woman. A constant theme in her robustly expressed columns was the West's moral decay, though she could surprise readers with articles about the joys of detective fiction. Trevor Phillips, the former chairman of the Equality and Human Rights Commission, became a regular contributor and a critic of "woke culture". Other additions included Clare Foges, a chief speechwriter for David Cameron and for Boris Johnson when he was mayor of London, who became a columnist in 2015. Iain Martin, a Brexit supporting former editor of *The Scotsman*, was signed up in 2016; and Gerard Baker, Obama-sceptical former US editor of *The Times* and the former managing editor of *The Wall Street Journal*, rejoined the pages in 2018, adding a muscular right-wing viewpoint from the other side of the Atlantic. In 2021, William Hague, the former foreign secretary and Conservative Party leader, joined the team and rapidly built up a loyal and appreciative readership.

Other changes to the Comment line-up were rare, however. Matthew Parris, Libby Purves and Ben Macintyre had been writing for the pages since the 1990s. Others, such as David Aaronovitch, Giles Coren, Daniel Finkelstein and Janice Turner, were close to the 20-year mark when Witherow's term as editor drew to a close in 2022. When James Marriott, who mused on bookish and cultural matters, was made a columnist by Witherow in 2021 at the unusually young age of 28, colleagues calculated that, if he followed their example, he would still be writing columns for *The Times* in middle age and beyond. Witherow's *Sunday Times* had published a weekly books section of 10–12 pages and was regarded by the publishing trade as the most important newspaper for review coverage. One of his first acts as editor of *The Times* was to double the number of pages it gave over to books, bucking the trend in newspapers of shrinking book review space and giving his old paper some competition. Erica Wagner, the literary editor, left in the summer and the section's emphasis moved from debut novels and anthologies of feminist writings to more mainstream fiction and many more non-fiction titles. Out went columns about the power of storytelling or reading aloud. The literary editor's column musing on bookish matters was axed.

Wagner was succeeded by Robbie Millen, who had been deputy editor of the op-ed pages. With Millen came a punchier, more irreverent tone. Witherow made it clear that the mission of *The Times* was to win the Hatchet Job of the Year prize for the "angriest, funniest, most trenchant" book review of the past 12 months. In the event, the Hatchet Job was won by *Sunday Times* reviews in both 2013 and 2014 but then, to Millen's frustration (or perhaps relief), the prize was no more. Its sponsor had been a short-lived news aggregator website called The Omnivore. Millen said his only rule for his reviewers was to try to be honest:

> That's the hardest thing. It's a weird job because we pay people not very much to possibly make an enemy for life if they're a freelancer. The literary world in Britain is actually quite small now a lot of book reviewers make a living by compering at literary festivals, and [I asked] them to be really honest and know that for their £300 Ian McEwan will hate them forever and they're going to have to hide from him in the green room. I'm actually impressed how honest the reviewers I use are.

Millen's first exposure to the self-importance of the literary world came in November 2013 when he provoked it by replacing the long-serving children's book critic, Amanda Craig. More than 400 literati – including the leading children's writers Julia Donaldson,

Philip Pullman, Neil Gaiman and Malorie Blackman – signed an open letter condemning his decision as "incomprehensible". The novelist Susan Hill came to Millen's defence: *"The Times* literary editor hasn't killed Bambi. He is more than capable of finding good people to review children's books in-house."

Though Bambi was not killed, reviewing was sometimes treated as an opportunity for blood sports. AN Wilson dismissed Jacob Rees-Mogg's *The Victorians* as "a dozen clumsily written pompous schoolboy compositions about 19th-century characters" and "a staggeringly silly book" (*The Sunday Times*, May 19, 2019). One new regular reviewer, Roger Lewis, biographer of Anthony Burgess, Peter Sellers and Charles Hawtrey, was particularly enthusiastic in mocking pseudery. The "laborious, exculpatory pages" of a long-winded biography of Philip Roth had "all the fun of a surgical procedure for inflamed third-degree piles". His tongue-in-cheek review of a book of Iris Murdoch's letters caused an inevitable kerfuffle on social media. He wrote of the novelist, whom he had known, that "in her prime she was a nymphomaniac, and had she been from the working class, instead of a fellow of an Oxford college with heaps of honorary degrees, she'd have been a candidate for compulsory sterilisation. From the moment she left school and arrived at university in 1938, she seemed to have felt obliged to sleep with everyone she met, particularly dreary ugly foreign intellectuals." (Saturday, November 14, 2015).

With the growth of the subscription-paying online readership came an evolution in what the books pages offered them. A weekly *Times* and *Sunday Times* newsletter for subscribers was launched in October 2014. First Edition, a Facebook group for readers of the books pages, was set up soon afterwards. It meant a chummier approach, in which recommending titles became more important than appearing as aloof guardians of literary virtue. It allowed for some demystification about the editorial decision-making process – how, for instance, were the 15 or so books covered each week chosen out of the thousands published or reissued each year. Digital analytics systems also began to affect some of the choices of which books to review, allowing editors to see not just which articles were the most read, but which most engaged their readers. In the main, the data reinforced previous editorial hunches about what people wanted to read: biographies, particularly of old rockers; royals bonking aristocrats (in fact any book with sex in the title); history, especially that of the Second World War; crime thrillers; and books about ageing and sleep. A review of contemporary poetry or a short story collection could be relied upon to stir up apathy. But surprises emerged: theoretical physics did well in attracting and engaging readers. Nature books, despite their popularity with publishers, tended to be dead ducks.

CHAPTER SIXTEEN

The most senior journalist to leave after Witherow took over was Keith Blackmore, deputy editor and a *Times* man for 25 years, who followed James Harding to the BBC in a newly created post of managing editor, news and current affairs. Witherow picked Emma Tucker, editor of Times 2, to replace him. She was one of the cohort of smart FT journalists poached by Robert Thomson in 2007 and a features specialist.

Andrew Knight, in admiring Witherow's passion for news, also noted his shrewdness in ensuring that other areas of the paper were not neglected: "John picked out Emma Tucker and others to make the 'soft' side of the paper every bit as questing, and broad, as James's had been." Principal among the "others" was Nicola Jeal, who had arrived from *The Observer* in 2008, having previously done stints at *The Daily Mail*, the London *Evening Standard* and as editor of *Elle* magazine. Both Jeal and Tucker were approachable meritocrats, energetic, full of ideas and with a deserved reputation for hiring young, particularly female, talent. Between them, they shaped *Times* feature content for more than 15 years.

In 2020, Tucker became editor of *The Sunday Times*, which she briskly brought into the "digital-first" era while shepherding staff through the Covid-19 lockdowns, before moving on again to *The Wall Street Journal*. The tireless Jeal remained, her remit stretching across features content on both titles and her influence evident almost everywhere. Caitlin Moran, the columnist, described her as "the boss of bosses".

There were not many male writers on the paper who did not, at some stage, succumb to Jeal's extraordinary powers of persuasion to be photographed in compromising, embarrassing and even unclothed poses. Rueful groups of Jeal 'victims' would occasionally congregate in the men's lavatories, swapping stories. Inspiration (and humiliation) could strike at any time. Besides the usual culprits – feature writers Damian Whitworth, Robert Crampton and Ben Machell – august heavyweight columnists David Aaronovitch, Daniel Finkelstein and Hugo Rifkind all appeared variously in unflattering regalia and states of undress, undergoing diets, miracle cures, spa treatments and the like. Chief leader writer Simon Nixon modelled his wetsuit for a feature about cold water swimming. Matt Chorley dressed up as Theresa May. Not that some of those writers took much persuading. One repeat offender, Robert Crampton, was happy to lay claim to – indeed, actively sought – the title of least camera-shy hack in *Times* history. Since he joined the paper in 1991 aged 27 he had been pictured trying to get a six pack; giving up drinking; sunbathing; synchronised swimming; synchronised diving (with Tom Daley); forming the back end of a pantomime dragon; impersonating Daniel Craig; road-testing a high-tech luxury Japanese lavatory that cost £12,000; skateboarding; cooking; weightlifting; tree-bathing; foraging; tree-planting with Chris Packham; shaving; going for a haircut from Nicky Clarke; doing breathing exercises; attending a tantric sex workshop; soul-cycling; boxing; road cycling; BMX cycling; ice-skating; having Botox; pretending to be a Victorian father complete with top hat and cane; and attempting (and failing) to chat women up in a Hackney cocktail bar employing solely corny one-liners from James Bond films.

The serious point about such first-person, writer-centred revelations was that in an age when the celebrity interview had become increasingly anodyne, neutered by demands for copy and picture approval, one ingenious solution was to make the journalist the star. A classic of the genre was when Jeal decided it would be instructive to task two writers to spend a day downing the same amount of alcohol, at the same time of day, as Don Draper & Co did on Madison Avenue in the early 1960s, as depicted on the hit TV series *Mad Men* A drinks trolley and several bottles were procured. Speculation (and competition) raged over who would get the job, although in truth the female lead was only ever going to be given to Carol Midgley, a survivor of both the *Mirror* and the last days of Fleet Street's drinking culture. Her junior male partner, Tom Whipple – later the renowned and award-winning *Times* science editor, then a fresh-faced reporter without Midgley's years of drinking practice – was significantly less match fit. They both became tired and emotional, Whipple rather more rapidly than Midgley; but, top professionals both, they filed bang on time.

Celebrity interviews were still keenly sought, and in the hands of skilled professionals such as Polly Vernon, Janice Turner and Alice Thomson could provide great insights, not just into particular personalities in the public eye but into the prevailing culture and mood. That cultural insight came increasingly to be reflected in the *Times* news pages too. Jeal played a key role in the editing of the Saturday *Times*, attending news conference and helping to ensure that the massive Saturday news run had strong human interest and the mix of light and shade that a weekend audience required.

A significant change at *The Times*, consolidated under Witherow, was this gradual integration of the various departments, both in terms of subject matter and writers. Formerly, in large part due to the physical layout of the Wapping offices, the various sections had been unhealthily isolated prisoners of geography. Between 2002 and 2010, in the rabbit-warren *Times* building facing onto The Highway in Wapping, the magazine, listings and arts departments were separated from daily features, in turn separated from News, Comment, Business and Sport. This balkanisation persisted even in the new office at Thomas More Square, occupied between 2010 and 2014, where news and features were two floors apart, in separate worlds. In features, weeks might pass without sight of the editor or his deputies, or so it could seem. It was possible for a designer, sub-editor or writer to spend a long career on features and never talk to anyone from news, and vice versa. Some news specialists were openly hostile if they detected feature writers trespassing on their territory by independently setting up interviews with politicians or sports stars, regarding such efforts as amateurish intrusions. Some features staff were similarly sniffy about mere jobbing hacks on news.

The move in 2014 from Thomas More Square to 1 London Bridge Street, combined with Jeal's influence and the arrival of Witherow as editor, changed everything. The various departments found themselves sharing the same space. The environment of the new building – lighter, cleaner, open-plan – was instantly more conducive to the cross-pollination of talent. Ancient and outmoded demarcations melted away. In the *Times* magazine under Jeal, a 5,000-word dispatch from Anthony Loyd in Syria or Ukraine might sit alongside a profile of a new celebrity chef and a first-person account of individual triumph or tragedy. Long-running columnists Caitlin Moran, Giles Coren, Robert Crampton and Melanie Reid had licence to be serious or surreal, frivolous or forensic.

Sport coverage was also recalibrated. Witherow felt that, while it was an important part of the paper and would remain so, it had become something of an obsession at *The Times*. There had been a tendency to celebrate any British (more likely English) sporting achievement with a special poster-style wraparound front page or even a pullout supplement, while a scene from the weekend's football had been a regular (almost a default) Monday morning front-page picture. As a keen follower of rugby, cricket and tennis, Witherow declined to simulate a blokeish interest in football and saw no reason for the often unbeautiful game to dominate the paper (or even the sport pages) to the extent that it had done. The coverage had to justify its space.

He knew that a lot of readers liked football more than he did, and that football reporting was an area where *The Times* had to compete. He poached Henry Winter from *The Telegraph* at considerable cost as chief football writer; revamped The Game, the weekly football supplement; and made sure big games always got the coverage they deserved. At the same time, however, he saw to it that his own sporting interests were covered to the highest standards and with adequate space by Mike Atherton (one of the paper's greatest assets), Owen Slot and Stuart Fraser.

One of the earliest manifestations of Witherow's reluctance to give sport the special dispensation it had previously enjoyed came with the departure of Simon Barnes, chief sports writer, in June 2014. Cost was a key factor in the decision. As Barnes (characteristically) described it, "their line to me was that they were selling their top striker because they could no longer afford his wages". He himself conceded that [the chief sports writer] "is one of the paper's more expensive assets; you fly business class long haul; you stay in decent hotels; you can, if you wish, eat at expensive restaurants." He was certainly well paid, with a longstanding contract that specified first-class rail travel and comfortable flights (he doesn't drive). But there may also have been a degree of impatience with a writer Witherow felt had been indulged (and who had indulged himself) for rather too long.

It was a firmly held view in the sport department that Barnes was one of the great jewels of *The Times*. At his best he was thoughtful, moving, colourful and sensitive. His critics felt, however, that at his worst he could be precious and pretentious and give the impression of writing chiefly for (and about) himself.

The opening pages of his book *The Meaning of Sport* gave full rein to his style. Barnes is sitting in a café in Lisbon after a good lunch and a couple of "very pleasant, crisp, cold beers", preparing to report on that evening's England–Croatia game in the UEFA Euro 2004 football championship. He is reading:

> the great Portuguese novel, Fernando Pessoa's *The Book of Disquiet*: rambling, brilliant, speculative, wise, above all, unpredictable. A phrase grasps me: ravishes me with its perfection. 'The more a man differs from me, the more real he seems, for he depends that much less on my subjectivity.' A writer's remark if ever there was one. And I who read, who digest, who sip and savour, am in a state of mild terror not because of what I must see but what I must write of Wayne Rooney and David Beckham, Michael Owen and Steven Gerrard.
>
> They are not like me, no. I do not possess the intellectual depth of a Rooney or a Beckham. I cannot compute the spin and curve of a football that Beckham has sought to perfect, the outcome of a collision of bodies at speed, Rooney's speciality. Tonight, at the moment the final whistle is blown, I must fire 700 words to London from my laptop in an instant of time. I am destined for the front page. The match is that important . . . I am the chief sportswriter – a dominance hierarchy thing – and in that I am a little like Beckham. We are both going to the Estadio da Luz to be brilliant, or at least try to be. But I am unlike him in many more ways: that is why he is so real to me, so enthrallingly un-dependent on my subjectivity. Not because I read Pessoa and presumably he does not; not because he can bend a free kick and I can't. But because he is the creator of tales and I am the teller of tales . . .

"One-nil to the Arsenal" it was not.

The quality of writing and reporting in the sport pages was what mattered most to Witherow. He wasn't particularly looking for – and didn't believe readers wanted – self-consciously "fine writing". But he saw no reason why writers and editors in sport should lazily assume, as he felt they too often had, that they were writing solely for a coterie of adepts and initiates and so were exempt from such basic journalistic requirements as telling a story clearly and explaining what was going on. Writing in the sport pages must be of the same high standard he expected everywhere else. He began a relentless campaign to improve its quality, enlisting Brunskill to explain to the sport department what was needed and to police it daily to ensure the message went home.

"The challenge for sport is the same as it is for business," Brunskill wrote in a memo to the sport editor Tim Hallissey. "You have readers who know a great deal about sport. You can't talk down to them. At the same time, you run stories that are – or should be – of interest to people who would never go to a football match. They're news stories and human interest stories, just as much as anything else in the paper. If you write them exclusively for the followers of a couple of football teams, you sell yourselves short."

The solution was something set out, at Witherow's insistence, in the *Times Style Guide* and often repeated by Brunskill in emails to all staff. Writers and editors in sport, no less than those in news or business, must grasp the importance of what's known in the trade as the nut par:

> We know that an intro (usually) tells the reader what has gone on: the *who, where, what, why, when* of basic journalism. The *nut par* [from nutshell] – sometimes called the *so what? par* – comes a bit further down and needs to explain why the story matters and what it means. Not by editorialising, but by giving readers a concise summary of whatever background information they may need if they're to understand the significance of what we're reporting.

The lesson was met at first with some bemusement. "Ah, the nut par man," was Mike Atherton's greeting to Brunskill at a party of Witherow's. The new editor, however, was firm. In sport as anywhere else, writers must write with readers in mind.

CHAPTER SEVENTEEN

Times obituaries were not immune to the Witherow revolution. On April 19, 2013, shortly after he took over, the paper was in large part given over to the death of Margaret Thatcher. Her obituary, which ran to 11,000 words over six pages, was unsigned as always but the thorough account of her life and analysis of her career was clearly the work of someone who was there and involved in events. It was, in fact, the work of a former Conservative cabinet minister whose own relationship with a prime minister he admired had not always been easy. Dispassionate and authoritative, it was peppered with telling epithets such as "abrasive, hard-working, intelligent without being intellectual, thrifty, combative, courageous and lucky, obstinate, narrow-minded, cautious, energetic, ruthless, militant, decisive, steely, outspoken, imperious and temperamental". It concluded: "Her record and her personality will be the subject of continuing controversy. But no one will ever doubt her sincerity and her courage, and most will concede that the far-reaching changes she made would have been impossible without her."

The Thatcher obituary, although unusually long and no doubt written well before Witherow became editor, proved to be the starting point for the changes he wanted. Obituaries became more anecdotal in style and more emphasis was put on visual display, with subjects depicted in their prime and looking animated. There was to be a lively mix of professions each day and, if possible, at least one of the three obits would be of a woman, though this was sometimes a struggle as obits usually feature people who are in their 80s and 90s when they die, so their lives reflect society as it was in the 1940s and 50s, when women had fewer opportunities. The same problem applied to ethnic minorities.

In a more liberal age, many of the euphemisms that had traditionally been used in obituaries, such as "confirmed bachelor", were no longer needed. Yet "code" was still considered a useful way of giving readers a wink. They could tune in to it and look out for phrases such as "convivial to a fault" by which was meant someone had a drink problem, or she "had an individual sense of style" meaning she had no dress sense at all. Other examples in the obits style guide included: a "voice that carried", "untroubled by self-doubt", and "an easy conscience". Writers were encouraged to come up with their own. "Euphemisms do not need to be well established, or strictly defined, they are more about conveying a mood in prose that is attractive, dispassionate and amused. The best examples of it are instinctively understood and create a pleasant sense of complicity between the euphemist and the reader." In the distant past there had been a tendency to regard them as an extension of the honours system, with few time-serving senior civil servants, public-school headmasters, or lords lieutenant excluded on the grounds that they were simply too dull. Or so it could seem. In the Witherow era, obit subjects had to earn their place in a more Darwinian fashion. They had to have made an impact, one way or another, which meant admirals and Nobel prizewinners more often rubbing shoulders with mafia bosses, soap stars and even, in the case of Charles Manson, a murderous cult leader. Traditionally war heroes had been the most popular obit subjects with readers, but as the war generation faded away, the new "Few" became the dissolute rock stars who had somehow survived the excesses of the Sixties.

Witherow's first obits editor was Simon Pearson, a white-haired military history buff and *Times* veteran whose previous roles had included night editor. He was succeeded by Nigel Farndale, a critically acclaimed novelist who had also been chief interviewer on *The Sunday* Telegraph for 20 years. Farndale had a bearlike, 6ft 2in frame that belied his equable manner. He brought a more writerly, features sensibility to the section, with more emphasis on "characterisation" and description. Although obituaries were a cross between a short biography and a character sketch, he believed, they could also be likened to a short story, with pleasing cadences and a natural "cradle to grave", beginning, middle and end. Other novelistic techniques could be applied, too, such as "show, don't tell" – don't just say someone was witty, give an example of their wit. The prose should be lively and evocative so that not only were the sights of a battle described but also its sounds and smells, and a subject's voice should be captured through idiosyncratic quotation and characteristic turns of phrase. It helped that Farndale had interviewed many of the big names, including Professor Stephen Hawking, Kirk Douglas and Dame Vera Lynn, who now crossed his desk as obit subjects.

Pearson had introduced certain modernisations, such as mentioning how the obit subject met their spouse and what their children did for a living. As well as keeping these, Farndale also kept the best of the freelance writers, including Martin Fletcher, Nigel Williamson and Valerie Grove, some of whom had written for Ian Brunskill and Anthony Howard when they ran obituaries. Long gone were the days when Oxbridge professors would write each other's obits, with all the compromise (and mischief) that implied. A small team of regulars was now preferred. Writing anonymously, they read unpublished memoirs and talked to experts in the field as well as colleagues, friends and family members, while making sure not to give them copy approval. Farndale also introduced a departmental style guide. *Times* obits should be life affirming rather than gloomy, he wrote, "full of colour, felicities and, where appropriate, humour, not dry CVs or lists of achievements, awards, book titles and so on.

They should also be a cool mixture of fact and assessment, detached and deadpan in style, alive to human frailty and gently subversive." He cited the opening line of the obit of Zsa Zsa Gabor, the Hollywood actress, as an example of this: "Provided that you were not married to Zsa Zsa Gabor – and many people were – she could be a lot of fun." Through anecdote and illuminating personal detail, the style guide continued, obits should weave a spell. They should tell the story of a life and give insight into character. Did the subject have a nickname or an unusual hobby? What made them tick? What quirks might make them come back to life on the page? . . . The judge who had a penchant for silk underwear . . . The army officer who took a rolled-up umbrella into battle in case it rained . . . The pioneering heart surgeon who was so competitive at board games he once made his grandchildren cry by sending a Monopoly board flying across the room. It remained important to be opinionated, "to leave the reader with a strong sense of whether you think the subject lived a good life or bad; whether they were right or wrong in the handling of their public affairs. If someone was pompous, vain or prickly (or for that matter a spiv, pseud or charlatan) the obit should reflect this. A little scuttlebutt can add to the flavour too."

Obits remained a keenly fought battleground between *The Telegraph* and *The Times*. When Lord Chalfont died aged 100 in 2020 the innuendo-laden closing paragraph of the *Times* obit of him went viral. "He served on the committee of the Garrick Club in London, where he played a part in excluding women from membership, even though he was fond of their company in more private surroundings." (Tuesday, January 14, 2020). Radio 4 interviewed Andrew Brown, the *Telegraph*'s obits editor about it, hoping he would say something disobliging. Instead he laughed and, to the evident disappointment of Mishal Husain, declared that *Times* obits were "excellent". He didn't mention that he had worked for a while under Brunskill on obits at *The Times*, or that he and Farndale were former colleagues who got on well.

Some things on the obits desk remained unchanged, such as the ban on the unlovely euphemism "passed away" and the problem of later wives wanting to airbrush out all mention of earlier ones. The tradition of honouring distinguished former *Times* luminaries also continued. Among them was a legendary figure known to the royal family as Mr Hamilton of *The Times*. Alan Hamilton, who covered the royal family for three decades, died of a heart attack at the age of 70 in August 2013. He had been an old-school reporter; he came to use a mobile phone only late in his career and never opened a laptop; he filed by phone to copytakers straight from his notebook from the most far flung parts of the world. He never deferred to the Palace, as was demonstrated when he discovered on the Queen's state visit to China in 1986 that Prince Philip had told a group of University of Edinburgh undergraduates studying in the city of Xian: "If you stay here much longer, you will all be slitty-eyed." Hamilton recalled in Philip's obituary, written long before either he or Philip died, that "under the rules of the game", he shared this gaffe with other royal reporters on the visit. "The tabloids could not contain their excitement, producing front-page headlines such as 'The Great Wally of China?' and 'Prince Philip Gets It All Wong'." When the Queen's press secretary appealed to him not to use the story, which had been intended as an ice-breaking joke – "surely *The Times*, of all people, are not going to use this?" – Hamilton replied: "Most certainly. But not until paragraph 14."

When the duke next saw Hamilton he commented: "So you've been at it again, have you, Mr Hamilton?" Spotting Hamilton talking to a local in tribal regalia at a High Commission garden party in Lagos, the Queen warned the dignitary: "That's Mr Hamilton. Don't talk to him; he'll only write terribly rude things about you." She then turned to Hamilton and gave him a knowing, sympathetic look before breaking into a smile. He said later: "I took this as a compliment."

Hamilton had joined *The Times* in 1969 as one of four labour correspondents, moved in 1975 to the Diary, and in 1982 became a home news special writer, covering the royal beat for the next 26 years, although the title of "royal correspondent" was not used. As an easy-going, gregarious colleague he made a natural leader in the royal press pack. He was a reassuring and conscientious presence, respected as serious-minded, fair, genial, occasionally exasperated but never losing sight of the duty to report professionally for his readers and not for the Palace. Always accompanied by a small bottle of whisky and a pipe, he took the confiscation of his "filing water" on arriving in an Arab country in good part. He wrote elegantly and swiftly and, whatever the subject, delivered his copy on time.

When Philip Howard died in 2014 at the age of 80, his obituary said that he "had served ten editors and represented the heart and soul of the newspaper". For half a century he had brought to *The Times* both intellectual seriousness and fun as leader writer, literary editor (for 14 years), columnist and expert commentator on philology, grammar, house style, manners and etiquette. "Howard was a character totally in touch with the world about him, whether through conversation, reading, writing, music, sport, dogs, friend or family," the obituary recalled. "In turn, he was one of the most loved journalists at *The Times*, admired as much by his colleagues as by his readers; indeed, from his sublime writing many of his readers felt as if they knew him personally." His office clothes were an eclectic mixture of pin-stripes, patched tweed, corduroy trousers with red braces and a quilted waistcoat. In this shabby-chic ensemble he resembled his fourth editor, Charles Douglas-Home, whose elbows could be seen protruding from ancient Jermyn Street shirts.

Howard's long life was a reminder of a bygone age both in British society and at *The Times* itself. A classical education – Eton King's Scholar, Major Scholar at Trinity College, Oxford and a First in Greats – shone through his limpid writing and led naturally to the presidency of the Classical Association. He wrote some 20 books on subjects as diverse as the Black Watch (his regiment), the monarchy and language; loved rugby and the Eton Ramblers, the Garrick, his beagles and Jack Russells; belonged to PEN International, contributed to the *Dictionary of National Biography* and was a fellow of the Royal Society of Literature.

He had joined *The Times* from *The Glasgow Herald* in 1964 as a reporter, taking a pay cut of £100 "for the honour of working for *The Times*", and always referred modestly to himself as a simple hack. His unstuffy attitude to colleagues and life in general was a trademark exemplified by jovial Bertie Wooster forms of address such as "dear boy" or "old bean". When he took over the Saturday Modern Manners column in 2000, some of his views seemed rooted in Eton mores circa 1950, but his advice on the social torments of his readers was always considerate and wise.

Howard was a big man with a carrying voice and a sporting pedigree: his father was capped eight times for the England rugby team at No 8 and his mother had won the Wimbledon women's doubles in 1932. He himself was a demon fast bowler for the *Times* cricket team. He never drove a car, relying on his beloved wife Myrtle to chauffeur him when needed, and his attitude to telephones and the editorial computer system at *The Times* was at best suspicious and at worst downright hostile, his obituary said. Assigned to cover the investiture of the Prince of Wales at Caernarvon Castle in 1969, he wrote his story by hand on sheets of paper and lowered it take by take in a basket on a rope to the ground, where a helper collected them and rushed to a public phone to dictate to the office copytaker.

He always seemed cash-strapped, though a desire to help his family was not the only reason he worked on well beyond his formal retirement in 1999. He took as much pleasure in his work as readers got from it. His last piece for the paper was his regular Word Routes column on July 19, 2014, less than three months before his death from prostate cancer.

CHAPTER EIGHTEEN

One of the paper's best-loved and most outstanding members of staff, Richard Beeston – "Beest", as he was known to all his *Times* colleagues – died on Sunday May 19, 2013, at the age of only 50. The son of a distinguished foreign correspondent for *The Daily Telegraph*, Beeston had gone straight from Westminster School into journalism without bothering with university. As a young correspondent for *The Times* in Jerusalem he had reported some of the Middle East's most harrowing stories and had been abducted in Lebanon. There was a picture of Beeston in his mid-twenties, impeccably dressed, notebook in hand, reporting a story that never left him – the chemical attack by Saddam Hussein on Halabja, northern Iraq, in 1988. As the paper's correspondent in Moscow he covered the Chechen wars, later becoming diplomatic correspondent, foreign news editor and in 2008 foreign editor. He once explained how he had managed to remain detached from the conflicts in Lebanon, Iraq, Bosnia and Chechnya: "I'm of the stiff-upper-lip school," he said. "What makes a difference is having a stable home to come home to . . . If I find something particularly hard, I spend a day fly-fishing to readjust my mind." (June 9, 2008).

Beeston's obituary filled seven columns. The prostate cancer he had borne since January 2007 had never deterred him: in between bouts of chemotherapy he had assigned himself to Iraq and Afghanistan and kept battle-fit with punishing sessions in the office gym. Even when terminally ill he had made his way into Syria to report, at some personal risk, on the uprising in Daraa against the Assad government at the beginning of the civil war. He found covering conflicts for *The Times* hugely therapeutic: "It is difficult to feel sorry for yourself," he wrote, "when you are confronted every day with people battling much greater tragedies with stoicism and courage." (April 6, 2011). When his cancer was diagnosed Beeston was offered hormone therapy as the only treatment available. That was not good enough for his wife, Natasha Fairweather, a literary agent. She scoured the internet for new treatments and emailed doctors in California to ask about their findings. Beeston embarked on a journey of discovery that took him to nine consultants in three different countries, exploring every possible treatment. A specialist in New York advised him to "throw everything he could" at the cancer. "Go for it." (April 6, 2011). So as well as the hormone treatment Beeston went on courses of chemotherapy and then radiation therapy. He kept working and was clear of cancer for two years, but it came back and he was able to get an American trial drug available in Britain. Soon after celebrating the success of the new treatment, he found the cancer had returned in his right lung.

> So here I am back on chemotherapy, wearing a cold cap to preserve my hair and waiting again to see if the cancer will respond to the poison being fed into my body. Whatever the outcome, a host of new treatments is becoming available which I am confident will help me to beat the disease. My main regret is that I can't be in the Middle East to witness the great story unfolding there. Maybe next time.

Throughout his illness Beeston kept filing news stories and writing analysis and comment. His last piece for the paper was a long commentary: "Arc we really winning the war on terror?" (April 17, 2013). He died a month later.

His memorial service was held at St Bride's (September 21, 2013), which was packed with colleagues and friends; tributes provoked laughter as well as tears. The inner core of the congregation was formed by war correspondents. Ben Macintyre, a close friend, told them in his address that Beeston took his job with intense seriousness but he never took himself too seriously. Passionate but balanced, never foolhardy but spectacularly brave, he never made the mistake of believing that he was part of the story. Witherow announced a new bursary in Beeston's honour with an award of £6,000 for an aspiring foreign correspondent under the age of 30 to spend six weeks abroad reporting on a foreign news story.

The value of first-hand foreign coverage of the kind Beeston had championed was confirmed for *Times* readers a year into Witherow's tenure. So too were the difficulties and dangers involved as Syria's civil war left much of that country splintered under the control of foreign armies, rebel brigades, bandits, kidnappers and outright terror organisations such as Islamic State (ISIS). *The Times* war correspondent Anthony Loyd and staff photographer Jack Hill were investigating barrel bombing by regime forces in Aleppo in the spring of 2014 when they themselves became the story. They were kidnapped and beaten, and in Loyd's case shot, but survived. "It wasn't what we set out to cover," Witherow said later, "but the tale of treachery, confusion and risk exposed the high price of western journalists and the modus operandi of local rebels and ISIS forces. It was war reporting at its finest."

Their ordeal began on Thursday, May 15, when, after several days in Aleppo, Loyd and Hill were driving back to Turkey with their "fixer", Hamza, and Avo, their close-protection bodyguard. A local rebel commander called Hakim, who Loyd considered to be a friend, was travelling ahead with his men as escorts. A BMW four-wheel drive overtook the car carrying Loyd, Hill, Hamza and Avo and waved them down. Armed figures sprang out, blindfolded and plasticuffed them and drove them to a lock-up garage. Before leaving them there, the gunmen took their possessions but did not find a memory card that Hill had hidden in one of his socks.

Hill and Hamza were in the boot of the car, which had been left open an inch to allow them to breathe. They managed to free their hands, jump out and overpower the guard, who they recognised as one of Hakim's gang: he had served them breakfast that morning. Hakim, far from protecting them, had double-crossed them in the hope of getting a ransom. Loyd and Avo, who were in the back seat of the car, leapt out and all four tried to escape. Hamza got away on a moped but Hill ran straight into one of Hakim's henchmen and they started fighting in the street. Hakim appeared and laid into Hill, ignoring his shouts of "You are my f***ing friend".

Loyd, his hands still bound, escaped across the rooftops until he ran out of roof. He scrambled down a ladder and into a private home. Clamping a kitchen knife between his teeth he tried to saw through the handcuffs. He had not got very far before two Kalashnikov bullets smacked into the wall beside him. Hakim's men burst in, dragged him outside and started beating him around the head with rifle butts. As Loyd lay on the ground, bleeding, Hakim arrived. "I thought you were my friend," Loyd said. "No friends," he replied, pulling out a silver automatic pistol and shooting Loyd twice in the ankle. A crowd was gathering and Hamza and Avo were rousing help from Islamic Front, an umbrella group of – in the Syrian context – moderate Islamists with considerable clout in the district. Hill was beaten up and taken to a police cell before being rescued by Islamic Front, but Loyd's torment continued: he was beaten again, punched and kicked and a stone was smashed across his head. His bloody ankle was stamped on. "After that," Loyd wrote, "they either had to kill me or take me to a clinic." The locals were unimpressed by Hakim's desperate claims that the *Times* men were CIA spies or ISIS volunteers, so he was taken to a clinic, still with his hands lashed together. As he lay on a stretcher surrounded by doctors asking who he was, a smiling civilian appeared. "It's OK," he said. "We know who you are. You are safe." An Islamic Front commander arrived, looked at Loyd and told Hakim's men to get out. Loyd, Hill and Hamza crossed into Turkey a day later. Hakim's treachery had failed. One source who handled their extraction told *The Times*: "The captors had dollar signs in their eyes when they realised they had two western journalists. What they did not anticipate was loads of the Islamic Front turning up on their doorstep to get them back."

The incident was being monitored throughout by an emergency team in an isolated control room at News UK headquarters. Roland Watson and his deputy, Suzy Jagger, were joined there by other journalists from *The Times* and *Sunday Times*, a hostage negotiation team was on standby and ex-forces personnel were active on the ground in Syria and Turkey. It was the first use of this new emergency response protocol established after the killing of the *Sunday Times* war reporter Marie Colvin in 2012, when it quickly became apparent that the greatly heightened dangers of the Syrian civil war required both greater protection for journalists going in and greater preparation for the task of getting them out in an emergency.

Rose Wild told concerned *Times* readers in her Feedback column after Loyd and Hill had reported their story that an enormous amount of preparation and due diligence took place before anyone was sent into the field; behind the bylines and the picture credits was a team of fixers and security help. "Everyone is aware how close a call it was for Loyd and Hill this week, but *The Times* has covered wars for 200 years and wherever possible will continue to do so," she wrote.

Loyd, who began reporting for *The Times* from Bosnia in 1993, talked about danger in an interview with Times Online as he was recovering from his injuries:

> The longer you do it the more chance there is of it going badly wrong. You can offset against that by being smart, but ultimately you can't offset against it as much as you'd like, so there does come a point of questioning how much longer you want to go through with it – but I'm not at that moment

yet. On a simple level I believe that war reporting matters and that Syria is a particularly important conflict . . . so it's important that people like me go in, in a very incomplete and imperfect way, to try to illuminate the picture of what's going on there.

As swathes of territory in Syria and Iraq fell under the control of ISIS, and a multidimensional war raged, the security team at News UK grew in size and its tasks multiplied. But reporters – particularly Loyd and Louise Callaghan of *The Sunday Times* – continued to brave the dangers and provide readers of both titles with insights into this most savage and bewildering of conflicts.

Their dispatches were leavened by the reporting of foreign affairs of a lighter kind. When the French president François Hollande was photographed arriving at the flat of the film star Julie Gayet wearing a motorcycle helmet and sitting precariously on the pillion seat of a scooter, writers and readers turned to his travails with gleeful relief. Adam Sage reported from Paris that, although Hollande's face and head could not be seen, his identity was given away by his distinctive black shoes, which he had worn on a well-photographed visit to Saudi Arabia the day before. Robert Crampton marvelled in his column that Hollande seemed to own only one pair of shoes (January 14, 2014). He'd done what might be called a reverse Imelda Marcos. Maybe Gayet, "a knockout French fox", appreciated a bit of podiatric parsimony in a man. There had to be some explanation of how such a babe had fallen for such a loser. The affair was also irresistible for Hugo Rifkind's My Week column. "Sacré bleu! If I had known that I was this attractive to beautiful women before I became the most powerful man in France, I might not have bothered, Wouf, wouf! Je suis le sexy, dirty chien . . . many of the pledges I made on the campaign trail were simply impractical. Such as les high taxes. And le fin de l'austérité. And le pecker staying in les trousers."

As all this irreverence showed, *Times* coverage of France had come a long way since the days of the exquisitely tailored and well-connected Charles Hargrove, known to President Charles de Gaulle as "Monsieur Hargrove du *Times*", who died at the age of 92 in September 2014. His obituary described how he believed journalism to be "un sot métier" (a stupid job) although it was almost inevitable that he would take it up (October 18, 2014). His father was a foreign correspondent for *The Times*, *The Wall Street*

Journal and *The Financial Times*, his mother was French and he went to school in Paris. He was as at home in the language of Molière as of Shakespeare.

As a 22-year-old lieutenant in the Royal Fusiliers Hargrove drove a jeep off a landing craft in the first wave of the D-Day assault on Gold Beach, but his principle task was not to fight but to act as a liaison officer "cultivating relations with the chatelaines . . . in whose manors the British officers set up their command". Having survived the war – and the chatelaines – he wanted to be a diplomat but twice failed the Foreign Office examination. After some paternal string-pulling, Hargrove was taken on by *The Times* as a trainee and was swiftly sent to its grand Paris office at 8 rue Halévy, near the Opéra. Mornings were spent reading the newspapers and the Agence France-Presse schedule and rewriting newsagency copy in *Times* style. The bureau's second crutch was the afternoon paper, *Le Monde*; its publication coincided with digesting lunch after a long break in a private room, usually at Drouant, the historic restaurant near the office. Gerald Norman, the bureau chief, would meet his deputies before penning his afternoon dispatch, which might have a snappy intro such as: "Monsieur Aristide Briand, minister of foreign affairs, today received Dr Gustav Stresemann, his German counterpart."

Hargrove thrived, also serving in Berlin, Bonn and Tokyo (where he flew a *Times* pennant on the bonnet of his car in the manner of a state dignitary) before returning to Paris in 1966 and settling in for the next 16 years as not just the chief correspondent but also as a kind of unofficial British ambassador. Having been appointed OBE and Commander of the Legion of Honour, he realised by the time of his retirement in 1982 at the age of 60 that he was anachronistic. When he joined *The Times* it had been "un journal de gentlemen pour les gentlemen", he wrote in his memoirs. He had become, in the words of a colleague, "an old-style correspondent for an old style of *Times* that no longer existed".

The diplomatic editor of *Le Monde* saluted his exit: "Hargrove always applied tact and insight to French affairs and Franco-British relations, which are eternally coloured by mésentente cordiale and entente acrimonieuse." Less tactfully, Brian Horton, managing editor of *The Times*, took him to lunch in a fashionable restaurant and told him bluntly that it would be best for the paper and for him if he were to leave Paris.

"I was a little heavy-hearted and I felt a mixture of bitterness and anxiety about my future," Hargrove wrote. He settled in Normandy but returned to 8 rue Halévy in February 2002 for a party celebrating the relocation of *The Times* after 71 years to less grandiose offices. Kate Muir, in her Fraught and Social column (February 16, 2002), was also there to say goodbye with her husband Ben Macintyre, Alastair Miller the office photographer, and Charles Bremner, the current bureau chief. *The Times* staff looked out onto the floodlit Opéra from the grand salon which glowed in the candlelight, and wept into their champagne. The partygoers agreed that three stories came around every year: "The beret story, in which we lament the closure of a beret factory and the lack of bicyclists bearing garlic; the café story, with them being destroyed by Le McDo; and the political scandal, involving either corruption or copulation. Other perennials are the Académie Française attacking Franglais and the latest scientific finding that lots of claret lowers cholesterol, always popular with the foreign news desk."

Hargrove returned to Normandy and after a retirement of 32 years – nearly as long as his 34 years as a *Times* correspondent – he was buried at Asnelles, where he had come ashore on D-Day.

Foreign correspondents, foreign editors, foreign governments may come and go, but for almost 20 years the beating heart of the *Times* foreign coverage was a diminutive figure whose name no reader would have known. Gill Ross, the foreign desk manager since July 1995, retired in June 2014. She was fondly remembered by her correspondents, who she always referred to as her "boys and girls".

When she joined *The Times* the paper had permanent bureaux in Beijing, Bonn, Paris, Delhi, Brussels, Rome, New York, Washington, Jerusalem, Johannesburg, Nairobi, Los Angeles, Tokyo, Moscow and Madrid. The department had one flak jacket and two satellite telexes, each the size of a medium suitcase. "It's hard to imagine the amount and weight of the kit my troops took out when reporting from locations with little or no infrastructure," she said. "We had several wonderful and slightly built female correspondents but somehow they coped and being true professionals never complained. By the time I left, all the correspondents had their own dedicated satellite equipment and flak jackets and helmets." Ross's first memory was of receiving a call from Anthony Loyd.

He was reporting from Bosnia and found himself on the wrong side of a forest surrounded by bad guys, and had to dump most of his kit to get out of there as fast as possible. Hence no sat telex – not only an expensive piece of kit, but how would he file his copy? He was very nervous about telling me the bad news but my main concern was for his safety, and then I set about sourcing a replacement sat telex and getting it out to him so he could carry on reporting.

Replacing stolen cash – usually US dollars – after correspondents had been captured or simply run out of readies was another regular challenge. When Stephen Farrell was seized while driving to Baghdad in his armoured Mercedes and held for eight hours by Shia bandits during the first battle of Fallujah in 2004, Ross broke off dinner in the West End to join the rest of the foreign desk. The headline on Farrell's splash: "A Kalashnikov in my face, a knife in my ear, a masked thug screaming you're finished" (April 8 2004), conveyed the alarm felt in the office. His car had been sprayed with bullets – "Fallujah hail" – and a tyre shot out. Farrell had lost $15,000 and his flak jacket. Once he was safe, he was characteristically disinclined to leave Iraq and return to his base in Jerusalem. Ross paid a freelance photographer bound for Iraq to reimburse him.

CHAPTER NINETEEN

John Witherow's close attention to reshaping the hinterland of *Times* pages – away from his first love, news – extended to bringing back the *Times* Diary, which had been in what its new editor Patrick Kidd described as a "period of hibernation" since 2002. The Diary had begun life on May 3, 1966, the day news first appeared on the *Times* front page. Sir William Haley, editor at the time, reassured readers it would not contain mere tittle-tattle, but he was frank about the reasons for introducing a note of lightness and frivolity in a paper that had long seen itself as above such things. "Some people have expressed the dark suspicion," he wrote, "that *The Times* is modernising itself to get more readers. Of course it is."

Kidd was a Diary veteran. Initially, while working as a parliamentary researcher, he had supplied so much political gossip to the Diary in the days before blogs and social media that the paper thought it would be cheaper to hire him. He joined *The Times* as a reporter on the Diary in 2001, when its corner of the Wapping office was seen as a bit of a children's playground. Boxes of champagne, given out in thanks to colleagues for tips, were stored under the desks and there was a dartboard on the wall.

As editor of the resurrected Diary, Kidd had no interest in writing society stories about what he called "posh girls in pretty frocks at garden parties" but was keen on political gossip and theatrical anecdotes. He was much happier picking up stories over lunch at the Savile Club or in the corner of a Westminster pub rather than at parties where, as Hugo Rifkind once lamented, "celebrities either ignore you, which is humiliating, or are desperate to speak to you, which is embarrassing". The column's primary purpose was simply to amuse readers and encourage them to send in their own stories and entries for running series on things like funny road signs or people with apt names for their jobs.

Kidd had a prominent success when the Diary reported in March 2016 that "Boaty McBoatface" was leading an online poll by the Natural Environment Research Council to find a name for its new £200 million Arctic survey ship. Within a month, after the rest of the world's media had followed the Diary's scoop, the joke name – first thought up by a BBC Radio Jersey presenter –

finished in first place with 124,000 votes. Sir David Attenborough, the distinguished broadcaster and naturalist, was fifth with 10,000. On May 11, 2016, David Cameron became the first prime minister to use the words "Boaty McBoatface" in the Commons. He noted that, although this had been the runaway winner of the poll, it was felt better to name the ship after Attenborough. As a consolation, one of its remote-controlled submarines was named Boaty McBoatface, instead.

It was an example of Kidd's ideal Diary story: something completely frivolous and trivial that amused readers and took on a life of its own. Not only did the story come to the prime minister's attention, but the science minister was called before a Commons committee to account for what had happened. Links were even drawn between the will of the people having been ignored over Boaty and the resounding raspberry delivered to Cameron by voters only six weeks later when he was defeated in the EU membership referendum and resigned.

As it always had done, the new Diary became a nursery for emerging talent. Of its deputy editors, Kaya Burgess became the paper's religion correspondent; Grant Tucker, to whom Kidd gave the nickname "the Hobbit" because of his ability to pop up out of nowhere as much as for being short and hairy, went to *The Sunday Times* as an arts correspondent; and Jack Blackburn added the brief of history correspondent. There was also a network of freelance "elves", who would be sent to parties and events to find stories, many of whom used their Diary experience to land a staff job on Fleet Street. Some readers wondered why the new Diary was called TMS. Kidd explained in a Diary note that when *The Times* first ran a Diary column in the mid-1960s it appeared under the name PHS, a reference to Printing House Square, the building near Blackfriars where the paper was then based. So when reviving the Diary, "we decided to give a nod to our heritage by calling it TMS after our current address in Thomas More Square. TMS can also be regarded as an abbreviation for TIMES (as London gets abbreviated to LDN). It has nothing to do with Test Match Special."

Just as the PHS label had endured until the late 1980s despite relocation of *The Times* to Grays Inn Road and then to Wapping, so the name TMS survived the next office move to the News Building next to the Shard at London Bridge in 2014. The 17-storey building was designed by Renzo Piano, the architect of the Shard, and developed to give about 430,000 square feet of highly efficient light and open office space. The floors were arranged around a central concrete core with floor-to-ceiling windows all round giving spectacular views across London. Excellent transport links made the lack of car parking unimportant. With the vibrant Borough Market across the road it was a welcome move for many of the staff.

Those old enough, like Witherow, to remember working in Grays Inn Road or Pennington Street may have missed some of the atmosphere of the grade II listed rum warehouse that *The Times* had occupied, alongside *The Sunday Times*, after Rupert Murdoch moved the titles to Wapping in 1986. Built in 1805, the year of Trafalgar, and subject to only rudimentary conversion, it was a long, low-ceilinged open-plan bunker which allowed the editor a virtually unobstructed view of everyone in the office from his mezzanine quarter-deck. It was also possible to walk the entire 280 metre length of the building underground. Here dusty leather-bound back numbers were stored, as well as obscure pieces of machinery. There were the remnants of the old *Times* reference library of newspaper cuttings and books. The "stone" was down here, too, where newspaper pages were physically made up by compositors, using film and paper and scalpels and glue instead of hot metal type. Maintenance men might be glimpsed mysteriously at work in the brick vaults, and an explorer could surface at various points to emerge unexpectedly in different departments upstairs. For years the area around the Wapping plant was something of a wasteland, inhospitable and bleak. Staff were warned of the danger of mugging. By the time News International moved out, the area had been transformed and, while the warehouse was converted to more comfortable office space, the rest of the site was swiftly razed to make way for a huge housing development.

No one missed Wapping's lack of windows, Heath-Robinson air conditioning or leaking roof, but the most disconcerting thing about a modern newspaper office was the near silence. Witherow was not entirely joking when he decreed that the sound of old-fashioned typewriters should be piped into the new office through speakers to simulate the noise and excitement of an old newsroom, in a nod to the industry's past.

"The problem with newspapers now is that keyboards are so silent you could be working in a bank or an insurance company," he explained. "But newspapers are different." He was perhaps inspired by the Hollywood actor and typewriter enthusiast Tom Hanks, who had developed a popular app that made an iPad keyboard sound like a typewriter. The "playful idea" was reported by Radio 4's *Today* programme and drew puzzled coverage in *The New York Times*.

The piped clattering sound could be played at different speeds, with the tempo seeming to increase the closer the newsroom got to deadline. Reporters were generally amused, if bewildered, by the noise, but it was opposed by some of the sub-editors, who preferred to work in monastic silence. For a time there was a running battle between one or two who turned the speakers off and the editor's secretary, who would turn them back on, until eventually the monastic tendency prevailed and the typewriters finally fell silent.

Robert Thomson's ambitions for the new building were summarised in one sentence: "Our new London location will allow us to realise one core objective as the new News – to work more closely and creatively and leverage our collective resources." Key to the realisation of that objective at London Bridge was Paige Ames, a specialist in executive project management, client engagement and workplace delivery. Eliminating individual offices was central to the approach taken by Ames and Jane Viner, global head of facilities and real estate transformation. Although some executives rebelled and had offices built later, initially only the editors of *The Times* and *Sunday Times* and the managing editors had offices with doors.

Witherow decided the shiny new home of *The Times* on the eleventh floor needed a visible link with the paper's ethos and long history. The solution was a wall with a gallery of heroes (and, as every good gallery requires, a few rogues) known as the "Makers of *The Times*". Researched by Anna Temkin, the deputy obituaries editor, and Nick Mays, the long-serving chief archivist of News UK, the wall features portraits of famous names and faces associated with the paper and a host of lesser-known figures, past and present, who made significant or unusual contributions to *The Times*.

One such was the mayor of London – and future prime minister – who opened the new building on September 16, 2014.

On the day after the opening ceremony, Kidd wrote in the *Times* Diary: "Boris Johnson popped into our new office, 26 years after he was sacked as a *Times* trainee for making up a quotation. 'Widely misreported cock-up,' he insisted. Shown a wall of books published by HarperCollins he was delighted to spot one of his own but added: 'You could build a much larger wall with some of [my] unsold copies.'"

Unreported by Kidd, however, was Johnson's more peppery response to finding himself one of the rogues in the "Makers of *The Times*" gallery, with his sacking recorded in the caption to his portrait. The visiting mayor of London turned to Witherow, who was standing next to Rupert Murdoch. "You bastard," he said.

CHAPTER TWENTY

The Times's parliamentary office had been since time immemorial a decrepit hut on the roof of the Palace of Westminster. It was far from comfortable but had a certain charm with a view from one side of a vast field of grey slate, the roof of Westminster Hall, while its other window offered a prospect of the palace's crumbling guts. In June 2013, with Roland Watson's move from political editor to the foreign desk after Richard Beeston's death, responsibility for the output of the hut passed to Francis Elliott. He had worked there before and had written a biography of David Cameron but had left Westminster to become South Asia editor shortly after the Tory leader became prime minister in 2010. Some aspects of the book, such as a previously unseen picture of Cameron in Oxford's notorious Bullingdon Club, had caused him political grief, and the prime minister had no difficulty containing his enthusiasm when introduced to *The Times*'s new political editor.

Elliott found a changed world at Westminster. Liberal Democrats, whom it had once been safe to ignore, now had to be courted as a party of (coalition) government, while Cameron and George Osborne, the chancellor, waxed more powerful as the economy started to recover and the pain of their initial round of austerity started to fade. The most significant story broken by *The Times* that summer of 2013 wasn't to do with the Tories or the Liberal Democrats, however, but concerned Labour and its relationship with the Unite union under its powerful general secretary, Len McCluskey.

A member of the lobby team, Laura Pitel, exposed the union's efforts to fix the selection of Labour's parliamentary candidates for McCluskey's acolytes and strengthen his hold over Ed Miliband, the Labour leader. It was political reporting at its best: detailed, robust, but fair. After a month Miliband cracked, announcing a series of measures that he said would reduce the party's financial dependency on Unite and other unions. This was to have unforeseen consequences: by greatly increasing the party membership and giving it a much greater say in Labour leadership elections, the reforms paved the way for Jeremy Corbyn to be opposition leader and potentially prime minister. Miliband's relationship with *The Times* had been poor since – with Unite's backing – he had won the party leadership race in 2010, narrowly beating his brother, David. The Ed camp were suspicious of Phil Collins, the Blairite *Times* leader writer, who was close to David Miliband. Relations were further complicated by the fact that Tom Baldwin, former deputy political editor and Washington correspondent of *The Times*, was Ed Miliband's media chief. Baldwin appeared to take Alastair Campbell, Tony Blair's media handler, as his model for dealing with the press. But Miliband wasn't Blair, and what *The Times* saw as Baldwin's blustering attempts at Campbell-style bullying made a tricky situation worse. Not for the first or last time a political leader saw bias where there was none, preferring to carp than engage. When Cameron called a general election in 2015, Elliott was unable to persuade Miliband to give an interview, breaking a long tradition in which the paper had big sit-down pieces with all the leaders during the campaign.

Although poor relations with the Labour team played a part, Miliband's refusal was part of a wider trend in campaigning in which print media lost ground to broadcast. Although Cameron did consent to an interview with *The Times*, it was short and tightly controlled like the rest of a thoroughly "de-risked" drive for a Tory government after five years in coalition with the Liberal Democrats. The opinion surveys (including those in *The Times*) pointed to the failure of Cameron's strategy, but as dawn broke over the new *Times* offices at London Bridge on May 8 the paper was reporting on the first outright Tory victory in 17 years.

For Cameron success came at a price. He had to deliver his manifesto promise that he would renegotiate Britain's relationship with the European Union and put the outcome to a referendum on membership of the bloc. Witherow and Elliott, summoned for a private meeting with Cameron in No 10 shortly after his triumph, left with the strong impression that the prime minister wanted to get on with this tricky vote as quickly as possible. Much of the conversation that day in summer 2015 was about Europe's migrant crisis. Wars in Syria, Libya and elsewhere in Africa were fuelling large flows of people into EU states, causing a series of humanitarian and political crises. It wasn't an ideal backdrop to make the case that the UK should stay in the bloc.

The renegotiation, the referendum and its aftermath were often hard to report but they also presented an opportunity for *The Times*. While others charged into set positions, Witherow insisted the paper play to its strengths by providing comprehensive but balanced coverage that allowed readers to reach their own conclusions. The paper had been resolutely Eurosceptic and retained its concern about the direction of the EU. It also favoured a low-tax smaller state over the European welfare model. But it had never favoured leaving the EU because of the market friction it would create and the loss of diplomatic clout. The consensus in leader conference was strongly for Remain. That was broadly the view of *Times* readers as well, and it would be reflected in the line the paper took in its leader on referendum day. The paper's neutral and balanced coverage continued to the end of the campaign, however, with a pair of supplements setting out a detailed case for each side in the days before the vote on June 23, 2016.

In a private briefing for senior executives in the midst of the campaign, Dominic Cummings, the iconoclastic mastermind of Vote Leave, had suggested that a huge turnout of the disaffected might happen on referendum day. Invisible to polling companies and the professional politicians who relied too heavily on them, a section of the electorate would power Leave over the line. Critical to that strategy was persuading Boris Johnson to support the campaign. Cummings could see that Johnson's celebrity helped him transcend traditional party allegiance – crucial in attracting those repelled by the Tory backers of Brexit and not as divisive as the other potential populist figurehead, Nigel Farage.

As *The Times* political team gathered on the evening of June 23 to report the results as they came in, Elliott was beginning to have serious doubts about the received wisdom that Remain would win. He had spent the day talking to Labour MPs canvassing in constituencies in the Midlands and North of England. The message was clear: in a mass vindication of Cummings's strategy, people who rarely if ever voted were coming out in droves. It was unlikely they were doing so to preserve mutual recognition of qualifications or student exchange programmes or any of the other benefits of EU membership that the elite running the Remain campaign thought so attractive. Just how fateful were the pairings of Cummings and Johnson, disaffected Labour voters and Brexit, was beginning to become clear as last light bled from the skies over central London. Witherow asked Elliott for his prediction, a mischief the editor enjoyed visiting on his staff before such set pieces. "Leave will win," Elliott replied with more conviction than he felt. A few hours later as early trends became overwhelming indicators that verdict looked less and less outlandish.

Next morning Cameron resigned and the blame game began. An informal post-mortem concluded that *The Times* had failed to learn a key lesson from the election just over a year previously: that opinion polls were not a safe foundation for coverage. There were some mitigations – sampling and weighting are much harder without the scaffold that previous elections provide the inexact science of modelling likely results from surveys – but it might have been better to listen to the reporters returning from places like Sunderland and Grimsby than pay too much attention to the latest surveys that almost universally showed Remain on course for a comfortable victory.

It also became clear that, at the same time as the UK's future had been put into question by Cameron, another significant factor had affected the outcome of the referendum. After Labour's general election defeat in 2015, the party's internal election reforms triggered by the Unite story in *The Times* in 2010 had swept the unlikely figure of Jeremy Corbyn into the leadership. The far-left Islington North MP, a marginal figure for decades, caught a wave of discontent that consumed Labour members. His victory was a shock of such magnitude that little effort was made to take him seriously. He was treated as an eccentric, even a genial figure, his leadership a fever dream from which the Labour Party would awaken at any moment. Corbyn's media chief, Seumas Milne, a former *Guardian* executive, rarely if ever engaged with Elliott or anyone else on *The Times*. That didn't help with the effort to explain to readers "The Project", as Corbyn's collection of socialist and "anti-imperialist" positions was called by his team. Following Corbyn's first speech as leader to a Labour conference, which included a long diatribe about the evils of "neoliberalism", Milne refused to say whether Corbyn's Labour believed there was any place for capitalism in the UK. Nor was his position on the EU clear. Although the party was officially in favour of continued membership, Corbyn's personal opposition to it as a capitalist club showed in his muted approach to the referendum. Paradoxically, however, the very fact that Labour was under the control of the left while campaigning for Remain drove patriotic, working class voters further into the Leave camp.

Corbyn was not alone in his ambiguity towards the referendum. Theresa May, Cameron's home secretary, had at first sought to avoid taking a side in the campaign. She broke cover only once, to make a speech in support of membership so half-hearted it was seen as more helpful to Leave. It may have lacked integrity but it was a skilful piece of politics that helped her to become prime minister in the chaos after Cameron's resignation.

Her path to the top was smoothed considerably by a car-crash interview in *The Times* between Rachel Sylvester and Andrea Leadsom, the last full-blooded Brexiteer standing in the leadership election after Michael Gove had forced Boris Johnson to pull out. Leadsom's campaign imploded the moment she met Sylvester in a Costa coffee shop in Milton Keynes for the hastily arranged interview. Asked what the difference was between her and May, Leadsom replied, "economic competence and family". Despite her later protestations, the implication was clear: Leadsom believed that May's childlessness was a relevant factor. The resulting story under the splash headline, "Being a mother gives me an edge on May – Leadsom", led to accusations of a crass lack of judgment and sank her leadership bid, leaving the way clear for the home secretary to become prime minister unopposed. It was a terrific scoop that once again showed the influence of *The Times* on the political scene.

Taking office, May inherited a small majority and a massive problem: how to interpret the vote to leave the EU. "Brexit means Brexit," she averred, ducking the critical question of trade-offs between sovereignty and preferential trading relations with the UK's biggest economic partners. *The Times* had backed Remain, but Witherow was adamant that it could not ignore the referendum result. From the moment the vote was announced the paper was clear that it must support implementation of the result, even if one or two leader writers were unhappy about doing so.

Simon Nixon, the business journalist who became chief leader writer later that year, was relentless in his exposure of Brexit's inconsistencies and faults. Occasionally he would come in pink and cross from another bout of early-morning outdoor swimming and express his frustration volubly in leader conference. Witherow, always laconic, would listen, smile and tell him: "We aren't writing that." Nixon would then frame a very elegant argument along the agreed lines. He had his work cut out. Over the coming months and years it sometimes seemed that every element of the UK economy was being exposed and reassessed, as if a vast, complex machine lay disassembled on the factory floor awaiting reassembly to a plan that was at best a work in progress. Each sweeping question, such as whether the UK should diverge from EU customs rules, bristled with subsidiary thorny issues.

The paper was very fortunate that it had recruited Oliver Wright to help navigate this morass. Wright had been a popular and highly rated member of the news desk under Thomson but had left for a more senior role at *The Independent* during Harding's editorship. Witherow lured him back and put him in charge of Brexit coverage. Wright's discrimination and ability to render comprehensible and even entertaining Brexit's myriad sub-plots were a major element of the paper's strength at this time.

Within six months it was becoming clear to May that she needed a bigger majority to drive through the compromises she believed struck the right balance between respecting the Brexit vote and preserving the country's economic and security interests. Corbyn's Labour, furthermore, appeared to be the softest of targets. The party was divided at all levels, with splits between its MPs, members and voters. By Easter 2017, May had convinced herself Labour was there for the taking and she called a snap election. That turned out to be a spectacular miscalculation.

The Times had its share of embarrassingly inaccurate miscalculations. In the aftermath of a decent set of local election results for the Tories, it forecast that May was on course for a three-figure majority at Westminster. Blushes were spared, however, thanks to a novel technique that YouGov, the paper's pollsters, had trialled in the US and were keen to debut in the UK. The statistical technique – multilevel regression and post stratification (MRP) – effectively allowed pollsters to model likely outcomes at constituency level. It was claimed it had helped predict Donald Trump's victorious insurgency in the United States in 2016, but no one really knew whether that was a one-off or whether it could be applied to Great Britain and its 632 constituencies. Sam Coates, deputy political editor, nervously broached the question at one of the team's weekly political meetings with the editor and other senior executives. He stressed the dangers but said the risks could be mitigated if it was given only a modest show. Witherow commissioned an MRP poll and put it on the front page. It was a sensation. It showed that although the Tories had a consistent lead in national polls, MRP indicated that the race was much tighter.

In fact, the model suggested, the UK was on course for another hung parliament. The backlash was fierce. Jim Messina, the Tory's election chief, tweeted: "Spent the day laughing at another stupid poll". Vindication came eight days later when, just as the MRP had predicted, the Tory majority had evaporated. The country was stuck at the crossroads, committed to leaving the EU but unable to agree how and with a substantial minority desperate for a second referendum.

For much of the next four years, the centre of the story was the chamber of the House of Commons, where every vote counted and party discipline broke down. A "par" day at *The Times* would see a political splash and two to three spreads. The demand was for comprehensive, authoritative and balanced coverage. The political team, which had been three when Elliott took over from Watson in 2013, grew to six. In addition to Coates and Wright, Elliott and Witherow had recruited Henry Zeffman and Lucy Fisher, both winners of the Anthony Howard Award. The prize, which included a two-month stint in the team, proved to be an excellent way of sampling emerging talent in political reporting, and poaching the best of it.

Zeffman was supposed to be a leader writer but Elliott persuaded Witherow he would be the ideal person to help Wright cover Brexit. He proved his worth fully in that brief but really came into his own exposing Corbyn's shameful relations with antisemites. *The Times* had done some solid reporting on claims that allegations of antisemitism weren't being properly dealt with by Labour's HQ, where some of Corbyn's allies believed they were motivated by spiteful factionalism. The leader's own culpability was harder to prove and it took a patient and thorough excavation of his career in fringe politics to draw out his serial failure to challenge the antisemites with whom he spent so much of his time. It was Zeffman who, in the summer of 2018, kicked off that work with a scoop that Corbyn had hosted an event in the Commons in which the Israeli government was likened to Nazi Germany.

It was Zeffman too who in late 2018, as the Brexit saga descended to new depths of parliamentary complexity, began sketching on the back of an envelope the various options available to May. Zeffman was initially amusing himself and his colleagues but his "flowchart" showed just what a mind-bendingly difficult challenge May was facing to land a deal. She was trapped between a hard-core of her own party that would accept nothing less than full sovereignty and a larger but fissiparous group prepared to dilute or indeed cancel the Brexit vote. Tidied up by the graphics department, the back-of-an-envelope flow chart appeared in all its glory as a double-page spread (December 6, 2018). It was pinned up on walls in Westminster and embassies, went viral and was soon being copied by others.

Of all the many scenarios contained within it, the final outcome was one of the more prosaic: having tried but failed three times to force a compromise through the Commons, May was forced from office. Aides sometimes made a point of telling Elliott that *The Times* was her newspaper of choice. If it was meant to inhibit criticism it failed, but she nevertheless made a point of ensuring that news of her final decision to resign was handed exclusively to the paper she read.

The frontrunner to replace her was Johnson; a figure of outward bonhomie, Johnson could be thin-skinned, even petulant, when criticised, quick to see a slight and slow to forgive. These flaws, and many others, were put to one side in July 2019 by the Tories. Facing an existential threat posed by Nigel Farage's Brexit Party, they opted for Johnson as their saviour. Once in Downing Street, he rapidly secured the outline of a deal with the EU – which postponed rather than settled critical questions but allowed him to claim an end to the years of rancorous division – and called another general election, the third in four years.

For this election Elliott was without Coates, who had left for Sky Television, but with a new deputy, Steve Swinford, who had been poached from *The Daily Telegraph* where he had been giving *The Times* team a run for their money. Too often for comfort they had been scrambling to match Swinford late at night. "We're just going to have to employ him," sighed Elliott one morning, enviously reviewing his rival's latest scoop. Swinford quickly started delivering the sort of essential in-the-room detail and colour that helped make the *Times* coverage stand out. A Saturday "long-read" of the political week became a staple of the weekend output, setting up a (mostly friendly) rivalry with Tim Shipman's similar effort for *The Sunday Times*.

Elliott had a head start in understanding Johnson's plan of attack. Months earlier, while May was still in her political death throes, Elliott had taken Dominic Cummings, the former director of

Vote Leave, to dinner near where both lived in north London. As it had been a fairly bibulous occasion and had taken place quite some time in the past, Elliott's memory of it was hazy. But he recalled that the former director of Vote Leave had told him that he had spent months in focus groups exploring further the new "coalition" of voters revealed by the Brexit referendum. Cummings believed on the basis of this analysis that a party that was pro-Brexit, pro-NHS and hardline on security would scoop the electoral jackpot. He had initially believed it might be necessary to start a new party to harness this support, but he had concluded that under Johnson the Tories could do so. Now he had shot to the heart of power as Johnson's chief of staff and was putting his strategy into practice. The winter election campaign was attritional. Johnson, submitting to the discipline of Cummings, had just one message: "Get Brexit Done". Although he agreed to an interview with *The Times*, it was heavily policed by his spin doctor, Lee Cain. Labour again refused an election interview. Corbyn was, nevertheless, finally run to ground over his failures to address the outbreak of antisemitism that he had allowed to infect the main opposition party under his leadership. Zeffman negotiated and secured an unprecedented op-ed from Ephraim Mirvis, Britain's chief rabbi, which said that Corbyn was "unfit for high office" and that the "very soul of our nation is at stake".

The result indicated that many former Labour voters agreed. Johnson secured a landslide victory via a swathe of gains from Labour in "red wall" seats in the Midlands and North. For the first few months of 2020 it seemed possible that he would radically change the UK, sweeping away anything and anybody he believed was an obstacle to achieving his vision for the country. The details of this vision were hazy but the broad brush was a combination of "levelling up", grand infrastructure projects, a rolling-back of judicial activism and other checks on executive power, and exploiting the economic opportunities afforded by escape from the EU's regulatory and tariff orbit. Barely had he taken office, however, than the outbreak of a novel coronavirus in Wuhan, China, threw Britain – and the world – into an unprecedented crisis. Johnson's handling of the Covid-19 pandemic, and subsequent revelations of a culture of internal rule-breaking at 10 Downing Street during national lockdowns, would ultimately destroy his premiership.

CHAPTER TWENTY-ONE

The *Times* business section acquired a new sense of urgency after Witherow took over as editor. One of his early moves was to hire Richard Fletcher, a dogged news fanatic, from *The Telegraph*. "Fletch", as he was universally known, was likened to the Duracell Bunny by colleagues. He never stopped. He was in the thick of things on the business news desk, constantly floating new story angles, barking instructions, pushing reporters to "hit the phones" and get better reaction to events. The atmosphere in the department became significantly more urgent. The news coverage became sharper and more immediate. More often than not, by the time of the morning meeting of all business reporters, Fletcher knew as much about the story as his specialist writers did and was already pushing for reaction stories, follow-up angles and follow-ups to the likely follow-ups.

While Fletcher was chivvying his news troops to Stakhanovite levels of story output, more space was given over to new business columnists. Alistair Osborne, a waspish, pun-loving business writer from *The Telegraph* with a forensic ability to drill down into the numbers, was hired to set the commentary tone. Paul Johnson, director of the Institute for Fiscal Studies, injected his encyclopaedic understanding of the government's tax and spending plans. Mark Littlewood, head of the right-leaning Institute of Economic Affairs, provided his libertarian, free-market take on the world. Sathnam Sanghera, a writer already familiar to readers of *The Times* features pages, offered his whimsical views on business, the world of work and his own experiences as a private investor.

Witherow could scent a great opportunity to poach new readers as *The Financial Times* increasingly ignored or downplayed UK-focused business stories. Globalisation and investor diversification had persuaded it to shift its focus away from domestic matters. Even FTSE 100 companies were sometimes reduced to a mere paragraph in the Pink Un's pages. Smaller companies, second-liners in the jargon of the City, were often ignored completely. Witherow and Fletcher were determined to exploit that neglect. They adopted a "desert island philosophy" for the business pages: even if readers were stranded on a desert island with no other media available to them, they should be able to count on not missing a single story of any significance. A Need to Know page of condensed bullet points was launched: if it wasn't in Need to Know, it wasn't worth knowing. At least that was the idea.

Another major innovation was the business spread – more in-depth reporting of a big story over two pages, perhaps running to 1,500 words and, more often than not, accompanied by explainers and other sidebars and graphics. Business was getting ever more complicated, more regulated and more opaque – and readers expected more help in making sense of it. "We started to do what the Sunday papers did in the old days," recalls Fletcher. "You used to have to wait until Sunday for the in-depth treatment of the big running story. Now you'd get it the next day."

The shift to digital was accelerated too. Commuting business readers in particular were in the vanguard of those keen to abandon a physical newspaper and shift to reading *The Times* on a smartphone or tablet. Some digital innovation, like business podcasts, soon fell by the wayside. Others proved to be big winners. One innovation was a tightly written summary of the day's new business stories delivered by email at 8am – quite a feat since most company announcements only came out at 7am. By 2022, 40,000-plus readers a day were subscribing to the business email, making it the most popular email service offered by the paper after the main general service. Official company results statements had got ever longer and windier, sometimes extending to tens of thousands of words or more, but ever less useful – with the key points for investors and users buried or obfuscated in jargon. Readers desperately needed something to tell them the headline angle and what had happened overnight in overseas markets; the *Times* business email hit the spot in a few hundred crisp words.

It was a rich era for business and economic news. The global financial crisis was over, but the years of relative austerity started to expose the frailties of some of Britain's biggest and most important businesses and the self-serving nature of some of their owners too. The collapse of BHS, the department chain store – and revelations of how its controlling shareholder, Sir Philip Green, tried to wriggle out of his obligations to its pension scheme members by selling to a thrice bankrupt with no retail experience – became a byword for irresponsible capitalism. The long-running scandal only simmered down when Green, under pressure from Westminster and Fleet Street, agreed to write a large cheque.

The demise of Carillion, one of Britain's biggest services and construction companies, in 2018 was another meaty story for *Times* business reporters. As a major contractor to the government, it caused massive embarrassment to ministers – and its own auditors KPMG – when it suddenly imploded, leaving hospital building and other public sector contracts in limbo. It turned out to have £7 billion in liabilities but just £29 million in cash, leading to criticism of both the board and KPMG, which had given it a clean bill of financial health only months earlier. The role of auditors in many business failures was a constant theme in the business pages, as was the timorous approach of their regulator, the Financial Reporting Council.

Then there were the big personality clash stories, as when Sir Christopher Hohn, a billionaire hedge fund manager, locked horns with Sir Donald Brydon, chairman of the London Stock Exchange Group in 2017. Xavier Rolet, the chief executive of the exchange, was in the process of being eased out by Brydon over his "abrasive" management style. Hohn wanted Rolet to stay and Brydon to go. It was a telling story about how capitalism was changing. The big traditional managers of pension funds were losing influence in the way the City was run: more swashbuckling and less accountable figures at hedge funds and so-called activist funds were increasingly prepared to make waves, and to do so publicly. The traditional City eventually won and Rolet departed, but only after the intervention of the governor of the Bank of England, Mark Carney. And in a telling coda, Brydon departed too.

The small-business world was of increasing interest to readers. Entrepreneurialism and self-employment were booming and a new section, Working Life, later renamed Times Enterprise Network, was launched to tap into that interest. Self-employment in the UK grew from 2.3 million in 2000 to almost 4 million by 2019. The newly hired small-business editor, James Hurley, pushed hard in trying to illuminate and explain the world of small business. His beefed up coverage extended far beyond inspirational pieces on successful entrepreneurs to numerous "how to" pieces explaining the practicalities of raising finance, clinching exports deals and saving on tax. The era also spawned an insatiable demand for economics stories. The immediate banking crisis of 2008–9 was over and the eurozone debt crisis was calming down, but the era of super-low interest rates and money-creating stimulus policies prompted by those two crises was not. Arguments about the wisdom of that scale of money creation, known as quantitative easing, dominated the headlines. Super-lax monetary policy was not just a matter for policy wonks. It was feeding through into what became one of the greatest bull markets of all time. Wall Street boomed almost continuously from a low in 2009 to peak at the tail end of 2021, when inflation started to take hold and central banks switched off the magic sauce of quantitative easing and started to raise interest rates.

The bull market created a handful of technology-linked corporations with unimaginable values. The so-called FAANGs (Facebook, Apple, Amazon, Netflix and Google) dominated not just American business coverage, but the UK too, as London listed stocks fell out of favour in this growth-focused world. It became apparent that British pension funds and even ordinary retail investors in the UK had far more exposure to these new giants than old standbys like Shell, GlaxoSmithKline and HSBC. *Times* US business editors, first Alex Frean, then James Dean, then Callum Jones became key figures in reporting and explaining the rise of American business in general and Wall Street's titans in particular. By 2021, US stocks accounted for as much as 60 per cent of the entire world equity market. There was soul-searching in the City, which worried it was missing out to more tech-friendly financial centres: not only New York but also Shanghai as China's tech industries burgeoned. The City authorities in 2022 embarked on reforms to relax standards and increase the appeal of London to tech entrepreneurs. *Times* writers expressed caution and scepticism, and were right to do so. The pendulum came swinging back: suddenly, the FTSE 100's roster of unloved fossil fuel companies and miners were back in vogue, while the once-lauded tech sector came back to earth with a bump.

There were many morale-boosting exclusives in the *Times* business pages. Towards the end of 2019, Phil Aldrick, the economics editor, was tapping out his last story of the day. It was about 4pm and he was looking forward to the *Times* Christmas party that night when an email from the Bank of England came through, confirming – in elliptical central bank speak – an extraordinary sequence of events. He stared at his screen in astonishment. "I looked at it and I thought, oh my god, the Bank's been hacked," he recalled. This was to produce a great scoop for *The Times*. Aldrick had been doggedly on the track of it for two years since he had first become interested in the City phenomenon of high-speed trading. He was intrigued by the way traders were prepared to fork out for high-speed transatlantic cables that enabled them to receive price-sensitive information a fraction of a second faster than others. He wrote a story on traders who established an operation in Slough because of that town's proximity to a data centre used by the London Stock Exchange. Then came an announcement by the European Central Bank (ECB) in early 2018 that it was introducing a low-latency – i.e. ultra-fast – feed for press conferences especially to address the problem of traders receiving price-sensitive information a split-second before others. "I thought then, bloody hell, someone's been rigging the system at the ECB." He wondered whether the same problem might be occurring at the Bank and, egged on by some whistleblowers in the high-speed trading community, kept pressing Threadneedle Street on whether it might have a similar problem. Then, eventually, came that Christmas email from the Bank. Its problem, however, was distinctly old tech compared to the ECB's. In essence, outside traders had been paying to make use of a back-up audio feed installed in the conference room at the Bank. The feed gave those listening an advantage of as much as eight seconds over the wider market, which used the Bank's official video feed of press conferences to hear what the then governor Mark Carney and other officials had to say.

"I was hyper-excited but I knew it was going to be very difficult to tell the story because it was so complex," Aldrick remembered. He rushed over to Fletcher, who in turn told Witherow. Aldrick recalled: "Witherow's news judgment was amazing. It was an extremely complex story, but he saw straight away that one of the great institutions of Britain had in effect been outwitted by a bunch of spivvy traders." It was going on the front of the whole paper. Under the headline, "Hedge funds eavesdrop on vital Bank briefings", the splash set out how the Bank's grandees had inadvertently allowed price-sensitive news to go out to traders early and gave them the chance to make millions of pounds in improper profits. "That is an astonishing embarrassment for an institution that has a responsibility to maintain global investor confidence in London's markets," observed an admonitory *Times* leader. The story was followed up by every other news outlet. Questions were raised in parliament. The Bank was forced into launching a review of its processes and later issued a mea culpa, though no one at the Bank lost their job. Aldrick was later named Business Journalist of the Year.

CHAPTER TWENTY-TWO

For four months in 2017, Britain found itself confronted by repeated outbreaks of deadly homegrown terrorism, and *The Times* was in the front line of the story both in its reporting and literally. On March 22 an Islamist terrorist, Khalid Masood, drove a hired Hyundai Tucson along the pavement of Westminster Bridge killing four people and injuring 29 seriously. He then crashed into railings outside the Palace of Westminster, ran through the carriage gates and stabbed to death PC Keith Palmer, who was unarmed. Masood was shot dead by police in New Palace Yard. The whole of page 1 of *The Times* on March 23 was taken up with a dramatic picture of victims being tended on the ground, police running to and fro, and marksmen on the alert.

The following day, a photo taken by the deputy political editor Sam Coates, from his window in the *Times* parliamentary office, which showed Masood and Palmer lying dying on the ground, was also used on page 1. The Metropolitan Police's communications chief, Martin Fewell, said on Radio 4's *The Media Show* that officers were "extremely upset" by it (*Press Gazette*, March 29, 2017). Emma Tucker, deputy editor, put up a strong defence, telling the programme that the picture was used because "one of the key stories that was emerging was the story of a security lapse, the fact that an unarmed police officer had been murdered in the precinct of the Houses of Parliament and the gates remained open after the attacker had got in". The photograph, she said, had vividly conveyed that information, and she noted that it was taken from a distance and the people involved were not recognisable. Asked whether she regretted publishing the picture, Tucker said: "Absolutely not – this was a picture that was an important illustration of a story about a security lapse, I totally stand by the fact that we used it."

Two months later an Islamist suicide bomber, Salman Abedi, killed 22 people and injured 800 at a concert by the American pop star Ariana Grande at the Manchester Arena. The national terror threat level was raised from severe to critical for the first time in a decade, meaning that a further attack might be imminent: SAS soldiers were sent to Manchester and thousands of troops were deployed at high-risk locations.

Death came to the *Times* doorstep on the evening of Saturday, June 3, when three Islamist terrorists drove a hired van along the pavement over London Bridge, ramming pedestrians before crashing on the south side near Borough Market, across the road from the *Times* building. The men then ran into busy pubs and restaurants in the market stabbing people, before being shot dead by police. Eight people had been killed and 48 injured. The attack occurred shortly after the first edition of *The Sunday Times* had gone off stone. Two hundred of the paper's staff spent the night in the office while the News Building was locked down behind a police cordon. Their third edition led on the terrifying experience of Ian Houghton, 55, the newspaper's chief sub-editor, who told how he escaped death by leaping out of the way of the killers' van. He had left work before the incident and was walking over the bridge from the direction of the Shard on his way home. "I could see a van coming at speed over the bridge. People were screaming and leaping out of the way. There was debris flying everywhere, bits of the car and people's possessions. He was coming right at me, so I jumped into the middle of the road." The driver swerved at him and as he stepped back on to the pavement, the side of the van brushed his left hand (*The Sunday Times*, June 4, 2017).

The News building remained largely out of bounds on Sunday so Monday's *Times* was produced by a small group of staff from a disaster recovery site established a couple of miles away in Southwark. A dramatic photograph filled page 1, with the headline: "Massacre in the market". A further 14 pages of news from a team led by Fiona Hamilton and David Brown dominated a 68-page issue. Brown heard the news on his car radio at 1am while driving home from holiday. At 4am he was up and working from home and came in later that day.

The dilemmas posed to a liberal democracy by homegrown Islamist extremists were brought sharply into focus two years later by Anthony Loyd. The *Times* splash on February 14, 2019, was headlined "Bring me home", the words of Shamima Begum, 19, one of three schoolgirls from Bethnal Green who had run away in 2015 to join ISIS. Loyd found her in a Syrian refugee camp, heavily pregnant with her third child by an ISIS fighter, as a US-backed coalition of local forces was closing in on the last ISIS enclave in eastern Syria after a long military campaign.

Loyd told of the chaos in the camp of 39,000 refugees. Hour after hour he had sat in a reception office asking to see British nationals. At last an official brought in two unidentified veiled jihadi brides and said simply that they would talk. "Then came those words," Loyd wrote:

'I'm a sister from London. I'm a Bethnal Green girl.' So it was. I would love to claim that it was the result of a skilled forensic investigation that led me to meet Shamima Begum. It was not. Despite every piece of previous planning, in its final moments the search for the Bethnal Green girls had ended in this moment of total serendipity as a harassed Syrian official, keen to get rid of a journalist in his office, simply waded into a crowded transit section for new camp arrivals and asked if any women there would be prepared to speak to a British reporter.

But a reporter like Loyd makes his own luck: he got the break because he knew what he was looking for and pursued the story single-mindedly.

Despite the ISIS reign of terror and beheadings, Begum told Loyd that life in Raqqa, the Syrian city it had used as its "capital", had been largely "normal". It was "the one I wanted", she said. Seeing her first severed head in a bin, "didn't faze me at all". However, the group's oppression and corruption meant that "I don't think they deserved victory". She was aware that she might return to a hostile reception in Britain if she was allowed back there. "I know what everyone at home thinks of me as I have read all that was written about me online," she said. "But I just want to come home to have my child. I'll do anything required just to be able to come home and live quietly with my child." Should she be allowed home? *The Times* came out for Begum in a leader: now ISIS had crumpled, several European countries faced the dilemma of what to do with zealots who wanted to return. Given the savagery dealt out by ISIS – the public beheadings, torture, flogging, public amputations and rapes – many would recoil at the suggestion, it conceded. She had volunteered, after all, to side with a group that had taken British hostages, fought against the western alliance, and mounted attacks on European cities. However, *The Times* said, she should be allowed to return to her family in Britain and explain her actions. On arrival she should be detained and questioned by the security services to determine how exactly ISIS was able to spread its tentacles into Britain and other European countries. A judgment would have to be made as to whether she was more victim than perpetrator.

The paper also reported that after Begum and the other schoolgirls had left Britain their parents had been assured by senior police that they were unlikely to be prosecuted for terrorist offences. Bernard Hogan-Howe, the Metropolitan Police commissioner, and Sir Mark Rowley, the force's head of counterterrorism, agreed that the girls would be "returning to their families" if they decided to come back. "We have no evidence that these three girls are responsible for any terrorist offences. They have no reason to fear, if nothing else comes to light, that we will treat them as terrorists," Rowley had told MPs. Loyd himself felt that Begum should be allowed home. The day after his story appeared, however, Sajid Javid, the home secretary, told *The Times* that although ISIS, also known as Daesh, was on its knees in Syria, it continued to plan and inspire attacks both in Britain and abroad.

> I condemn anyone who has travelled to be part of this barbaric and brutal group – and we must remember that those who left Britain to join Daesh were full of hate for our country. My message is clear: if you have supported terrorist organisations abroad I will not hesitate to prevent your return. If you do manage to return you should be ready to be questioned, investigated and potentially prosecuted. The reporting in *The Times* has shone a light on to the complex issues we currently face in countering the terrorist threat . . . My priority is to ensure the safety and security of the UK, and I will not let anything jeopardise this.

When Javid revoked Begum's British citizenship six days later, legal experts argued that because individuals cannot be rendered stateless under international law he didn't have the power to stop her unless she was a dual national. Her family's solicitor, Tasnime Akunjee, said that although Begum's parents were Bangladeshi she did not have citizenship there and held no identity documents for any country other than the UK. The Court of Appeal ruled in 2020 that Begum should be allowed home. The ruling presented a path back for jihadists stripped of citizenship. The court said that she could appeal properly against the government's decision to revoke her citizenship only if she came home. Javid said that if Begum returned it would be impossible to remove her later, regardless of the outcome of the case. A *Times* leader (July 17, 2020) said that Javid's decision had always been legally and morally debatable given that it rendered Begum effectively stateless. The leader pointed out that, in a counterterrorism strategy document written the year before Begum was found, the Home Office had laid out the way in which people like her should be treated. It called for them to face interrogation and a police investigation into whether they had committed any crime. Although it might be hard to produce evidence of exactly what Begum had got up to in Syria, support for a death cult such as ISIS was itself a crime. That suggested that she was likely to have a criminal case to answer. The strategy also rightly called for returnees to enter a long deradicalisation programme, be electronically tagged and have their risk assessed by the security services, if necessary, for life. The leader stated:

> The hope must be that her experiences might yet turn her into a powerful voice against the cult she joined. When Loyd . . . first found her . . . that seemed unlikely. She showed little remorse and indeed some bravado. But she also expressed disillusionment with ISIS, who imprisoned and tortured her husband, and she mourned her infant children. By Loyd's final visit, the black robes had gone and she spoke of her regrets about what she called her 'brainwashing'. If she is truly contrite, few could do more to ensure that no other schoolgirls are seduced into ISIS's murderous embrace.

The government appealed, however, to the Supreme Court, which ruled that it would be too dangerous to public safety for Begum to return, and she remained excluded for the foreseeable future.

Loyd won the British Journalism Awards Scoop of the Year in December 2019 for his story. The judges described it as a "standout world exclusive" that Loyd "had to go out and find", adding that the story was "so big that everyone had to follow it". He was also named Print Journalist of the Year at the London Press Club Awards in October 2020 for his "stunning exclusive". Loyd said: "There is never a better alternative for a foreign correspondent in getting scoops or breaking stories than being on the ground."

It was a measure of the breadth of coverage *The Times* commanded and the stature of its specialists that they included both the bearded, war-scarred Loyd and a neatly dressed mother-of-three with an eye for the absurd who brought down one of the mightiest judges in the land and successfully campaigned for a change in the divorce laws to the benefit of millions.

Frances Gibb, who retired as legal editor in 2019, was only the third incumbent of the post, much the longest-serving and, to the surprise of some in the legal profession, not a lawyer. She joined *The Times* in 1980 as a 29-year-old home news reporter – starting on the same day as John Witherow – and, when the post of legal affairs correspondent became vacant two years later, persuaded her editor Charles Douglas-Home that her lack of legal training would be an advantage. She argued that she had to explain the legal world to the layman, and was better placed to do that as a journalist rather than as an insider.

It marked her out as a contrast to her predecessor, Marcel Berlins, a lawyer who had been compiling law reports in the Lord Chancellor's department when he applied for the post in 1971. He was interviewed by John Grant, the managing editor, who concluded their interview by memorably asking Berlins "Are you a shit?", explaining that there was no place for such a person on *The Times*. Assuring Grant that he was no such thing, the affable and cultured Anglo-French Berlins joined the paper and under the editorship of William Rees-Mogg spent a little more than a decade as legal correspondent and leader writer, covering not only his own field but topics such as cricket and pop music, including a *Times* leader on the death of Elvis Presley (August 18, 1977).

His successor was certainly no "shit" either – Witherow remembered her fondly as "the Blessed Frances Gibb" – though for years consternation persisted in some quarters that she was not a lawyer. She recalled a phone call to the notoriously rude Mr Justice Harman. He had taken 20 months to deliver a ruling. Gibb wanted to know what he had to say. "Clearly not a man given to swift responses, he paused – then asked if I was a member of the Bar. I said no. There was a longer pause. Was I a solicitor? Again I replied that I wasn't. Finally, with evident disdain, he said: 'I am so sorry – I thought you were the *Times* legal correspondent'."

Soon after her appointment, she triggered the retirement of one of England's most famous and distinguished judges, Lord Denning, the 83-year-old Master of the Rolls. She picked up a story from his new book *What Next in the Law*, in which he had criticised the use by defendants of their right to challenge jurors (later abolished) during the trials of the leaders of the Bristol riots in 1981, saying that they were trying to secure "as many coloured people on the jury as possible – by objecting to whites". He went on:

> The underlying assumption is that all citizens are sufficiently qualified to serve on a jury . . . I do not agree. The English are no longer a homogeneous race. They are white and black, coloured and brown. They no longer share the same standards of conduct. Some of them come from countries where bribery and graft are accepted as an integral part of life: and where stealing is a virtue so long as you are not found out . . . They will never accept the word of a policeman against one of their own.

Gibb's report (May 22, 1982), a scrupulously neutral single-column story on page 5, prompted the Society of Black Lawyers to call on Denning to quit, saying the remarks were insulting and degrading and "couched in terms virulent enough to destroy any remaining credibility he may have as an unbiased and impartial interpreter of the law". Gibb recalled: "Early next morning (my husband and I were still in bed) the phone rang. It was Denning, deeply aggrieved that I had run the piece, which he knew would give his comments wider prominence and fuel controversy." The book was withdrawn a week later. Denning, then 83, apologised and announced that he would retire. It was, Gibb wrote, the end of an era.

Serving under nine editors, Gibb greatly developed the *Times* legal coverage to reflect the changes in the justice system, which, as she wrote on her retirement, was "transformed beyond recognition" during the 27 years she reported on it. Initially, she had a couple of law pages in the business section and was able to have three spells of maternity leave,

> because in the 1980s the job was far less mainstream and I could return to work each time on a part-time basis. But working from home one day a week brought its own stresses. I had to interview Lord Hailsham of St Marylebone, the Lord Chancellor at the time, by telephone

with a seven-month-old baby lying on the bedroom floor. I had a bagful of toys at the ready, but almost from the start of the interview my son began to cry in a full-scale crescendo. Lord Hailsham pressed on regardless on the niceties of legal aid reforms, apparently totally impervious.

Legal coverage was given a boost by Simon Jenkins in 1991 when specialist columnists were taken on. Then in 1999 Peter Stothard enhanced it further, giving Gibb the new title of legal editor and proposing the Law supplement, a weekly pullout reflecting the volume of advertising that was distorting the pagination of the paper on Tuesdays. It flourished for a decade alongside a Student Law section three times a year before being incorporated into the main book. Law Online was launched in 2008 and then in 2016, under Witherow, The Brief was born – a daily (later weekly) legal bulletin modelled on the politics newsletter Red Box.

In 2017, Gibb launched a successful campaign in *The Times* for the modernisation of family law after a report by the Nuffield Foundation, Finding Fault, condemned divorce laws in England and Wales for forcing couples to make false and exaggerated allegations of adultery or bad behaviour, causing bitterness and harming the mental health of children. The *Times* Family Matters campaign called for sweeping reform, including the abolition of the need during divorce proceedings to allege fault or blame, which had caused people to remain locked for years in loveless marriages; the end of the so-called meal ticket for life maintenance awards; and statutory backing for prenuptial contracts. Gibb wrote that senior judicial figures had called for an end to "unjust" and "outdated" divorce laws (November 17, 2017). Lord Mackay of Clashfern, the Lord Chancellor to two prime ministers, and Baroness Butler-Sloss, the former lord justice of appeal and president of the High Court family division, had joined other legal grandees to condemn the "antediluvian, damaging" 50-year-old laws governing marital break-ups. Sir Paul Coleridge, for ten years a family judge in the High Court and founder of the charity Marriage Foundation, which was working with *The Times*, said that the current system was expensive for couples, fuelled acrimony and damaged the possibility of long-term relationships in the interest of children.

A leader said that divorce laws ought to make it easier for couples to remain on civil terms after separating. "Today *The Times* joins the charity Marriage Foundation, senior judges and leading family law experts to campaign for the urgent reform of the nation's divorce laws. This is for the sake of children and spouses locked in loveless marriages, and for the institution of marriage itself . . . Whoever may be to blame, it is not vulnerable children. For their sake, and for the good name of marriage, the law must be reformed."

The campaign quickly gathered pace: a week later dozens of top lawyers and judicial figures had weighed in. They included Baroness Shackleton of Belgravia, the leading divorce solicitor whose many clients included the Duke of Cambridge and the Duke of Sussex, Sir Paul McCartney and Madonna. Lord Falconer of Thoroton, Lord Chancellor in Tony Blair's government from 2003 to 2007, added his voice to the campaign and a month later the justice secretary, David Gauke, agreed to examine the case for reforming divorce laws that force couples into damaging and false allegations of blame. The reforms finally came into force in April 2022.

By then, Gibb had been in retirement for three years but was still writing for *The Times* and sharing her fund of stories about legal bigwigs. A favourite concerned Lord Irvine, Tony Blair's notoriously vain first Lord Chancellor. Soon after stories appeared in 2004 that he had spent £650,000 on wallpaper for his official residence, Gibb reported that he had compared himself to Cardinal Wolsey, Henry VIII's mighty chancellor. "Irvine was livid. He launched into a torrent of abuse when I was seated opposite him at a dinner shortly afterwards: I had 'no soul', he told me, and I was a 'silly goose'. I declined to take him on, mindful of representing *The Times*. It was in any case behaviour fitting of a fuming Tudor cardinal, if not a modern Lord Chancellor."

CHAPTER TWENTY-THREE

On January 9, 2020, Didi Tang reported from Beijing that China had identified a new strain of coronavirus following a pneumonia outbreak in the central city of Wuhan. It came from the same family as the deadly Severe Acute Respiratory Syndrome (Sars) virus that had killed 349 people in China in 2002–3, but the authorities had assured the public that there was no evidence of human-to-human transmissions. That assurance was wrong. Cases were confirmed in Thailand, Japan and South Korea on January 20 and the first case in the US, in Washington State, was reported next day. On January 23 Wuhan was closed off by Chinese authorities. On January 31 the first cases of Covid-19, as the coronavirus had been named, were announced in Britain. The first UK death from Covid-19 was announced on March 5. World financial markets plunged on March 9. On March 26, a nationwide lockdown came into force in Britain.

Since the Brexit referendum in 2016, its chaotic aftermath had dominated the news agenda at *The Times*. Now suddenly this had been shunted aside by an almost unfathomable threat. For the next two years the newsroom dedicated itself almost entirely to reporting – and living with – the Covid-19 pandemic. Such was the dominance of the coronavirus story that between February 28 and June 13, 2020, there was only one day when the splash was not related to Covid-19. From mid-March headlines announced a series of grim milestones as the death toll steadily rose.

The Times office on the 11th floor of the News Building at London Bridge was almost empty. Only a few key volunteers came into the newsroom where light flooded through the floor-to-ceiling windows onto ranks of abandoned desks. Anyone entering the building put on a face covering and gave a floor number to a similarly masked and gloved security operative in the lobby, who pressed the lift button for the required destination. Outlines of footprints inside the lift invited passengers (only four at a time) to face into the corners. On arrival at the eleventh floor the usual swipe pass admitted staff to a one-way system. Meeting rooms were off limits. Hand sanitisers and disinfectant wipes were everywhere. At times cleaners outnumbered journalists.

Tony Gallagher, the former editor of *The Daily Telegraph* and *The Sun*, had become deputy editor of *The Times* when Emma Tucker moved to *The Sunday Times* at the end of January, just as the pandemic was taking off. He was frequently seen in the office, keeping morale high among the few others there. "Our lovely canteen staff keep us fed all day, and chocolate and crisp consumption appears to be on the rise," he said.

Staff who could work from home had to learn about videoconferencing, hangouts and data-sharing platforms. They met colleagues only as rows of heads and shoulders on a screen in virtual meetings or heard them as disembodied voices as the daily news conference went remote (with sound but no video). At the height of the pandemic at least two issues were produced with their respective duty editors and all other staff at home and not a single person in the office. Deadlines had to be brought forward to accommodate the new working pattern, which made life especially tricky for the subs, designers and graphics staff, Gallagher noted. "Their home kit is never going to be as fast as what we have here [in the office]," he said, "which makes it all the more impressive that they get the job done with an hour less to do it in. It's amazing really." Aside from the technical issues, there was also the challenge of setting up a home office. An invitation to staff to send in photos of their new workstations revealed some impressive creativity, incorporating coffee tables, deckchairs, two ironing boards and at least one cat. Josh Glancy, Washington correspondent for *The Sunday Times*, had several useful suggestions for tackling life outside the office: "Do . . . all the civilised things. Open your blinds, get dressed, shave, put make-up on. The first hour of working from home sets the tone for what comes next. If you roll downstairs and start eating cereal in your pyjamas, doom awaits."

A month or two into the crisis, John Witherow addressed his staff, most of them via their screens at home. Since Britain went into lockdown we have had to rethink almost everything about how we make the newspaper," he said. *The Times* had faced disruption before and had come through. When a bomb hit the paper's offices in September 1940, it had taken only 18 minutes to get the presses in the basement up and running again.

[More recently, terrorists had attacked] virtually on our doorstep, with significant upheaval but no interruption of production. On those occasions, however, disruption was finite and caused by a tangible threat. The real challenge in the present crisis, for us as for everyone else, has been the uncertainty. We've had to tackle the difficulties of remote working, restricted communications, earlier deadlines, without having any idea how long they might last.

In congratulating *The Times* on continuing to publish through the Blitz, Winston Churchill praised 'the resourcefulness and adaptability' of the paper's staff. Those same qualities have been much in evidence this time round. There are a dozen or so people in the office most days, safely social distancing in a space that would normally accommodate 400 or more. News conferences and editorial meetings are conducted via Google Hangouts, with editors phoning in. Writers file their copy from home, and designers, sub-editors and their colleagues work remotely to put it on to pages. Thanks to the enterprise and enthusiasm of everyone involved, it works astonishingly well. I'd like to think that readers will scarcely have been aware of the peculiar conditions in which their paper is being produced. It's important that we carry on. In troubled and uncertain times the job of the press is to provide clarity, understanding and knowledge and to hold those in power to account. Now, more than ever, we must do all we can to provide our readers with reporting and analysis they can trust.

Tom Whipple, the *Times* science editor, had moved out of London recently and was an enthusiast for working from home. Now that all his interviews had to be conducted by phone or FaceTime, his view was rather tempered by the fact that his house also had three children stuck in it. "What I have enjoyed about this crisis, though – and it's only a small silver lining given the wider tragedies – is that we have all had to come to accept the background noise of children. This idea, perpetuated by office culture, that people come without families is now untenable. I hope when this is over we have a rethink of how we once worked. But I also hope that my children get back to school soon."

Whipple, who had a maths degree from Cambridge, had started writing for *The Times* in 2006, specialising in offbeat stories about such things as anti-fart pants and punting in Tower Hamlets at the less salubrious end of Regent's Canal, for which he was bylined as punting correspondent. Now he led the daily pandemic coverage in *The Times*. He later recalled the moment when he realised for the first time what lay ahead.

> At a research conference, over a glass of wine with a Nobel-winning biologist, I asked him whether the press was over-egging this new virus. Were we scaring people unduly? He took a crisp from a nearby plate of nibbles and looked me directly in the eye. 'I've got a house in the country with a moat,' he said, 'and I'm stockpiling corned beef.' So it was that I truly began my [life] in Covid and the biggest story I will ever cover.

He not only reported every grim twist and turn of the unfolding story for the next two years but also produced a remarkable series of in-depth background pieces, serious and authoritative yet always lively and highly readable, in which he made accessible the often difficult science behind key developments and explained the challenges ahead. It was science communication at its best, "as engaging as the best thriller writing", in the words of the citation when Whipple won Science Journalist of the Year at the Press Awards in 2021. Roger Boyes, diplomatic editor, caught coronavirus early in the pandemic when doctors were struggling to fight the mystery illness and the death toll was rising. Notes written by NHS staff in a critical care patient diary while he was in the St Thomas' Hospital intensive care unit helped him to piece together the ten days he spent in a coma on a ventilator. The nurses in the unit were encouraged to keep the diary, he wrote, so that "when the patient wakes up he or she is left with something that can anchor their memories. If they don't, well, then they don't."

At the fag end of the night shift when backs were bowed with exhaustion, staff nurse Catherine Whitley had settled down to write him a letter.

> 'Dear Roger,' she wrote in a rounded schoolgirl script, 'unfortunately you came to us at handover tonight. You have got a nasty chest infection and you are being supported on one of our ventilators. You are being kept asleep with sedation so your lungs can rest. Apart from keeping you stable and giving you lots of medication I have given you

a little wash, cooled you down, brushed your teeth and documented and kept your property safe.'

Boyes recalled a succession of physical crises, a desperate shuttling between ventilators and the levels of sedation needed to keep the process going, of buying time with oxygen and feeding tubes and catheters while the virus was beaten off. "You're rarely the participant in this battle," he wrote, "merely the battlefield . . . I had never been a patient in a big city hospital before, was unfamiliar with the beeping of machines, the regular policing of blood pressure; the heavy traffic of healing. In the ward after nightfall grown men call out for their mothers . . ."

How does the psyche adjust to a succession of near-death moments, Boyes asked.

Coronavirus is a disease that does real cognitive damage and leaves survivors like me struggling to explain something that has hit them with the force of a truck. It should make us think again about the place of death in life, its random brutalities . . . John Donne talks of a 'preternatural birth in returning to life from this sickness'. All of us corona returnees should celebrate our escape, rejoice in the moment – but also think hard about what the hell has just happened to us (April 18, 2020).

For Steven Swinford, deputy political editor, who like other staff was working from home, "one of the most surreal moments that I've had as a reporter was during the pandemic". The date was Friday, November 4, 2020: "For some reason, in the pandemic, things always happened on Fridays," Swinford later told Times Radio's Matt Chorley.

I had been working on a story all day that Matt Hancock [the health secretary] was pushing for stronger, another lockdown, basically a second lockdown. But Boris Johnson was resisting . . . Sitting in the bedroom on my fold-out desk with my laptop, because that's what the pandemic was like, I was calling around as many people as I could, and something didn't smell right about the story. Something wasn't good and it just didn't chime correctly. And it got to 6 o'clock – and we have early copy deadlines on a Friday – and the editor started calling me and saying, 'You need to file your story now, Steve.' I said I just need a little bit more time. Something's not quite right with the story. 'Well, then we're going to go late off stone. You need to file your story.' I said, 'Hang on, John.' And then I managed to put in a few more calls and I discovered that there had been a secret meeting that afternoon between Boris Johnson, the then prime minister, and all the most senior cabinet ministers, and they had decided to put the UK into a second lockdown that was going to start the following week. And I sat there and I thought, 'This is utterly incendiary.' And I rang a few more people, managed to stand it up and to crash it into the paper for first edition that evening.

And I remember sitting there after doing this, and the adrenaline from that kind of reporting is quite an extraordinary thing as you are reporting on it. And I was just sitting there in my bedroom, on my fold-out desk, on my laptop, and just thinking this is absolutely extraordinary. We're going down to a lockdown. I remember going downstairs and saying to friends and family, so just so you know everyone, we're going into lockdown. And when the front page came out, when the story came out that evening, *The Times* was the first to break that story. And it actually accelerated the moves the government then had to do, because it was all true. The government had to bring forward a press conference to Saturday – Boris Johnson did a press conference on Saturday. Johnson told the nation: 'Christmas is going to be a little different this year . . .'.

All it was is reporting on what was happening. But at the same time, it's extraordinary sometimes the extent, the kind of influence, that reporting can have when you're just literally someone with a phone at a computer on a fold-out desk. And a lot of the pandemic was like that. We were finding out about things that would affect the lives of millions and millions of people very significantly, just literally on our own, in our bedrooms, doing our reporting because we couldn't go into work. And it just it really has stuck with me as one of the most surreal moments of my career.

He was promoted to political editor three months later.

While the pandemic dominated both the news pages and the lives of the staff charged with filling them, it was vital that the paper continued to report on issues that would still be important when Covid-19 was gone. In May 2019 *The Times* had launched a campaign demanding "Clean Air for All". It was calling for a new Clean Air Act to give everyone the right to be protected from the toxic air that contributed to an estimated 40,000 early deaths a year and particularly threatened the young, the elderly and people with lung conditions.

The government claimed to be tackling air pollution under a clean air strategy published in January but analysis of official projections revealed that almost 4,700 schools with 1.9 million pupils would still be over the limit by 2030. Leaders of Britain's doctors said that ministers were ignoring medical advice and doing the "minimum possible" on air pollution. The Royal College of Physicians and the Royal College of Paediatrics and Child Health said the government had focused on a "series of distractions" such as wood-burning stoves to avoid the real problem of traffic fumes.

The initial impetus for the campaign came from an exclusive investigation which showed that 6,500 schools educating 2.6 million children were in areas with dangerous levels of fine particles in the air. The total included 3,900 nursery and primary schools, where the younger children were most vulnerable to air pollution because their lungs were developing and their relative size meant that they were closer to low-lying exhaust emissions. Fine particles, known as PM2.5, were the most dangerous form of air pollution because their microscopic size allowed them to penetrate deep into the lungs and enter the bloodstream. Every school in London was over the World Health Organization's recommended limit of 10 microgrammes per cubic metre; in Birmingham 234 schools were over the limit and more than 100 in other large cities such as Nottingham and Leicester. One of London's most polluted schools, St Mary's Primary in Chiswick, had reduced outside playtime because of fumes from the six-lane A4, which carried 80,000 vehicles a day and was less than three metres from the playground.

A *Times* leading article said that Britain, which had cleaned up its pea-souper smogs with a landmark piece of legislation in 1956, should be a world leader in addressing the issue of clean air. Instead, as a UN environmental representative had told *The Times*, it had become a "laggard and a scofflaw". Frustrated by the government's foot-dragging, the paper was launching a manifesto for policymakers and planners, school teachers and parents. Britain urgently needed a new act of parliament giving everyone in the country a legal right to clean air. *The Times* set out a five-point manifesto majoring on a new Clean Air Act to replace the Act of 1956. The other points were a ban on sales of new diesel and petrol cars from 2030 and reversing the cut to green car grants; temporary traffic bans outside schools at drop-off and pick-up times; extending pay zones for pre-2010 diesel and pre-2000 petrol cars to other cities; and pollution monitors in every postcode.

In a unique experiment *The Times* provided portable pollution monitors to a dozen people with varying lifestyles and occupations. When analysed, the monitors showed that people who spend much of the day travelling in cars and lorries are exposed to far more air pollution than those who use other transport; a quieter cycle route to work could reduce pollution exposure by 90 per cent; London's deep Tube lines were far more polluted than those near the surface – passengers on the Victoria, Northern and Jubilee lines were exposed to up to four times more pollution than those on the Metropolitan, Circle and District lines; and scented candles in the home caused more exposure to pollution than standing beside a busy road.

All that was before the pandemic, which inadvertently demonstrated how quickly air pollution could dissipate. By mid-2020 the City was visibly less polluted because its streets were almost emptied of traffic and people during the first three-month lockdown imposed by the government. Throughout the country, one of the most memorable aspects of the period – apart from the tragically high death toll from Covid-19 – was the clean air that resulted from people staying close to home while their movement was curtailed by the three national lockdowns and other curbs imposed by the government. It was evidence of what could be achieved permanently if lower pollution targets were hit by less draconian restrictions.

In the course of 2021, as Britain emerged from the Covid-19 crisis with a greater awareness of the relationship between health and environment, *The Times* built on the Clean Air for All campaign to broaden its coverage and help readers to play their part in reducing the UK's carbon emissions. A new digital hub was created where they could find all news about the planet, climate change and sustainability, including problems, initiatives and solutions. Times 2 ran a series headed by Lucy Siegle, a journalist specialising in ethical living and environmental issues. The theme of her first piece was "start at home". A spread suggested tracking your own carbon footprint: the average per person in the UK was 12.7 tonnes of CO_2 a year, or the equivalent of eating a thousand beef steaks. Remedial steps included turning down thermostats, changing light bulbs, reducing deliveries and growing your own vegetables. Special supplements looked at the future of energy and of transport (June, July 2021). Another looked at the ways in which businesses were responding to the challenge of climate change. An eight-page supplement on Green Food featured Siegle again, with recommended green restaurants and tips to find them. Greener approaches to property and personal finance were explored in further supplements. A 32-page pullout was produced for COP26, the UN climate change conference held in Glasgow that November. For Witherow the important thing about this increased coverage of climate change and the environment was it should be constructive. There was no merit or mileage in instructing *Times* readers to put on hair shirts or terrifying them with apocalyptic tales of flood and drought. The focus should be on solutions: what governments, businesses and individuals could do (and were doing) to bring about change. This reflected an approach that had become increasingly important to Witherow. Encouraged by Emma Tucker and the digital team, he had grown steadily more interested in what had become known as constructive journalism. Witherow explained:

> Journalists often have a story that's 80 per cent positive, say, and 20 per cent negative, and the knee-jerk reaction of a journalist, probably including me at one stage, is you go for the negative because it gives you a better headline. But, in fact, the story is generally positive, and we want to turn that around and make news reflect the world more accurately because the world is getting better, people are living longer.

Disease is in retreat, violence is down over the decades . . .
If you read the newspapers, you think everything is worse.
It's not, and we want to change that direction.

To that end, he called in Ulrik Haagerup, founder and
CEO of the Constructive Institute, to address the newsroom.
Haagerup was formerly executive director of news at the Danish
Broadcasting Corporation, Denmark's public service broadcaster.
His mission was now to change the global news culture and
promote constructive journalism in response to what he saw as an
increased negativity bias of the news media. It aimed to provide
audiences with a fair, accurate and contextualised picture of
the world, without overemphasising the negative. Constructive
journalism, Haagerup explained, complemented breaking news
and investigative journalism. "Breaking news is about today,
investigative journalism [about] yesterday and constructive
journalism about tomorrow. Constructive journalism is about
inspiring readers, it asks the questions what now? and how? It
provides solutions and best practice." The approach found fruitful
application at *The Times* in the field of education. The pandemic
had placed the education system under severe strain because of the
temporary closure of schools, but it also presented an unparalleled
opportunity for change. *The Times* Education Commission was
established at the suggestion of Sir Anthony Seldon, former
headmaster of Wellington and vice-chancellor of the University of
Buckingham. Seldon said: "We still have a factory-depersonalised
model of education which is not satisfying employers, not
satisfying universities, not turning out young people capable of
adjusting and living harmoniously in the world today. It's failing
a third of our young children who are deemed a failure by the
system, which is totally disgraceful."

Chaired by the *Times* columnist Rachel Sylvester, the
commission was launched on May 24, 2021. Its members were
experts in education, business, science and technology, the arts and
politics. Bringing together a wide-ranging team of experts, it would
sit for a year and examine every aspect of education in Britain and
around the world with a view to proposing radical reform. A leader
explained that a final report would be published in June 2022 after
investigating the future of education in the context not only of the
disruption suffered by schools and colleges over the past year,
but also of changes in technology, society and work that would

ensure the education system produced the skilled and adaptable workforce that Britain needs. There were to be fortnightly evidence sessions, with witnesses including leading figures from the worlds of business, science, culture and the arts, as well as politics and education.

A year later the commission's 96-page final report proposed a 12-point plan for education, building on best practice around the world, including proposals for a British Baccalaureate; an "electives premium" for schools to be spent on activities such as drama, music and sport; a significant boost to early years funding; a laptop or tablet for every child; and a greater focus on well-being in school. Within days of the report being published, Nadhim Zahawi, the education secretary at the time, had backed the commission's proposal for an army of undergraduate tutors to help pupils who had fallen behind to catch up, and several other ideas had won cross-party support.

CHAPTER TWENTY-FOUR

The Covid-19 pandemic highlighted the need for two developments that were already well underway when it began: more sharing of editorial resources between *The Times* and *Sunday Times*, and a greater emphasis on digital publishing. Those developments went hand in hand. Print circulations across the newspaper industry had long been in steady and irreversible decline.

Future growth in readership would be digital. The two *Times* titles shared a website, and as they moved more purposefully towards digital-first publication there would be clear economies of scale in integrating departments to remove duplications and facilitate more continuous publication through the week. It had been a long haul since *The Times* first "went digital" on January 1, 1996, when a paragraph on page 1 announced that "*The Times* is available from today on the internet, the worldwide system of interlinked computers". On page 4 a down-page story by the technology correspondent explained that the paper would be available to read on a personal computer around the world for the price of a local telephone call. A leader set out the paper's hopes for the new format: "We expect that those with the choice of an electronic or printed edition will long prefer the more familiar form. But for readers who live or work abroad the impact can be immediate. And for the benefit of those closer to home we are determined that the heart of *The Times* should be as rapidly instantiated in the new electronic media as it has always been in other great technical changes of the past."

In 2004, News International had spent close to one billion dollars on the new printing plants at Broxbourne, Knowsley and Glasgow. Graham Stewart's volume 7 of *The History of The Times*, published in 2005, devoted fewer than four pages to digital operations. That was also the year, however, that, in a speech to the American Society of Newspaper Editors, Rupert Murdoch warned that the newspaper industry would be "relegated to the status of also-rans" unless it woke up to change. "I venture to say that not one of the newspapers represented in this room lacks a website," he said. "Yet how many of us can honestly say that we are taking maximum advantage of those websites to serve our readers, to strengthen our businesses, or to meet head-on what readers increasingly say is important to them in receiving their news?" Murdoch's response to his own question was the introduction of an online paywall in 2010 on what was by then the joint *Times* and *Sunday Times* website. Charging for access to online news ran counter to the prevailing media zeitgeist that "information wants to be free". The decision was slammed by media pundits – The *Guardian* columnist Jeff Jarvis said it was "simply insane". They would be proved wrong. Journalists steeped in print traditions but quick to adapt were picked to manage the shift to digital dominance. Alan Hunter, a genial giant and Oxford swimming blue, was picked in 2013 to lead the transformation as cross-title head of digital. He had been with *The Sunday Times* for 12 years, latterly as executive managing editor, but when he was offered his new role by Witherow and Martin Ivens, the *Sunday Times* editor, he told them that he didn't really know very much about digital. They replied that he was a good journalist, which was the main thing. "It became very quickly apparent to me that I had to learn a lot from my team," he recalled.

Witherow told an interviewer in 2017 that it had been a very slow, tough battle to get digital subscriptions working, but gradually the world of newspaper media was moving towards paywalls. *The Wall Street Journal, The New York Times, The Financial Times*, and *The Economist* were all subscription models by then, and *The Telegraph* was partial subscription. *The Guardian* was holding out but asking for donations from readers to fund its journalism, or as Witherow put it:

> *The Guardian*'s begging: at some stage they'll have to face up to it and just start charging, and that's a good thing. One of the reasons that we can maintain good journalism is that we're charging for content online. There's so much free content out there the only way you can get people to pay is if you have different and, we hope, better content. So it's a virtuous circle. It's a merit of the policy we've been pursuing for seven years now of charging online. We believe this is the only way you are going to sustain newspapers in the future.

Two years later, in a 2019 lecture to the Society of Editors, Witherow spoke of the most challenging environment newspapers had ever confronted and of the breathtaking digital disruption facing newsrooms. What subscribers still wanted, he said, was distinctive comment, analysis, exclusives and investigations. But while print had served the industry well, younger people were coming to *The Times* through search engines, with no knowledge of the print edition. In that context the language of "a splash" or "a quirky page 3 story" had no meaning. They all still had to be good stories, but they had to survive on their own, untethered from their position in the print edition. He said:

> The good news for *The Times* is that, in the quest for new audiences, we do not have to fundamentally change who and what we are. We just need to remember that the only thing that will survive the revolution will be quality. And that we must adapt to the new technology, to make it our friend, to put it at the service of our journalism. One of the most invigorating things about journalism is that no two days are ever the same [. . .] There is a clue in the word 'news'. We have a privileged vantage point as stories unfold. It is the prospect of change that keeps us interested, keeps us honest. I feel the same about the way the industry is changing as I do about the daily news cycle . . . It's still an exciting place to be. It always will be.

Edward Roussel succeeded Hunter as head of digital in 2021. He too came from a journalistic rather than technological background. He had spent 11 years with Bloomberg as bureau chief in London, Paris and Brussels, and had been chief innovation officer with Dow Jones in New York when he was invited to London in March 2021 to assess Times Online by Witherow and Tucker, who was by then driving digital transformation as editor of *The Sunday Times*. He submitted reports on the newsroom and budgets to the two editors and asked them to let him know if these resonated with them, failing which he would stay in New York. Within two months he was back in London. His brief could be gleaned from a speech that Tucker had made to the International News Media Association at the beginning of the year. Journalists, she said, now had to have more skills than simply being able to write a news story: "Today's journalists must know video and multimedia storytelling, SEO, data, etc. There's a lot more responsibility lying on one person's shoulders." At *The Times* and *Sunday Times*, she said, staff were no longer divided into print and digital journalists. "Everybody does everything, for all the platforms. We don't set individual targets, but we do expect them to be . . . across the data and I talk to them endlessly about engagement. What I'm always saying to the newsroom is, you concentrate on keeping the subscribers happy, and let marketing chase after the subscriptions."

Smart publishers, in Tucker's view, were asking several key questions: "Are you commissioning the right kind of content for the audiences you want and are they coming in, liking what they see and staying? Are you looking at what the data is telling us about how people read stuff, when they read it, how they read it, what they like to read and are you using that information to inform what you commission?"

Winning the hearts and minds of print journalists to embrace digital involved starting to talk about this data.

> You need to start giving regular data feedback; you need to show those print journalists that you're looking at the data to see how successful their journalism is. Getting people used to the idea that if they play their cards right, if they listen to the digital teams, if they think about social and search, then a piece that might once have just been read by your print readers could end up going all over the world. Every journalist likes to think they're being read.

Roussel started work at the News Building on May 17, 2021, the day the government lifted pandemic restrictions in England. He had just spent a week quarantining in a cramped Notting Hill bedsit after his arrival from New York. With many people still working from home, he was unsure if he would meet anyone he knew on day one of the new job.. But as he exited the lift in the News Building, there was the familiar face of *Times* star political reporter Matt Chorley, who had recently moved into broadcast journalism working for Times Radio, launched in the throes of the pandemic. "So you're here to run the paramilitary wing," Chorley said, deadpan.

Roussel inherited the digital editorial team of *The Times* and *Sunday Times*. It was a skilled group of specialists ranging from video to data graphics, search and social media, but he found that it seemed to operate in a parallel world to the news desk, the beating heart of *The Times*. There seemed to be a cultural chasm between digital and print journalists. While the news desk was focused on the core journalism for the daily output in print and the website, the digital team was more interested in long-range projects, such as graphics-driven features or video documentaries.

In Roussel's view, *The Times* had got more things right than wrong in the transition to the digital era. It had never lost sight of its purpose to publish well-reported, factual journalism that was informative and entertaining. It had always believed in editors and editing, when rivals including *The Telegraph* were experimenting with publishing reporters' copy straight to the web. Under Hunter's direction, *The Times* had also stood out from the crowded media market by focusing on fewer stories, better told. Most journalists believe that readers will love you more, the more stories you write. Hunter's insight was that readers wanted constraints. In print, the constraints imposed by column inches were clear. Creating constraints digitally required more discipline: the endless scroll of a web page had done away with word-count limits. And the vertical swipe on the home screen of a phone could produce an endless list of story options, leaving readers feeling defeated by information overload. Hunter had imposed story limits and reduced the publishing times to four in a 24-hour cycle, at 9am, noon, 5pm and midnight, a so-called "edition" model. Roussel's first radical decision, however, was to retire the concept of "edition-based publishing". In his view, a shift towards "live news" coverage, combined with a growing number of overseas subscribers, accounting for 20 per cent of the total, highlighted the need to be able to respond to news that readers cared about at any time of the day or night, seven days a week, anywhere in the world.

The primary focus was on a different, more innovative approach to storytelling. This meant focusing on three trends. One was visual journalism. "In the era of Instagram," Roussel explained, "readers of all ages – and particularly younger readers – are increasingly drawn to visual stories. For *The Times*, this means excelling at some combination of graphics, photography and video as a key component for any big story." Another was reader interaction. "Social media has conditioned readers to take an active interest in stories – literally. *The Times*'s own data shows that reader comments topped 20,000 posts daily in 2022, while one in five readers take part in opinion polls gauging their views on everything from politics to how to respond to the threat of war." The third trend was "live" journalism.

Two thirds of digital subscribers use mobile phones to access *Times* journalism. This has created an expectation that big stories will be covered as they unfold, with an average Briton looking at his or her phone more than 100 times a day. When we surveyed readers, we found that 74 per cent wanted big stories covered in a timely manner. No media organisation in the Twitter era can claim to be first with a news story that isn't an exclusive. But being able to update readers as events unfold – be it war in Ukraine or a political crisis in the UK – had to become part of the *Times* journalistic arsenal. Hence the launch of two new newsroom tools: a 'live article page' that can be updated with key developments in real time, and breaking news notifications – to be used sparingly for major news and story exclusives only.

Greater focus on "intraday" reporting, enriched by visual journalism, had a big impact on the newsroom, including how stories were commissioned, edited and published throughout the 24-hour cycle. To accommodate the changes, *The Times* launched in September 2021 a new digital commissioning hub, bringing together all the critical skills needed to cover stories throughout the day. A commissioning editor was flanked by specialists in search engine optimisation, social media, data journalism, audience engagement, graphics, video, photography and the sub-editors who pulled it all together.

The early results were promising, with audience levels rising in five of the next six months, and an increase in reader engagement, with the majority of digital subscribers returning daily. Revenue in the year to the end of June 2021 rose 5 per cent to £327 million, and profits tripled, as the growth in digital revenue more than offset a decline in print. In 2022, *The Times* broke through 400,000 digital-only subscribers after adding a net 60,000 in the previous 12 months. The financial strength opened the way once more for newsroom expansion, and the *Times* newsroom opened 50 new positions.

Roussel commissioned a monthly digital performance report, which quantified reach and audience engagement, listed the most read stories and dominant themes and reported on new subscriptions. It was not a question of allowing data to replace old-fashioned news judgment, he insisted, but of using one to inform the other. This demanded a whole new approach.

Paradoxically, the other hugely successful innovation at *The Times* during the pandemic involved a medium that had been around for more than a century. "Good morning and welcome to a new voice in British radio" were the first words spoken on Times Radio as Aasmah Mir launched the digital speech station at 6am on Monday, June 29, 2020. It was the first time that a British newspaper group had started a current affairs radio station. A leader in *The Times* pointed out: "In times of national ferment, exemplified by Brexit and Covid-19, hard news leavened by the art of conversation can help to make sense of the whole. Times Radio is ready to provide it."

Chris Longcroft, then chief financial officer of News UK and later publisher of *The Times* and *Sunday Times*, explained that Times Radio grew out of the purchase four years earlier of the Wireless Group, a Belfast-based broadcaster that News had relocated to London. "We'd bought Wireless in 2016," he said, "primarily for Talksport, which was complimentary to *The Sun*. We realised it was similar but different to *The Sun*, and both brands could benefit from the collaboration. We saw it was a repeatable business model, and we had the studio capability, radio could be part of the marketing mix for *The Times*, a free product as a taster. We were spending £5–6 million on external marketing with Classic FM and ITV. We decided to shut that off and start Times Radio."

Longcroft compared this to the former marketing practice of distributing "bulks", free sample copies of the print edition. "Sampling *The Times* is difficult," Longcroft said. "Twenty years ago you could read a free copy in a hotel, a train, a library, a university union. Such bulks don't make economic sense in this day and age. Times Radio is a digital bulk."

It soon proved to be more than an effective marketing device for the newspaper. Staff were proud of it and journalists presenting or guesting on the shows broadened their skillsets, learning to tell stories, inform and entertain in different ways – and promoting their own stories. Roger Mosey, a former BBC editorial director, applauded the "investment in intelligent speech radio". In 2021 Rajar, the official body in charge of measuring radio audiences in the UK, produced its first report since the pandemic struck. Times Radio had 637,000 weekly listeners tuning in for an accumulated 3.5 million hours or an average of 5.5 hours. Tim Levell, the station's programme director, said the figures exceeded expectations and surpassed the weekly reach of 450,000 for TalkRadio, the more established speech station run by News UK's Wireless Group (October 29, 2021).

All of these developments – from Witherow's initial cost-cutting at *The Times* to the move to digital-first and the launch of Times Radio – were associated with a transformation in financial performance. Longcroft saw Witherow's move from editing the more commercially minded and viable *Sunday Times* to editing the daily *Times* in 2013 as a key factor in this. Longcroft said:

> Profitability coincided with John making *The Times* a more attractive proposition to more people. It's not for the corporate side to dictate content, it's church and state, but certainly previous editors had been more traditional and more wary. John accepted there was no future for *The Times* if it wasn't profitable. He wasn't afraid to take a commercial view. He also saw there was still a layer of people in the newsroom who didn't need to be there. Productivity and efficiency went up after he arrived.

Between 2002 and 2013 inclusive, Times Newspapers Ltd had made a total net loss of £505 million, roughly £40 million a year. "Revenues went up and down," said Longcroft, "advertising went up and down, the cost of newsprint varied, there was a recession, but the only constant was making a loss." From 2013 onwards, however, Times Newspapers was making a profit – and by the end of Witherow's tenure at *The Times* in 2022, record profits driven by strong growth in digital subscriptions and advertising revenue. Pre-tax profit rose by 229 per cent to £34 million in the year to June 27 2022, up from £10.4 million the year before.

The Times had made a loss throughout most of its history, propped up by wealthy proprietors and then, in recent decades under Rupert Murdoch's ownership, by a subsidy first from *The Sunday Times* and latterly from *The Sun*, a very profitable business. Many employees, both in editorial and on the corporate floors, were resigned to working for a loss-making newspaper. Some staff, indeed, maintained a certain gallows-pride in doing so. Moreover, this was a period of huge disruption right across the newspaper industry with print circulations declining and managements struggling to shift their focus from newsprint to the challenges of digital publishing.

When, in 2010, Project Walter (named after the first editor of *The Times*, John Walter) was outlined to the News Corp board as a plan to make *The Times* profitable, one senior executive, over from New York to hear the presentation, laughed so hard he reportedly fell off his chair. The ridicule was understandable: the paper had sustained a record loss of almost £90 million in 2009. "Not many people would have allowed *The Times* to continue to exist having racked up such immense losses," said Longcroft. "It's a testament to Rupert's love of journalism."

There were other, more traditional, restraints on profitability. The after-effects of the recession triggered by the 2008–9 global financial crisis were still being felt. Plus, in 2011, *The News of the World* was closed down. It had not been hugely profitable but it had soaked up a huge amount of overheads, which afterwards had to be spread across three titles rather than four. Yet by 2022, with 430,000 digital subscribers, *The Times* had arrived at scale. Businesses were all about scale, or allocating costs over as many units sold as possible. "You begin to see a return on investment. You begin to see profit and the opportunity to reinvest," said Longcroft.

How did the transformation come about? Partly by traditional means: working to ensure revenue outstripped costs. The biggest cost was labour; even the most militant hacks recognised the *Times* newsroom was overstaffed. The headcount was nowhere near as high in 1981 when Harry Evans, newly arrived from *The Sunday Times*, failed to sack one notoriously indolent specialist because the culprit could never be found in order to be fired. There were culls later in the 1980s and 1990s, but still, in 2002, some reporters, writers and critics were seriously underemployed. One veteran recalled that one year he published 19 articles in *The Times*: "They were long articles, but even so . . ." Twenty years on, he averaged five bylines a week, albeit most of them on somewhat shorter pieces.

As for expenses, at the start of the 21st century, first-class rail travel and, for some big names, first-class air travel, was still standard. Entertainment allowances were generous, interpreted very broadly and then only cursorily checked before being signed off. Many well-paid executives departed their Wapping cubbyholes not long after noon, hailed a black cab back to their former watering holes in Fleet St, and returned well-refreshed after 3pm, the whole business paid for by their employer. By 2022 such jollies had stopped, partly because the drinking culture had evaporated, mostly because everyone was too busy to indulge.

Savings were not just found in the editorial workforce. Right across the board – in marketing, admin, printing and advertising – numbers were steadily reduced through the first two decades of the century. The secretary fetching a coffee for her boss was by 2022 almost a thing of the past. The process was greatly helped by rationalisation between the back offices of the daily and Sunday papers. Duplication of executive and clerical roles was steadily phased out and, gradually, the editorial side began the long transition towards a seven-day operation.

The second huge driver on the journey towards profitability was the decision to impose an online paywall in 2010. Until then, in common with almost all other newspapers worldwide, *The Times* and *Sunday Times* had been giving away their digital content, such as it was, for nothing. Indeed, the digital platform had been not only free but largely unimagined as an alternative to print, let alone its successor. There was no advertising market for online news content. Even when one gradually developed, agency fees meant the paper received a far smaller slice of the spend than it did for a print display. Print advertising remained a remarkably efficient proprietary mechanism for focusing millions of eyeballs on a company's products. With a circulation of around 700,000 for *The Times* and around 1.1 million for *The Sunday Times*, News International had considerable leverage over price with wholesalers, print suppliers and advertisers alike. A less innovative company might have been prepared to rest on its laurels, hoping the challenge of new technology would somehow fizzle out.

"At that stage," said Longcroft, "intuitively you would have said 'focus your resources on print, because print is making money, and digital is losing it'. But we didn't because we knew that [attitude] was the past." Had the company ignored the shift to digital news, pretty soon someone else would have stepped in and, once the newcomer had got it right, news would have gone the same way as many local newspapers did. "If we hadn't deliberately and consciously started to cannibalise ourselves, someone else would have and we wouldn't have had a business."

Thanks to excellent journalism, sales of both papers held up rather better than did rivals, yet the decline was inexorable. That was reflected in reduced print advertising revenue, declining ever since 2007. The average age of a reader buying *The Times* print edition in 2010 was about 51. It increased by a year with every following year. Readers bought fewer copies – perhaps three rather than four or five each week. The move to an online subscription model felt like a giant gamble. "No one knew if readers would be prepared to pay for content," said Longcroft. It gave rise to "reams of articles saying 'this is the death of *The Times*!'" There was stiff competition for reliable news and comment from the BBC, which employed as many journalists as the whole of Fleet Street put together and had ramped up its free online reporting offer. Mail Online also emerged as a competitor. *The Times* could not compete with the resources of the BBC nor did it want to tread the breathlessly populist route followed by the Mail. "We had to steel ourselves and state very clearly that our content was worth paying for," said Longcroft.

Predictably, numbers accessing the website dropped off dramatically following the imposition of a subscription fee, even one as affordable as the initial £2 a month. It was an anxious time, but also exciting. A 225-year-old business was seeking to reinvent itself, and even tiny incremental successes such as the acquisition of 50 or 100 new subscribers in a day were greeted triumphantly by management. One enormous game-changer was the advent of the iPad edition. Previously, online content had only been accessible on a website via a laptop or desktop computer. Now, as Longcroft pointed out, "You could carry a digital device and keep a newspaper stored on it. You didn't have to be connected to the internet." The iPad edition also swiftly surpassed the design excellence of the print edition in a way the website had yet to do. The development and refinement of a dedicated app for mobile phones in 2013, a platform with which customers had previously struggled, persuaded another tranche of subscribers to sign on the dotted line.

Still, there was a long way to go to scale. In 2010, the initial costs of customer management, access control, data collection, financial organisation and a nascent advertising effort meant there was no scale. When the huge start-up costs of the new digital platforms combined with the tiny numbers of initial subscribers, the marginal cost of each unit of product was enormous. "The costs of the first paid-for digital newspaper were extravagant," Longcroft said with a degree of deliberate understatement. Designing, filling, curating and maintaining a website accessed by one person cost the same as one accessed by a million. "The first subscriber bears all the costs. After that each new subscriber brings the marginal cost down, at first dramatically, until you get scale. That's what business is all about. That's why *The Sun* is such a spectacular success," said Longcroft.

"Rupert says newspapers are a pennies business," he continued. "You get small amounts from lots of people. That's *The Sun*'s model. It doesn't work quite the same for *The Times* – we don't like using the word but it is a niche product, not a mainstream product. Only a certain number of people will have affinity with the content. But people who value that content have understood that to get it you have to pay for it." Some readers – Longcroft cited his own father-in-law – would not make the transition from print, however cheap a digital sub, however much the various apps continued to improve across platforms. "We've realised some people are just committed to staying with print, and that's fine."

The next step on the path to scale was to experiment with subscriptions. As of 2013, online readers were asked to pay more while print readers paid less, although online remained considerably cheaper than print. "We discounted the price of a seven-day print subscription to £5 when it was £9 on the newsstand. We were going for long-term loyalty over short-term cover price revenue. Our digital subscription reinforced that same habit but we had to experiment, we had to find out how much the consumer was willing to pay. We wanted to get to what we called 'the point of indifference', where we didn't mind whether someone bought us in print or digital. The only way to get to that was to take the price of a digital sub from £2 to £4 to £6 per month, which we did in nine months." Steady online growth continued. When digital subscriptions hit 430,000 in 2022, Longcroft raised his target to at least one million. Was that realistic? "As a way point, yes," responded Longcroft bullishly. "*The New York Times* has eight million subscribers in a country 4.5 bigger than ours. Arguably we should be above two million. We'll see. The digital product certainly keeps on getting better."

As digital grew, so print continued to decline; yet with the pressure off the old technology to maximise gross sales, so paradoxically a degree of stability was brought to the venerable platform through price rises that loyal print subscribers seemed willing to shrug off. "As we've lost scale in print," said Longcroft, "and the ad market erodes, we've accepted that we maintain revenues by increasing the price as volumes decline. It means we can map out the pricing in a more scientific way, as opposed to just doing it haphazardly or when Rupert says we can." He predicted that the print version of *The Times* would, over time, become, if not a premium product, then certainly one priced as a niche product for those who do not want to make the change to digital. Another factor in the financial success of Times News Limited after 2013 was the vital matter of an organisation simply getting better at doing something through the experience of doing it. Just as print journalists over the past decade had learnt to be online bloggers, videographers, broadcasters and photographers, their colleagues in finance and administration had learnt new skills too. "We had to professionalise ourselves delivering a new business model," Longcroft pointed out. Thanks in part to "stealing a lot of people from Sky", which had pioneered subscription television in Britain, executives learnt quickly about such things as cost per acquisition and lifetime value. The subscription business was about data, which was accumulated in-house or bought in as appropriate. "You can quantify everything," said Longcroft. Whereas back in 2002, marketing was the equivalent of firing grapeshot via an 19th-century cannon and hoping some of it hit the target, seeking out new customers 20 years later could be done with laser-like precision. "We know if it's worth contacting this demographic with this offer at this time of day to give us the best chance of a long-term subscription," said Longcroft. "It's no use calling someone with kids at 8am. We can be incredibly precise about how and when we approach customers. The days of the billboard on the motorway are long gone." Much effort was expended on dedicated training at call centres, what script to follow if someone rings to cancel and so forth. "We've had to learn a lot of human science."

That process of refining data, and in time possibly differentiating the product, continued. Would subscribers pay more if they got more? Would new subscribers be tempted if they were to pay less to get less? What were the dangers of thus unbundling the product? Would new customers be attracted by cheaper offers to receive content on just one device? That they were then, perhaps, prevented from sharing? To what extent would people who paid less initially build an affinity to the brand so they were willing to pay more later? "We're about making marginal gains," said Longcroft.

"There wasn't one thing we corrected to start to become profitable. There were lots, and there will be many more in the future."

For Jeremy Griffin, executive editor, profitability was providing great benefits to his news operation:

> This revenue, combined with the position of *The Times* as a truly global brand, has encouraged greater imagination and investment into our storytelling capabilities. That has to be a good thing for journalists. Look at all the different ways in which we can tell our stories: words, video, radio, social media, events – far from being limited to page leads and the occasional splash, reporters can lead our digital platforms, have the story in the next day's paper, talk about it on our own radio station and promote (or even construct a different version of it) on TikTok, Instagram, X and elsewhere. So, as someone who ran *The Times* online news operation in 2008–09, when it was quite often seen as an encumbrance by those resistant to change, I'm very optimistic about the future of the newsroom. Through our new ways of telling stories, we are never off deadline! And that makes us all sharper.

A further significant breakthrough came in November 2021 when, 40 years after Murdoch had bought the two *Times* titles, News UK was formally released by the government from the undertakings that he gave in 1981 to keep the two titles separate. This resolved a long-running grievance, with important financial consequences for the company. Witherow and Tucker reassured staff that "editorial independence continues and is enshrined in the editors' contracts. *The Times* and *The Sunday Times* remain as separate newspapers and there are no plans to merge the titles."

CHAPTER TWENTY-FIVE

What nobody realised was the extent to which the transformed, financially profitable, digital-first, 24/7 operation on the 11th floor of the News UK building would be tested by the extraordinary events of 2022, the year of three prime ministers, two monarchs, a war in Europe and, as it happens, two editors of *The Times*.

The first challenge came with the Russian invasion of Ukraine on February 24. The *Times* foreign desk stepped up, combining first-hand accounts from correspondents on the ground with expert analysis of what was happening and what it meant. Times Radio also showed its value. "At one point we were able to boast of seven foreign correspondents covering the story, each of them bringing a distinctive voice and authority to *Times* journalism, often talking down the line from bomb shelters, live on Times Radio," said Jeremy Griffin.

Digital-first publication brought a new intensity to all this. Dramatic words and pictures from the front line were in London and ready for publication within minutes, with stories on the paper's digital platforms updated throughout the day. The result was an immediacy unimaginable to reporters covering previous major conflicts. There was always someone, somewhere, at home or in the office, working on the *Times* war coverage, whether it was handling breaking news or preparing overnight copy that would be fresh as soon as readers in Britain were awake. This forced the issue on the hiring of editors and sub-editors who could oversee the website throughout the 24-hour cycle, seven days a week.

During the last major war in Europe, the Yugoslav Wars of the 1990s, video had been dominated by major media and heavy camera equipment that was lugged from one location to another. The result was that there were few images from many of the hot spots such as the persecution of Kosovo Albanians. The most memorable videos from the Ukraine war, by contrast, were shot on mobile phones, car dashcams or CCTV. With this abundance came a new challenge: how to check the veracity of each video, and how to stitch disparate videos together into a coherent package. The Ukraine war also brought to the fore a new form of media footage: satellite imagery from companies such as Maxar Technologies and Planet Labs. This proved critical in terms of validating the build-up of weapons before the war, undermining Russia's claim of peaceful intentions.

Data graphics had come into their own in newsrooms across the world during the Covid-19 crisis, when readers became accustomed to tracking healthcare data in their local areas, nations and across the globe. This nascent skill set proved critical during the Ukraine war in ways including mapping Russia's advance, comparing weaponry and tracking fatalities. As with citizen video, the sourcing of data proved critical and journalists relied on independent groups, such as the Institute for the Study of War and the Centre for Information Resilience. Readers' comments peaked above 25,000 during the early days of the Ukraine crisis, and as many as one in four readers took part in e-polls. That prompted the newsroom to innovate with other ways of engaging readers, including digital Q&As with readers and expert writers, such as Larissa Brown, *Times* defence editor, and Maxim Tucker, a foreign correspondent who had recently lived in Kyiv. Ukraine dominated the news for a month, but the Partygate scandal over lockdown-breaching parties at 10 Downing Street during the pandemic was fast overtaking it. For the political editor Steven Swinford, 2022 became a year he would never forget. Looking back on this time in an interview with Matt Chorley of Times Radio, he gave an insight into how much politics – and the reporting of it – had changed. It was "the most incredible period in politics of political violence". His biggest shock had been to realise that the lobby, the political editors who by tradition attended confidential briefings in No 10, was being fed a series of lies. Swinford said that Francis Elliott, his predecessor, had once told him that "the great thing about *The Times*, Steve, is you get to tell the truth". Swinford saw his job as "to give readers a ringside seat on events without fear or favour and literally just tell them what is happening". He discovered, however, that "the truth" was an alien concept in Johnson's 10 Downing Street.

> One of the most interesting things from my perspective about covering that period is the total erosion of trust in No 10 [. . .] it relies on trust. It relies on when it says something is not true, that people report that. But because things had happened and it was issuing very firm denials that there had been any parties, that there had been any issues in No 10 at all, it just became apparent that these were lies,

that there were real issues with what was emanating from the building in No 10. And there was almost during Boris Johnson's premiership a total breakdown in trust between the lobby and No 10."

Chorley pointed out: "Lots of people will say that politicians have always lied, but there has been this sort of agreement, this unspoken rule between special advisers and ministers and the press – journalists – that you don't lie. They might obfuscate, they might not return your calls, but you don't tell straightforward lies. And that was quite a breach, wasn't it, in that unwritten rule?" Swinford agreed:

It was a huge breach of that unwritten rule. And for a lot of Boris Johnson's premiership and the aftermath of it we have been in a debate about what is a lie, what is misleading, is it intentional, is it unintentional, is it knowing, is it not knowing? But either way, you ended up in a situation where effectively the lines from No 10 were just untenable and unsustainable; and that went right to the top ultimately, because you had the prime minister standing up in the Commons, Boris Johnson, saying that there were no parties and there were no events that happened in No 10, and these lines turned out to be wrong.

So how did he get to the truth of what was going on? Swinford explained:

One of the misconceptions about politics is it's all about the principles, it's all about the kind of big figures, the leaders, the cabinet ministers. It's not. Westminster is a kind of interconnected spider's web, almost, of lots of people, and many of them are very small players. People won't know the names, they won't know who they are. And occasionally you find someone and they know everything and they're really interested in it and they know the whole wider picture. And so often the very biggest, some of the very biggest, stories that I have broken have come from people who are minnows . . . No one knows their names. But that's the point: the people that know what's going on in the rooms of power and where things are happening are much lower down the food chain than you think. And it's a lot of those people that are relatively anonymous that are incredibly useful to me and always have been. That's not to say that the cabinet ministers and all the other players aren't important, but it's a much broader network than people think.

As No 10's lies were exposed and ministers deserted Johnson en masse, Swinford said, the infighting became deeply personal. A "senior ally" of the prime minister briefed him that "that snake" Michael Gove, the leading cabinet minister and fellow Brexiteer who had stymied Johnson's first attempt to be prime minister in 2016, was now knifing him again. Johnson resigned on July 7, but emotions remained so high that a few days later Swinford saw two Gove and Johnson aides, Josh Grimstone and Guto Harri, nearly come to blows at *The Spectator*'s summer garden party. He recalled that "literally they physically squared up to each other in the garden. The violence, the political violence nearly ended in fisticuffs in front of me and several other journalists at this very serene, cerebral event. So it was just – there was a kind of undercurrent of violence throughout it all that even in its dying days was still there."

Also present at the garden party were Liz Truss and Rishi Sunak, the leading candidates to succeed Johnson as Tory party leader and prime minister. Truss won the leadership election among party members that summer and entered 10 Downing Street on September 6 for what would be the shortest and possibly most tumultuous premiership in recent British history.

At the *Times* office on September 8, the focus in the morning editorial conference was on an announcement Truss was due to make in parliament on an "energy price cap" to keep down the cost of household heating that had shot up because of the effect of the Ukraine war on gas prices. Jeremy Griffin recalled that the conference was unmemorable,

> until the very end, when the meeting was about to break up, and an executive producer from Times Radio asked if anyone had heard that the Queen was ill. I don't know Molly Guinness well, but she will remain forever etched in my memory as the first person in an extraordinary chain that helped to produce one of the greatest editions of *The Times*.

Molly is one of several broadcast journalists in the building to have worked at the BBC. At some point towards the end of conference, she heard from a former colleague that there had been contact between Buckingham Palace and the corporation with regard to the Queen's immediate health, and that this time it was serious. The last thing any journalist wants is to look like they are not in control of a story, especially if it's a big one. However, if what we were hearing from Molly was true, we were about to put in place one of the most detailed plans ever to have been drawn up at *The Times*, with huge logistic and editorial ramifications, in the knowledge that our work would be judged as historical record and saved for the ages. And there was a big problem: we didn't know when, or even if, we'd be publishing any of it that day.

Tony Gallagher, acting editor in the absence of John Witherow, who was convalescing after a serious illness, ended conference by asking that staff be prepared for the announcement of the Queen's death should it arrive. Information about how the official announcement would be made, the succession of the Prince of Wales to the throne, events up to and including the funeral and the differing scenarios depending on the location of death, had all been briefed by the Palace to correspondents. Everything had been planned for decades. The *Times* royal writer Valentine Low knew enough about the protocol of Operation London Bridge, as the Palace called its masterplan, to be able to construct a basic news story in advance, one that would inevitably form the splash should the Queen die. There was just one problem: Low, in the time-honoured tradition of specialists when the biggest story of their career is about to unfold, was away somewhere on a day off. Much messaging ensued and, despite nervous looks on the faces of the news desk, he jumped back in readily.

Low had been de facto royal correspondent since the retirement of Alan Hamilton in 2008. He once observed that there were two crucial differences between writing about royalty and the other specialisms in the newsroom. One was that no one ever set out to be a royal correspondent, de facto or titled. And if they did, they should be banned immediately from doing the job, because they were quite clearly far too interested in the royals and therefore in danger of becoming a full-blooded sycophant. The other was that, unlike fields such as politics, sport and the arts, the people you were writing about don't actually talk to you. Not if they could help it. Some members of the royal family were, he admitted, more personable than others. "William says hello from time to time, and even Harry has been known to be friendly, before he decided that he hates all representatives of the media, however respectable. Charles has been known to be chatty: he once engaged me in conversation during a downpour in the Indian rainforest while I sheltered under one of his flunkey's umbrellas."

Low's favourite royal was the former Camilla Parker-Bowles, who as Charles's wife became Duchess of Cornwall and later Queen. While touring Australia with Charles and Camilla in 2012, Low had written a piece as part of his "non-royal" duties about the death of a key character in the latest episode of *Downton Abbey*, the hit television series about the tribulations of an aristocratic family. In a remote corner of Queensland, Camilla walked over. "How nice", I thought, "my favourite member of the royal family has come to say hello. She looked at me with a sorrowful expression. 'Valentine,' she said, 'you totally ruined my Downton.'" She had seen his article before having the chance to see the episode in which the character died. "Ah well," Low thought, "at least she reads my stuff." And now this Downton fan was set to be Queen. Witherow had a warm memory of meeting the late monarch herself at a Buckingham Palace reception, as he would later reveal in his retirement speech:

> I was chatting to Geordie Greig, the editor of the *Mail*, and Rachel Johnson. A flunkie came up and said Her Majesty would be along in a moment so, basically, behave yourselves. This tiny woman came up and Geordie immediately bowed and said 'Ma'am, what an honour. My grandfather was Silver Stick in Waiting to your father.' 'Yees,' said the Queen, looking distinctly unimpressed. Then Rachel said: 'Ma'am, my husband's father was a close aide to your sister.' 'I don't think so,' said the Queen, looking even more unimpressed. Rachel then made the mistake of correcting the monarch. 'No, he really was,' she said. The Queen turned to me, and I said: 'Am I the only person here with absolutely no royal connections?' And the Queen gave me a beaming smile and walked off.

They don't like commoners pretending they have royal connections you see.

Events at the *Times* office were moving rapidly.

We knew by 12.30pm that doctors were 'concerned for Her Majesty's health', an unprecedented alarm signal, said Griffin. The whereabouts of Charles, William and other senior royals were being tracked, as were those of the Duke of Sussex. There were whispers and grim faces at the dispatch box in the House of Commons, and the BBC adopted a sombre tone to what by then was rolling news coverage comprising long-range views of Balmoral, where the Queen was staying. Indeed in our very own Times Radio studio three floors above the newsroom, breakfast presenter Stig Abell had returned in the early afternoon to help anchor the story. One didn't require a sixth sense to conclude that we needed to plan firmly for the likelihood that the nation's longest-serving monarch was about to die.

There was an immediate recognition that, unlike the fast-moving Westminster stories and the Ukraine war that had dominated the year so far and shown *The Times* at its digital best, this was an occasion when print would come back into its own. Readers would want a tangible souvenir of a solemn landmark in the history of the nation. Griffin said:

At around 1pm I discussed the structure of the next day's edition with our colleagues in publishing, who oversee timely delivery of *Times* pages to our print sites. This was part of a process that was in many ways the opposite of modern newsroom operations. *The Times* has become increasingly digital-first in recent years, in the knowledge that the vast majority of its subscribers have paid for online access to its journalism and expect accurate, informed and speedy insight into world events. However, we knew that the death of the Queen would result in a massive uplift in print sales – and as we were producing something that would end up in the nation's archives, we had to ensure it was a newspaper that we could be proud of in decades, not just the following day.

There had for many years been a schedule of stories in place for the death of the monarch and for a series of posthumous daily print supplements in the week leading up to the funeral. They had been updated, finessed or sometimes completely overwritten on several occasions over the previous two decades. Several journalists who had since moved to rival publications, retired or even died had had a hand in the work. The task of having this package ready for the eventuality of the Queen's death had fallen on Ian Brunskill, associate editor and master of detail, and Bridget Harrison, a highly experienced features executive. Some ingenuity had been needed. Commissioning the content had been easy. There was no shortage of royal experts happy to write about Elizabeth II's life and times. The problem, for many years, had been getting anyone to work on production, editing or design. It was well-nigh impossible to persuade busy staff to drop what they were doing for a project that (with luck) might not be needed for years. Something more pressing always got in the way.

The Queen's 90th birthday in 2016 had offered a solution. The *Times* syndication department decided there was a market for a *Times* "bookazine", a substantial glossy magazine celebrating Elizabeth's life and reign, to be sold on newsstands at a premium price. A generous editorial budget was available, and there was a date by which the finished product had to be on sale. Brunskill and Harrison seized the opportunity. The copy commissioned from writers such as Hugo Vickers, Valentine Low and Sally Beddell Smith for the (still unproduced) death supplements could easily be repurposed for the birthday tribute magazine. Suddenly there was a deadline for editing, design and picture research.

With tenses changed from past to present and some cheerful illustrations thrown in, the bookazine duly came together in fairly short order, and was well received. Its internal sections corresponded roughly to the division of the planned run of posthumous daily print supplements. It was then a relatively straightforward job for a small team to dismantle it, change all the tenses back from 'is' to 'was', replace some of the jollier photographs and reshape the whole thing back into the planned run of supplements for publication when the Queen's death eventually came. "The work was done. At last, the supplements were ready for immediate publication whenever the moment might come. Relief all round," Brunskill recalled.

Harrison ensured the print supplements were kept up to date over the five or more years until they were eventually needed. Brunskill meanwhile, with news editors Lindsey McIntosh and then Seb Mann, prepared 14 spreads of print coverage to run in the main newspaper on the day after the Queen's death. Mann worked closely with the digital team to turn this into an effective package of online coverage for publication the moment the announcement came.

As *The Times* was one of several news organisations owned by News UK, there was an obvious need for coordination. A "gold command" meeting was called to discuss each title's plans and the likely demands on the printing and circulation operations. Griffin recalled: "We knew that we wanted to make a commemorative wrap for the newspaper, and after discussing production capability it was agreed – and I've checked my notes – that we would run a 168-page edition. This comprised a main book of 96 pages, an obituary supplement of 40 pages, and the usual supplements of Times 2 and Bricks & Mortar. Quite some undertaking, meaning we absolutely had to hit our deadline and get the paper off on time. But we still didn't know when the news would break."

By mid-afternoon, thousands of members of the public were massing at the gates of Buckingham Palace and other royal residences. "Although we later learnt that the Queen had died at 3.10pm," said Griffin, "the official announcement of her passing was not until 6.30pm, which meant that for most of the day we were working to the possibility that 80 per cent of what we were doing was not going to be needed. When the news finally arrived, the team – and by that I mean the entire newsroom of reporters, subs, picture researchers and editors – had three hours to ensure it conjured a newspaper worthy of the story while giving our digital readers everything they required, too. The planned running order was modified to take account of events, with news executives Dan Parkinson and Tom Payne working closely with Tony [Gallagher] and me as we agreed on both the scale and detail. Senior designer Dinesh Mehta took charge of the look of the Queen pages. Senior sub-editor Tom Leece, who had worked closely with Brunskill on preparations, became the go-to person for the gargantuan task of subbing. And everybody else piled in."

That night *The Times* beat both *The Telegraph* and the *Mail* to the presses, enjoyed a very good print run and doubled its usual sales figure; in fact, it sold out. "Everyone involved realised that Operation London Bridge was extraordinary in many ways, but one that should not be overlooked is that it was a last hurrah for print editions," Griffin pointed out. "There won't be too many more of those; indeed it would be a surprise if the number of actual newspapers sold in Britain on September 9, 2022, the day after the Queen died, is ever again surpassed."

The editorial and production team behind this achievement were all horrified two days later when Tom Leece, the senior sub at the heart of their successful coverage, died in a road accident at the age of 32. The huge edition marking the Queen's death was remembered as a fitting memorial to this dedicated and hard-working young journalist.

At Westminster, all political activity was suspended until after the Queen's funeral on Monday, September 19, but it re-erupted furiously on the Friday of that week, September 23. Truss's newly appointed chancellor of the exchequer, presented to parliament a £45 billion package of tax cuts with which they proposed to boost the British economy and tackle the cost of living crisis caused by rising inflation. World markets were shocked by the amount of government borrowing that would be required to fund the measures. The pound collapsed to near parity with the dollar; bond markets dumped British debt; and the home mortgage market dried up. Truss's grip on reality was called into question and open plotting to get rid of her began among Tory MPs. After ten days she started to reverse the most contentious tax cuts, and a week after that she dumped the chancellor himself while he was flying home from a visit to the International Monetary Fund in Washington.

Steve Swinford was in the thick of it, wielding one of the tools of digital journalism, his Twitter account, as he told Matt Chorley:

> I picked up a suggestion that was really incendiary that Liz Truss was about to sack Kwasi Kwarteng. And it's the kind of thing you have to be very careful with. So I did some more checking and I got it confirmed. And then I thought, What do I do with this? This is politics happening at hyperspeed. It's not like we wait for newspapers anymore. We have live blogs. We have Twitter. So I thought, let's just get out there. So we did the Tweet and we put it at the top of the *Times* live blogs and everything just exploded because, at this point in time, Kwasi Kwarteng was

completely unaware that he was going to be sacked and he learnt that he was going to be sacked reading that Tweet and the *Times* live blog.

Kwarteng himself confirmed this course of events: "I actually learnt on Twitter, on Steve Swinford's Twitter . . . I was in the car on the way to Downing Street and my special adviser said, 'Have you seen this?' And I looked at it and it said, 'Kwasi Kwarteng has been sacked' or 'will be sacked'. I can't remember which tense it was. And I was very much of the view that, well, that's interesting."

For Swinford, it showed how much politics and political journalism had changed: "We're in this era now where . . . things were happening almost minute by minute. You were getting entire budgets reversed in a matter of hours. You were getting successive cabinet resignations, appointments. And it's just the sheer pace of it that is one of the biggest changes in covering politics." Truss herself lasted only 49 days in office, resigning on October 24 under pressure from Tory backbenchers and facing widespread public ridicule. She was replaced by the rival she had beaten in the Tory leadership contest, Rishi Sunak. Chorley asked Swinford if she would have survived if it had been the 1970s. Was there something about the modern "relentlessness of rolling news, social media, live blogs and actually the fact the Westminster village feeds that beast the entire time", whereas in the 1970s the pace was so much slower with just one deadline to meet at the end of the day?

Swinford thought not: Truss had been brought down not by the press but by her risk-taking with the economy and by the fact that she had been elected Tory leader by party members not by MPs:

So when you get those two things – you've got her choices, you've got these very risky choices on the economy that she took, with the consequences, allied with the fact that there were so many people who didn't want her to be prime minister in the first place – that meant it was totally unsustainable, and that would have been as unsustainable back then [in the 1970s] as it was now. Twitter, the way we report things, accelerates all of that. It means that things happened faster. Hence it was a 49-day premiership. But all of those seeds of her destruction were there almost from day one.

In the throes of the Truss debacle, when the pages of *The Times* were dominated by the noise and fury over her mini-budget, some readers might not have registered that the paper reported some news of its own on Tuesday, September 27: "John Witherow, the editor of *The Times*, has stepped down after a decade in charge." With characteristic self-effacement, Witherow had picked an extremely busy news day to slip out his announcement without fanfare. Tony Gallagher was confirmed next day as the new editor. There were many tributes to Witherow's 42 years with *The Times* and *Sunday Times*. Rupert Murdoch called him one of the great editors of his generation. Robert Thomson recalled when he was himself editor of *The Times*:

> I admired the journalistic excellence of *The Sunday Times*, which was an artful blend of headline-snatching scoops, the finest writing and superior craft under John's sage leadership. He brought those same enduring qualities to *The Times*, which was much enhanced under his editorship and patently became a global beacon of editorial integrity at a time when journalistic standards around the world have slipped perceptibly and profoundly. John's positive impact on journalism and on society will resonate for many, many years to come.

Charles Moore, former editor of *The Daily Telegraph*, *The Sunday Telegraph* and *The Spectator*, said Witherow had "always been a consummate professional. Because he doesn't promote his own ego he is excellent at bringing out the talents of his journalists." Sarah Sands, a former editor of the *Today* programme and the London *Evening Standard*, agreed: "He knew that great editors do not need to be particularly visible and voluble – they can be brilliant conductors. I have never known *The Times* in better shape." The most weighty encomium, however, came from Paul Dacre, editor-in-chief of DMG media, who had been editor of *The Daily Mail* for 26 years. Witherow was often said to resemble this Fleet Street "big beast", taking a similarly single-minded approach to editing (though not using Dacre's famously profane newsroom language).

Over the decades, *The Times*' eye-watering losses – while being a remarkable tribute to Rupert Murdoch's awesome commitment to journalism – called into question whether it would ever make money. That the paper is now both profitable – and excellent – is, in no small way, down to John. As an editor, he was a master craftsman, possessed of the all-round journalistic skills that are beginning to die in a digital age – an age that John was also hugely successful at coming to terms with. I salute him, his huge achievements and his decision to stand down while he was well ahead. He is one of the great, professional editors of his age.

INDEX

BIBLIOGRAPHY

Ayres, C. (2005). *War Reporting for Cowards*. London: John Murray.

Barnes, S. (2006). *The Meaning of Sport*. London: Short Books Ltd.

Brown, G. (2018). *My Life, Our Times*. London: Vintage.

Bryson, B. (1996). *Notes from a Small Island*. London: Black Swan.

Cameron, D. (2019). *For the Record*. London: William Collins.

Grabbe, J.W. (2017). 'Sudoku and changes in working memory performance for older adults and younger adults', *Activities, Adaptation & Aging, 41*(1), 14–21. https://doi.org/10.1080/01924 788.2016.1272390.

Ellman, L. (2019), *Ducks, Newburyport*. Norwich: Galley Beggar Press.

Hargrove, C. (2001). *Un Gentleman du Times*. Paris: Tallandier.

Hinton, L. (2018). *The Bootle Boy: An Untidy Life in News*. London: Scribe UK.

Horner, A. and Rowe, A. (eds) (2015). *Living on Paper: Letters from Iris Murdoch 1934–95*. London: Chatto.

Kalia, V., Fuesting, M.A., & Cody, M. (2019). 'Perseverance in solving Sudoku: role of grit and cognitive flexibility in problem solving', *Journal of Cognitive Psychology, 31*, 370–78. https://doi.org/10.1080/20445911.2019.1604527.

Lewis, R. (2002). *Charles Hawtrey 1914–1988: The Man Who Was Private Widdle*. London: Faber & Faber.

Rees-Mogg, J. (2019). *The Victorians. Twelve Titans who Forged Britain*. London: WH Allen.

Stothard, P. (2003). *Thirty Days: Tony Blair and the Test of History*. London: HarperCollins.

The Times (2022). *The Times Style Guide* (3rd ed). London: HarperCollins.

Thomson, R. (1998). *True Fiction*. London: Penguin.

Wagner, E. (2001). *Ariel's Gift*. London: Faber & Faber.

Wagner, E. (2007). *Gravity*. London: Granta.

Waterhouse, K. (2010) *Waterhouse On Newspaper Style*. London: Revel Barker.

Webster, P. (2016). *Inside Story: Politics, Intrigue and Treachery from Thatcher to Brexit*. London: William Collins.